GREAT

FOOD

PUBS

GREAT FOOD PUBS

POCKET GOOD GUIDES

Edited by Alisdair Aird

Deputy Editor: Fiona Stapley

Managing Editor: Karen Fick
Research Officer: Elizabeth Adlington
Associate Editor: Robert Unsworth
Editorial Assistance: Fiona Wright

EBURY PRESS
LONDON

This edition first published in 2002 by Ebury Press,
Random House, 20 Vauxhall Bridge Road,
London SW1V 2SA

The Random House Group Limited Reg. No. 954009

www.randomhouse.co.uk

1 3 5 7 9 10 8 6 4 2

Copyright © 2002 The Random House Group Ltd
Maps copyright © 2002 Perrott Cartographics
Cover design by Nim Design
Cover photograph © Image Bank

A CIP catalogue record for this book is available from the British Library.

ISBN 0 09 188 5167

Typeset from author's disks by Clive Dorman & Co.
Edited by Pat Taylor Chalmers
Printed and bound in Denmark by Nørhaven Paperback A/S, Viborg

CONTENTS

INTRODUCTION   7

PUB CHAINS   8

GREAT FOOD PUBS   10

MAPS   215

To contact us write to:

> Great Food Pubs
> Freepost TN1569
> Wadhurst
> E Susssex
> TN5 7BR

or

Check out our web site!

www.goodguides.co.uk

INTRODUCTION

Great meals out at pub prices

The Good Guides team, responsible for the top-selling annual Good Pub Guide, have for the first time searched their database to bring you the country's most enjoyable food pubs. This hand-picked selection is based on the team's own detailed anonymous inspections, and on some 45,000 recent reports from readers.

Pub food has changed out of all recognition in the last few years. The pubs in this book serve food that's at least as good as restaurants in their area, and add two special ingredients – pub prices, which generally give much better value than restaurants; and a relaxed pub atmosphere, with a real sense of welcome. It's this friendly and informal atmosphere which now leads so ds so many budding young chefs to put their talents to work in the happy surroundings of a pub, instead of some stuffy restaurant.

As well as smart pubs where mouth-watering new recipes draw gourmets from many miles around, in this book you'll also find simple taverns where honest home cooking using the freshest local ingredients gives just as much satisfaction. From one extreme to the other, all these very individual places share one vital quality: whoever you are and however you're dressed, you'll go in to a real welcome, and come out feeling that you've enjoyed something rather special – and been treated as someone rather special.

Chain pubs may not have the same individuality. And they can't match the sheer food quality of our top food pubs. But at least you know what to expect from their standardised style and menus. And the best pub chains can be really useful, for a comfortable meal if you're in an unfamiliar area, and well trained friendly staff. So for this book the Good Guides team has included a special survey of some of the larger chains, including many that specialise in family dining, with facilities specially for children.

Alisdair Aird

PUB CHAINS

Here we sketch out what you can expect from the main dining pub groups. We have added notes on some of the more interesting smaller groups, too. Sometimes all the pubs in the chain use the chain's name, such as All Bar One. More often, each pub has its own separate name, but the name of the chain usually appears in its signage and on its menus and so forth. All these groups have no-smoking areas and – unless we say they don't – do provide for families. We have found all of them reasonably reliable, in providing pub meals to a consistent standard.

All Bar One Town bars often in interesting converted buildings, stripped down décor and a trendy feel, brasserie-style food served all day, and strong on wines. Six Continents. 53, nationwide.

Appletons Family dining pubs with emphasis on wholesome fresh produce (grow their own herbs), fair prices. Greene King. 6, mainly Surrey.

Bar 38 Young modern city bars with inventive contemporary food (served all day), trendy drinks and music; attractive prices. S&N. 13.

John Barras Large, comfortably refurbished traditional high-street locals with standard choice of low-priced food (served all day) – good value. S&N. 114, nationwide.

Beefeater Comfortable, neatly kept dining pubs with good steaks plus some interesting dishes (served all day). Nearly half are next to a Travel Inn. Whitbreads. 226, nationwide.

T & J Bernard Traditional city pubs, attractive choice of traditional food, served all day. S&N. 54, nationwide.

Brewers Fayre Comfortably furnished pubs with emphasis on good value meals (served all day) eaten in a relaxed atmosphere; child-friendly but perhaps more appealing to adults, with modern ideas such as juice bars, fresh bread ovens, and Weightwatcher dishes. Whitbreads. 271, nationwide.

Brewsters Aimed at parents with young children, with state-of-the-art play areas known as Fun Factories with team members trained to juggle, face paint and so forth (Playstations for older children), regular appearances by the mascot, Brewster the Bear, collectable toy with children's meals, tagging for children and ParentCam CCTV, and a good choice of reasonably priced meals (served all day). Whitbreads. 129, nationwide.

Chef & Brewer Country dining pubs, often attractive, with good furnishings, wide choice of reliable food on changing blackboards including individual chef's specials, served all day, and good value wines. S&N. 105, nationwide.

Country Carvery Useful budget family restaurants with emphasis on carvery, various meal deals; food served all day. S&N. 38, nationwide.

Davys Traditional old-fashioned food in thorough-going olde-worlde taverns – sawdust and candlelight; good wines, good fun. Independent. 37, mainly London.

Harvester Cheerful country feel, sensibly priced food (served all day) strong on chargrills and salads, some interesting buildings in pleasant surroundings. Six Continents. 150, nationwide.

Henry's Interesting modern food (served all day) and good drinks choice in stylish city café/bars; more young people's meeting place at night. S&N. 10.

Hungry Horse Huge helpings of straightforward meaty food on huge plates, low prices (especially Monday and Tuesday). Greene King. 119, spreading widely westwards from East Anglia.

Kings Fayre Standardised menu (straightforward and sensible, with some more interesting choices) and enjoyable wines in non-standardised pubs, often attractive. Greene King. 29, middle England.

Millers Modern furnishings, sensible food with skillet dishes and unusually good children's choice (served all day), and kids' electronic games, too. S&N. 12, likely to grow.

Old English Inns Generally very handsome old buildings, now each doing its own food; good wines. Recently taken over by Greene King: great potential. 134, mainly southern parts of England.

Original Pub Co Town pubs with airy modern facelift, cheap meals and some interesting snacks, served all day. S&N. 23.

Tom Cobleigh Comfortable, roomy pubs, especially aimed at families, with elaborate indoor play facilities and play barns, a good choice of straightforward food (served all day), plus a menu for hearty appetites, and children's dishes. Tom Cobleigh. 72, mainly Midlands and north.

Vintage Inns Typically well converted or rebuilt to give attractive olde-worlde feel with plenty of small areas; enjoyable food (served all day), good wine choice, pleasant, helpful staff, and log fires; generally among the best of the chain pubs. Six Continents. 186, nationwide.

Wetherspoons Another excellent chain. Typically, roomy, comfortably traditional pubs in well converted interesting buildings (even banks and opera houses); standard pubby food (served all day), good value, no piped music – but only a few allow children. Independent. 545, nationwide, growing.

ABERDOVEY Map 3 E1
Penhelig Arms

Opposite Penhelig railway station

In summer you can enjoy the high quality, generous bar food at this mainly 18th-c hotel on their terrace by the harbour wall which has lovely views across the Dyfi estuary. Fresh fish, delivered every day by the local fishmonger, is a big draw and there are usually 12 or so fish dishes to choose from in the evening, with a couple less at lunchtime. They serve the same menu in the bar and restaurant, and the very reasonably priced menu changes quite frequently but might include pea and mint soup (£2.50), sandwiches (from £2.95), duck slices with chicory and apple in pink peppercorn and balsamic dressing or griddled halloumi cheese with roast peppers (£4.25), grilled lambs liver and bacon or chicken cooked in lemon sauce with cardamon and ginger (£7.95), seared salmon fillets, roast pork wrapped in bacon with mustard and caper sauce, lamb cutlets with rosemary gravy or baked cod with a stilton crust with Italian salsa verde (£8.50); puddings such as rhubarb crumble or blackcurrant mousse with cassis (£3.25); good selection of British cheeses (£3.95). Their two-course Sunday lunch is a good deal (£9.95). The excellent, expanding wine list numbers about 250 bins, with over 40 half bottles, and about a dozen by the glass; they also have two dozen malt whiskies, fruit or peppermint teas, and various coffees. The small original beamed bar (which they plan to refurbish) has a cosy feel with winter fires, and three changing real ales such as Abbot Ale, Brains Rev James Original and Tetleys on handpump; dominoes. Service is friendly and attentive. The separate, newly refurbished restaurant is no smoking. Sea views from the comfortable bedrooms; new ones have balconies.

Bar food (standard food times) ~ Restaurant ~ (01654) 767215 ~ Children in eating area of bar and restaurant ~ Open 11-4, 5.30-11; 12-4, 6-10.30 Sun ~ Bedrooms: £61S/£108B

ALCISTON Map 2 E6
Rose Cottage
Village signposted off A27 Polegate—Lewes

In summer, this bustling country cottage is very pleasant with ducks and chickens in the back garden, and gas heaters for cooler evenings; the charming little village (and local church) are certainly worth a look. Inside, there are cosy winter log fires, and half a dozen tables with cushioned pews under quite a forest of harness, traps, a thatcher's blade and lots of other black ironware, with more bric-a-brac on the shelves above the stripped pine dado or in the etched-glass windows; in the mornings you may also find Jasper the parrot (it can get a little smoky for him in the evenings); it's best to arrive early to be sure of a seat. There's a lunchtime overflow into the no-smoking restaurant area. Made from fresh local produce wherever possible (fresh fish comes from a fisherman at Eastbourne, eggs from their own chickens, and venison from the landlord's brother-in-law), hearty bar food includes pâté (£3.25), ploughman's (from £4.75), Lincolnshire sausages (£5.25) and rib-eye steak (£7.50), with daily specials such as beef and ale pie (£6.75), chicken in white wine and mushroom sauce (£7.50), good vegetarian dishes (around £7.50), wild rabbit in cream and mustard sauce or whole local plaice with lemon and parsley butter (£7.95), venison braised in port and Guinness (£8.50), whole grilled bass with pickled ginger and soy sauce (£9.95), and roast Sunday lunch (£7.50); very good home-made puddings like home-grown rhubarb crumble, treacle tart or hot chocolate fudge brownie (£3.25). Well kept Harveys Best, winter Old, and a guest such as Rother Valley Level Best on handpump, decent wines including a 'country' of the month and six by the glass (or half litre), winter mulled wine, summer Pimms and sangria, and Biddenden farm cider; the landlord, whom we have known now for many years, is quite a character; darts, dominoes, cribbage, and maybe piped classical music. House martins and swallows continue their annual custom of nesting above the porch, seemingly unperturbed by the people going in and out beneath them. Nearby fishing and shooting.

Bar food (till 9.30; exc Sun) ~ Restaurant ~ (01323) 870377 ~ Children welcome in restaurant and eating area of bar but must be over 6 in evening ~ Open 11.30-3, 6.30-11; 12-3, 7-10.30 Sun; closed 25 and 26 Dec ~ Bedrooms: /£50S

ALDERMINSTER Map 2 A2
Bell

A3400 Oxford—Stratford

The licensees put in a huge effort to keep this comfortably smart dining pub flourishing by putting on lots of parties, food festivals, and classical and light music evenings throughout the year. There's some emphasis on the freshly cooked to order food from an imaginative menu which changes monthly. There might be soup (£3.50), filled baguettes (from £4.25), brie, bacon, garlic and mushroom tart (£4.50), pâté with cumberland sauce (£5.75), fisherman's crêpe with lobster and prawn sauce au gratin (£6.25), potato, leek, mushroom and stilton bake with tomato and sage sauce (£6.95), pie of the week or fishcakes with dill sauce (£8.95), stir-fried spiced duck breast with wilted greens and potato rösti (£10.95) and home-made puddings such as dark chocolate, almond and brandy torte, coffee and walnut cheesecake or blackcurrant sorbet (from £4). The communicating areas of the neatly kept spacious bar have plenty of stripped slatback chairs around wooden tables on the flagstones and wooden floors, little vases of flowers, small landscape prints and swan's-neck brass-and-globe lamps on the cream walls, and a solid fuel stove in a stripped brick inglenook. Two changing real ales might be Greene King Abbot and Ruddles County under light blanket pressure, alongside a good range of wines and champagne by the glass, freshly squeezed juice and cocktails. They have high chairs, and readers with children have felt particularly welcome. A conservatory and terrace overlook the garden and Stour Valley.

Bar food (standard food times) ~ Restaurant ~ (01789) 450414 ~ Children welcome ~ Open 12-2.30, 7-11(10.30 Sun) ~ Bedrooms: £25(£35S)(£45B)/£45(£55S)(£60B)

ALDFORD Map 3 D2
Grosvenor Arms

B5130 Chester—Wrexham

A real favourite with readers, this lively pub is popular for its enjoyable food and an impressive choice of beers, wines and spirits. There's a traditional feel throughout the spacious open-plan layout, and a chatty atmosphere in the huge panelled library with tall book shelves along one wall and long wooden floor boards with lots of well spaced substantial tables. Several quieter areas are well furnished with good individual pieces including a very comfortable parliamentary-type leather settle. Throughout there are plenty of interesting pictures, and the lighting's exemplary; cribbage, dominoes, Trivial Pursuit and Scrabble. Huge helpings of well presented imaginative bar food might include home-made soup (£3.50), sandwiches (from £3.75), roast duck leg with a red onion marmalade (£5.95), fresh salmon and horseradish pâté with a vinaigrette dressing (£5.45), spicy lamb kebabs with coriander yoghurt in pitta bread with mixed salad (£7.45), grilled cod with crab risotto and shellfish butter sauce (£10.95), and medallions of beef cooked in a mustard, brandy, cream and wild mushroom sauce (£14.95). Unusual vegetarian dishes might be baby corn fritters on stir-fried vegetables and noodles with a chilli and sesame sauce (£7.45) or ricotta, spinach and pine kernel strudel with a tomato and red pepper sauce (£7.25), and there are puddings such as coffee and whisky cheesecake and sticky date pudding with butterscotch sauce (£3.95). Up to five well kept real ales on handpump include Batemans XB, Flowers IPA and guests such as Shepherd Neame Best, Hanby Drawwell and Weetwood Eastgate, all 20 wines (largely New World) are served by the glass, and an awesome choice of whiskies includes 75 malts, 25 bourbons, and 25 from Ireland. There are canapés on the bar at Sunday lunchtime, and it's best to book on weekend evenings. The airy terracotta-floored conservatory has lots of huge low hanging flowering baskets and chunky pale wood garden furniture, and opens on to a large elegant suntrap terrace and neat lawn with picnic-sets, young trees and a tractor.

Bar food (12-10(9 Sun); not 25 Dec) ~ (01244) 620228 ~ No children under 14 inside after 6pm ~ Open 11.30-11; 12-10.30 Sun

ALDWORTH Map 2 C3
Bell

A329 Reading—Wallingford; left on to B4009 at Streatley

A favourite with many readers, this unchanging 14th-c country pub has been run by the same family for over 200 years. It is simply furnished with benches around the panelled walls, an ancient one-handed clock, a glass-panelled hatch rather than a bar counter for service, beams in the shiny ochre ceiling, and a woodburning stove. The timeless, welcoming atmosphere is helped by the ban on games machines, mobile phones and piped music. Apart from winter home-made soup (£2.50), appetising bar food is confined to exceptionally good value filled hot crusty rolls such as cheddar (£1.30), stilton, ham or pâté (£1.50), turkey (£1.60), smoked salmon, prawn or salt beef (£1.95), and delicious crab in season (£2), plus filled french bread (£2.50), and ploughman's (from £3); very good service. Particularly well kept and very cheap Arkells BBB and Kingsdown, Crouch Vale Bitter, and from the local West Berkshire Brewery, Old Tyler and Dark Mild on handpump (they won't stock draught lager); good quality house wines. Darts, shove-ha'penny, dominoes, and cribbage. The quiet, old-fashioned garden by the village cricket ground is lovely in summer, and the pub is handy for the Ridgeway. At Christmas, local mummers perform in the road by the ancient well-head (the shaft is sunk 400 feet through the chalk), and steaming jugs of hot punch and mince pies are handed round afterwards; occasional morris dancing in summer. It can get busy at weekends.

Bar food (11-2.45, 6-10.45; 12-2.45, 7-10.15 Sun) ~ No credit cards ~ (01635) 578272 ~ Children must be well behaved ~ Open 11-3, 6-11; 12-3, 7-10.30 Sun; closed Mon exc bank holidays, 25 Dec

APPLECROSS Map 4 C1
Applecross Inn
Off A896 S of Shieldaig

The drive to this welcoming inn over the pass of the cattle (Beallach na Ba) is one of the highest in Britain, and a truly exhilarating experience. The alternative route, along the single-track lane winding round the coast from just south of Shieldaig, has equally glorious sea loch and then sea views nearly all the way. More popular than you might expect from the loneliness of the setting, you'll usually find it has a number of cheerful locals in the newly refurbished bar with its woodburning stove, newly exposed stone walls, and upholstered pine furnishings on the stone floor; there's also a new no-smoking dining area with lavatories for the disabled and with baby changing facilities. Usually available all day, the very good, enjoyable bar food under the new chef might include sandwiches, rocket, sweet chilli and parmesan or slow roasted tomato and onion soups (£2.25), haggis flambéd in Drambuie, topped with cream (£3.95), local prawns in hot garlic butter or home-made macaroni cheese (£5.95), squat lobster Thai curry or fresh haddock in crispy batter with home-made tartare sauce (£6.95), king scallops in garlic butter with lemon and crispy bacon (£8.95), lots of daily specials, and home-made puddings such as vanilla panna cotta with red berry compote or chocolate and rosemary mousse (£2.95). You must book for the no-smoking restaurant. Pool (winter only), TV, and juke box (unless there are musicians in the pub); a good choice of around 50 malt whiskies, and efficient, welcoming service. There's a nice garden by the shore with tables. The bedrooms have been refurbished this year and all have a sea view; marvellous breakfasts.

Bar food (12-9; not 25 Dec or 1 Jan) ~ Restaurant ~ (01520) 744262 ~ Children welcome until 8.30pm ~ Traditional ceilidhs Fri evening ~ Open 11-12(11.30 Sat); 12.30-11 Sun; closed 1 Jan ~ Bedrooms: £25/£50(£60B)

APPLEY Map 1 C4
Globe

Hamlet signposted from the network of back roads between A361 and A38, W of
B3187 and W of Milverton and Wellington; OS Sheet 181 map reference 072215

Even on dismal winter evenings, customers are happy to brave snowy
conditions to enjoy the good food in this 15th-c country pub. Generously
served, dishes might include sandwiches, home-made soup (£2.75; smoked
haddock and bacon chowder £5.25), mushrooms in cream, garlic and
horseradish (£3.95), a light cold egg pancake filled with prawns, celery and
pineapple in marie rose sauce (£6.50), home-made steak and kidney in ale
pie (£7.25), Thai vegetable curry (£7.50), lamb curry with mint, yoghurt
and coriander (£7.75), steaks (from £9.25), chicken breast stuffed with
lemon grass, chilli and ginger (£9.75), half a crispy roast duckling with red
onion, orange and madeira sauce (£11.75), daily specials such as beef
stroganoff (£8.25), grilled fillet of pork with fresh sage, shallot, seed
mustard, cream and white wine (£9.95), fresh whole lemon sole or fresh
crab salad (£10.95), and puddings such as white chocolate and Malteser ice
cream or bread and butter pudding (£3.25); Sunday roast (£5.95) and
children's meals (from £3.75). The simple beamed front room has benches
and a built-in settle, bare wood tables on the brick floor, and pictures of
magpies, and there's a further room with easy chairs and other more
traditional ones, open fires, a collection of model cars, and *Titanic* pictures;
alley skittles and pool. The restaurant is no smoking. A stone-flagged entry
corridor leads to a serving hatch from where Cotleigh Tawny and guests
such as Palmers IPA or John Smiths are kept on handpump; summer farm
cider. Seats, climbing frame and swings outside in the garden; the path
opposite leads eventually to the River Tone. The lavatories are outside.

*Bar food (standard food times) ~ Restaurant ~ (01823) 672327 ~ Children
welcome ~ Open 11-3, 6.30-11; 12-3, 7-10.30 Sun; closed Mon except bank
holidays*

ASHLEWORTH Map 1 A5

Queens Arms

Village signposted off A417 at Hartpury

The courteous licensees in this attractive low-beamed country pub have worked hard during their four years' tenure to achieve their target of what a country village pub should be. They continue to add antiques to the civilised and immaculate décor, have a range of 15 real ales (with a rotating choice of 3), keep 10 wines by the glass, and use the best local produce for their popular home-made food. The comfortably laid out main bar, softly lit by fringed wall lamps and candles at night, has faintly patterned wallpaper and washed red-ochre walls, big oak and mahogany tables and a nice mix of farmhouse and big brocaded dining chairs on a red carpet. Good, imaginative bar food includes lunchtime specials such as freshly baked baguettes (from £5.25), salad niçoise (£5.50), chicken, ham and leek pie (£6.50), South African sausage with tomato and onion gravy (£6.75), and grilled salmon with cherry tomatoes and a lemon thyme butter (£7.75), with evening dishes like chicken topped with mozzarella and capers, served with a marsala, mushroom and cream sauce, or rack of spare ribs (£10.75), lamb noisettes with a garlic and rosemary stuffing with a red wine and wild mushroom sauce (£11.50), fresh monkfish and king scallops with a chilli, garlic and ginger dressing (£11.50), and wild boar with a rich fresh raspberry sauce (£12.95); puddings like cape brandy pudding (a South African speciality), raspberry crème brûlée or meringues with toffee cream and sugar bark (£3.95), and Sunday lunch (£6.95). The dining room is no smoking. The well kept real ales might include any of the following: Adnams Bitter and Broadside, Bass, Brains Bitter, Brakspears Bitter and Special, Donnington BB, Greene King Old Speckled Hen and IPA, Marstons Pedigree, Shepherd Neame Spitfire, Timothy Taylors Landlord, and Youngs Bitter and Special on handpump; a thoughtful wine list with some South African choices (the friendly licensees hail from there). Piped music, shove-ha'penny, cribbage, dominoes, and winter skittle alley. Two perfectly clipped mushroom-shaped yews dominate the front of the building, and there are a couple of tables and chairs and old-fashioned benches in the back courtyard.

Bar food (till 10 Fri/Sat) ~ Restaurant ~ (01452) 700395 ~ Well behaved children welcome ~ Open 12-3, 7-11(10.30 Sun); closed 25 Dec

ASHURST Map 2 D4

Fountain

B2135 S of Partridge Green

The main dining area in this welcoming 16th-c country pub has now been restored, and during building works, old plaster and panelling have been removed to show ancient brickwork and add to the pub's impressive collection of heavy oak beams. The neatly kept and charmingly rustic tap room on the right has a couple of high-backed wooden cottage armchairs by the log fire in its brick inglenook, two antique polished trestle tables, and fine old flagstones; there are more flagstones in the opened-up snug with heavy beams, simple furniture, and its own inglenook fireplace. Well kept Adnams, Fullers London Pride, Harveys Best and Shepherd Neame Bitter with a guest such as Ringwood Best or Shepherd Neame Spitfire on handpump; freshly squeezed apple juice from their own press in September (proceeds to a children's charity), and decent wines; cribbage, dominoes, shove-ha'penny, and an oak-beamed skittle alley that doubles as a function room. Good popular food includes lunchtime sandwiches (from £3.95), ploughman's (£5.50), and home-cooked ham with free range egg (£6.50), plus salads such as grilled goats cheese with sunflower seeds (from £7.50), steak, mushroom and ale pie or popular smoked haddock and prawns in a cheese sauce (£7.95), evening steaks (from £12.50), puddings like sticky toffee pudding, blackberry and apple pie or hot chocolate fudge cake (£3.95), and imaginative daily specials such as local pheasant and partridge casserole, leek, red onion and parmesan strudel, braised organic beef with mushrooms and shallots, fresh roasted bream stuffed with fennel and orange, or mahi mahi with a roasted pepper and dill dressing (from around £8.95). Service is pleasant and attentive. The prettily planted garden (including raised herb beds for the kitchen) is developing well, and there are plenty of tables on the wooden decking, a growing orchard, and a duck pond. No children inside.

Bar food (12-2, 6.30-9.30; sandwiches only Sun and Mon evenings) ~ Restaurant ~ No credit cards ~ (01403) 710219 ~ Folk music second Weds evening of month ~ Open 11.30-2.30, 6-11; 12-3, 7-10.30 Sun

ASTON Map 3 D3
Bhurtpore

Off A530 SW of Nantwich; in village follow Wrenbury signpost

There are up to a thousand beers a year at this deservedly popular roadside inn, which takes its name from a town in India where local landowner Lord Combermere won a battle. Though frequently dubbed a real ale enthusiasts' dream, there's a lot more to it: this year they've added a selection of fine wines to their already decent wine list, there's a choice of 90 different whiskies, and their menu continues to expand. The cheerful, willing staff remain cool under pressure and are not averse to a chat with customers. Nine handpumps serve a rotating choice of really unusual and very well kept beers, which might include Abbeydale Absolution, Durham Sanctuary, Hydes Dark Mild, Marston Moors Mongrel, Salopian Heaven Sent and Wye Valley Wholesome Stout, as well as European beers such as Bitburger Pils or Timmermans Peach Beer. They also have dozens of good bottled beers, fruit beers (and fruit-flavoured gins) and a changing farm cider or perry. The carpeted lounge bar bears some Indian influences, with an expanding collection of exotic artefacts (one turbaned statue behind the bar proudly sports a pair of Ray-Bans), as well as good local period photographs, and some attractive furniture. Enjoyable reasonably priced bar food includes sandwiches (from £2.25, hot filled baguettes £3.50), filled baked potatoes (from £2.95), locally produced sausages, egg and chips (£4.25), lemon sole fillets with parma ham in a cream and herb sauce (£8.95), steak, kidney and ale pie (£6.95), and very good home-made Indian dishes such as chicken tikka kebabs (£4.25), and a choice of about six curries and baltis (from £6.95). The licensees are constantly adapting the specials board, which might include fillet of bass and spinach in filo pastry with citrus sauce (£10.25), venison casserole (£8.95), a decent vegetarian choice such as leek and cheese cakes in a cheesy mustard sauce (£6.95) or ratatouille (£6.95), and puddings such as rhubarb crumble and local ice cream (from £2.95). At weekends it can get extremely busy, but at lunchtime or earlyish on a weekday evening the atmosphere is cosy and civilised. Tables in the comfortable public bar are reserved for people not eating, and the snug area and dining room are no smoking. Strictly no children. Darts, dominoes, cribbage, pool, TV, fruit machine; readers highly recommend their occasional beer festivals. By the time this book goes to press they will have two new bedrooms.

Bar food (standard food times; not 26 Dec) ~ Restaurant ~ (01270) 780917 ~ No children ~ Folk third Tues of month ~ Open 12-2.30(3 Sat), 6.30-11; 12-3, 7-10.30 Sun; closed 25 Dec and 1 Jan

ASWARBY Map 3 D4
Tally Ho

A15 S of Sleaford (but N of village turn-off)

This handsome, civilised place was built as a farm manager's house for the estate in the 17th c and became an inn in early Victorian times. The bar is more or less divided in two by an entrance lobby stacked full with logs, giving the feel of two little rooms, each with their own stripped stone fireplace, candles on a nice mix of chunky old pine tables and small round cast-iron-framed tables, big country prints on cream walls and big windows; daily papers, piped music. Real ales, appreciated by thirsty locals standing round the bar, include well kept Bass and Batemans XB and a guest such as Brewsters Serendipity on handpump and good house wines. The generous bar food includes soup (£2.75), Lincolnshire sausage (£4.75), ploughman's or filled french bread (£4.95), blackboard specials which might be four cheese tartlet or smoked mackerel pâté (£3.85), Mediterranean vegetable lasagne (£6.25), lambs liver and bacon in red wine gravy, salmon and spinach fishcakes or beef and ale pie (£6.95), chicken pieces in pepper and orange sauce (£7.15), rump steak (£10.50); carefully prepared home-made puddings might include lemon crumble and blackberry sponge (£2.75). Booking might be necessary if you want to eat in the attractive pine-furnished restaurant. Among the fruit trees at the back there are tables. The bedrooms are in a neatly converted back block, formerly the dairy and a barn. Over the road, the pretty estate church, glimpsed through the stately oaks of the park, is worth a visit.

Bar food (12-2.30, 6.30-10) ~ Restaurant ~ (01529) 455205 ~ Children welcome ~ Open 12-3, 6-11(7-10.30 Sun); closed 26 Dec ~ Bedrooms: £35B/£50B

AYCLIFFE Map 3 A3

County

The Green; just off A1(M) junction 59, by A167

Driving past, you could easily mistake this white pub, with its name emblazoned on the walls in big fancy script, as the sort of roadside local best left to the business of neighbourhood wakes, wedding receptions and pigeon club suppers. The reality is very different. Top-notch cooking by its young ex-factory hand chef/landlord (in the process of buying the place as we went to press) now brings diners from far and wide, including heads of government gnawing away at the BSE crisis over a good piece of local beef. A sensibly limited choice of reasonably priced bar food served at lunchtime and in the early evening (until the bistro opens) might include a choice of soups (£3), open sandwiches (£4.50), prawn cocktail (£3.95), sausage and mash or cajun chicken (£7), battered cod (£7.40) and seared salmon with chargrilled vegetables and prawn couscous (£10). Though the ingredients are good solid largely local produce, the style of cooking is light and deft (and all is cooked fresh, so there might be a bit of a wait). The evening bistro menu (best to book) is more elaborate, including dishes such as crab and prawn risotto with lobster sauce (£5.60), warm salad of black pudding, chorizo and spiced apple topped with a soft poached egg (£6.20), grilled leg of lamb steak with Mediterranean vegetable and mint couscous topped with cucumber raita (£13.45) and halibut steak with Welsh rarebit crust, pesto new potatoes and tomato salad (£13.95). Puddings are a high point, and might include lime and lemon cheesecake (£3.95), chocolate torte with Grand Marnier crème anglaise (£4.50) and a regional cheese selection (£5.95). Furnishings in the extended bar and bistro are fresh and modern, definitely geared to grown-up dining, and the minimalist décor gives a light and airy feel, but there's no mistaking the friendly and civilised mood brought by a happy mix of expectation and contentment. Four real ales on handpump include Charles Wells Bombardier, John Smiths Magnet and a couple of guests from brewers such as Daleside and Hambleton, and a good choice of wines by the glass; service too is good. There may be piped music. The green opposite is pretty.

Bar food (12-2, 6-9.30) ~ Restaurant ~ (01325) 312273 ~ Children welcome ~ Open 12-3, 5.30(6.30 Sat)-11; 12-3, 7-10.30 Sun

AYMESTREY Map 1 A5
Riverside Inn

A4110; N off A44 at Mortimer's Cross, W of Leominster

There are picnic-sets by a flowing river, and rustic tables and benches up above in a steep tree-sheltered garden as well as a beautifully sheltered former bowling green behind this idyllically situated black and white timbered inn. It's lovely out here in summer when big overflowing flower pots frame the entrances. In cooler months there's no shortage of warm log fires in the rambling beamed bar with its several cosy areas and good laid-back atmosphere. Décor is drawn from a pleasant mix of periods and styles, with fine antique oak tables and chairs, stripped pine country kitchen tables, fresh flowers, hops strung from a ceiling waggon-wheel, horse tack, a Librairie Romantique poster for Victor Hugo's poems, a cheerful modern print of a plump red toadstool. There's a big restaurant area, shove-ha'penny, cribbage and dominoes. Well kept own-brew ales on handpump include Kingfisher Ale, Jack Snipe and Red Kite; local farm cider in summer and decent house wines. The French chef provides a good mix of daily changing bar food, which might include filled baguettes (from £3.75), soup such as leek and potato or fish (£3.25), wild mushrooms and garlic fried greens with crème fraîche (£8.95), monkfish and mussels in brandy cream sauce, rack of lamb with rosemary jus or duckling breast with savoy cabbage and bacon and bramble sauce (£13.95), a few lunchtime daily specials such as pork and leek sausages, lasagne or fish and chips (£5.95) and puddings such as home-made ice cream (from £3), crème brûlée or fresh lemon tart (£3.95) and a local cheese platter (£4.95). Residents are offered fly-fishing (they have fishing rights on a mile of the River Lugg), and a free taxi service to the start of the Mortimer Trail. It does get busy at weekends, so booking would be wise.

Bar food (standard food times) ~ Restaurant ~ (01568) 708440 ~ Children over 8 in eating area of bar ~ Open 11-11; 12-10.30 Sun ~ Bedrooms: £25(£30S)(£30B)/£40(£50S)(£50B)

BADBY Map 2 A2
Windmill

Village signposted off A361 Daventry—Banbury

From businessmen to walkers, there's a friendly welcome for everyone at this well run, old thatched inn. The atmosphere is relaxed and civilised in the two chatty beamed and flagstoned bars, which have cricketing and rugby pictures, simple country furnishings in good solid wood, and an unusual white woodburning stove in an enormous white-tiled inglenook fireplace. There's also a cosy and comfortable lounge, and pleasant modern hotel facilities for staying guests (an unobtrusive modern extension is well hidden at the back). Good, generous bar food is served promptly by good-natured efficient staff and might include soup (£2.75), sandwiches (from £2.75 to £6.25 for tasty triple-decker ones), potato skins with yoghurt and mint dip (£3.75), crispy whitebait (£4.50), filled jacket potatoes (from £4.50), ploughman's (£5.50), aubergine stuffed with rice and nuts (£6.25), venison burgers with creamy peppercorn sauce (£8.25), fresh crab salad (£9.25), 8oz sirloin steak (£10.50), monkfish provençale (£11.25), duck breast with lime, mango, chilli and ginger glaze (£11.50); puddings (from £3.50). The pleasant restaurant is no smoking. Well kept Bass, Boddingtons, Flowers Original and Wadworths 6X on handpump; dominoes, quiet piped music.

Bar food (standard food times) ~ Restaurant ~ (01327) 702363 ~ Children in eating area of bar and restaurant ~ Open 11.30-3(4 Sat), 5.30-11; 11.30-4, 7-11 Sun ~ Bedrooms: £52.50B/£69B

BARNACK Map 3 E4
Millstone

Millstone Lane; off B1443 SE of Stamford; turn off School Lane near the Fox

Steady and reliable, this well liked old stone-built village local is run by a particularly friendly and accommodating landlord. It's especially popular for its enjoyable food, so much so that you may need to get there early for a seat, even during the week. As well as their famous home-made pies such as steak in ale, chicken and bacon, minted lamb or pork with apple and cider (all £6.95), there might be home-made soup like good carrot and coriander or broccoli and stilton (£2), sandwiches (from £2.95), freshly baked filled baguettes (£3.25), generous pâté (£3.45), ploughman's, stilton and vegetable crumble or liver and bacon hotpot (£6.95), mixed grill (£8.95), and home-made puddings such as white chocolate and rum torte or home-made blackberry crumble (£2.95); on Thursday and Friday, there's fresh fish from Grimsby (battered haddock or plaice, £6.25). Smaller helpings for OAPs, a straightforward children's menu, and maybe marmalades, jams, pickles and fruit cakes for sale with the funds going to a charity. You may find Stone the ancient pub dog sitting motionless on one of the cushioned wall benches in the traditional timbered bar, which is split into comfortably intimate areas, and also has a patterned carpet and high beams weighed down with lots of heavy harness. A little snug displays the memorabilia (including medals from both World Wars) of a former regular. The snug and dining room are no smoking. Beers include consistently well kept Adnams, Everards Old Original and Tiger and an interesting guest on handpump. They also keep a good choice of Gales country wines. In summer the window baskets and window boxes are attractive.

Bar food (standard food times; not Sun evening) ~ Restaurant ~ (01780) 740296 ~ Children in eating area of bar and restaurant ~ Open 11.30-2.30, 5.30(6 Sat)-11; 12-4, 7-10.30 Sun

BARNOLDBY LE BECK Map 3 C5
Ship

Village signposted off A18 Louth—Grimsby

Although this genteel pub, filled with such an amazing collection of Edwardian and Victorian bric-a-brac that it feels a bit like a museum, has changed hands, the new landlord says he doesn't intend to make any real changes. Comfortable dark green plush wall benches with lots of pretty propped up cushions face tables, many booked for dining, and there are heavily stuffed green plush Victorian-looking chairs on a green fleur de lys carpet. Heavy dark-ringed drapes and net curtains swathe the windows, throwing an opaque light on the beautifully laid out nostalgic collection of half remembered things like stand-up telephones, violins, a horn gramophone, bowler and top hats, old rackets, crops and hockey sticks, a lace dress, stuffed birds and animals, and grandmotherly plants in ornate china bowls. Only the piped music is slightly incongruous. Good bar food could include mushrooms with cream and garlic sauce (£3.45), Scotch salmon and prawns (£4.95), beef madras or vegetarian lasagne (£6.95), halibut steak with herb and garlic butter (£9.95) and mixed grill (£10.95) and daily specials (with lots of good fresh fish from Grimsby) such as vegetable stir-fry or stilton and mushroom crêpe (£6.95), lemon sole with salmon and prawns in a cheese sauce, fresh dressed crab or lamb steak with port sauce (£10.95) and puddings such as chocolate and brandy fudge cake or white chocolate crème brûlée (£2.95). Well kept Courage Directors, Castle Eden and Marstons Pedigree on handpump, and an extensive wine list with plenty by the glass. There are a few picnic-sets under pink cocktail umbrellas outside at the back, next to big hanging baskets suspended from stands.

Bar food (12-2, 7-9.30) ~ Restaurant ~ (01472) 822308 ~ Children welcome ~ Open 12-3, 6.30-11(10.30 Sun)

BEESTON Map 3 D4
Victoria

Dovecote Lane, backing on to railway station

Carefully converted from an almost derelict railway hotel, this friendly pub is popular for its imaginative food (with around 10 vegetarian choices a day) and good choice of real ales. The 12 changing well kept ales might include Everards Tiger, Ossett Silver King, Batemans XB, Burton Bridge Summer Ale, Whim Hartington IPA, Castle Rock Hemlock, Dark Star Cascade and Hook Norton Best on handpump; also, two traditional ciders, over a hundred malt whiskies, 20 Irish whiskeys, and half a dozen wines by the glass. The lounge and bar back on to the railway station, and picnic-sets in a pleasant area outside (with new heaters) overlook the platform where trains pass just feet below. The three downstairs rooms in their original long narrow layout have simple solid traditional furnishings, very unfussy décor, stained-glass windows, stripped woodwork and floorboards (woodblock in some rooms), newspapers to read, and a good chatty atmosphere; dominoes, cribbage, piped music. From a daily changing blackboard menu the popular, reasonably priced bar food (served in the no-smoking dining area) might include sandwiches (from £1.40) as well as vegetarian dishes such as Bombay pizza (£5.95), stuffed vine leaves with mozzarella and peppers or asparagus, taleggio and chive tart (£4.95) or Mediterranean platter (£6.95) and other dishes such as Lincolnshire sausages and mash (£5.95), pork kebabs (£6.50), seared salmon fillet with cajun spices (£7.95), Italian lamb meatballs (£6.95) and grilled monkfish and pancetta parcels (£10.50); puddings such as plum tart with amaretto ice cream and hot bananas with dark rum and ice cream (£2.95-£3.50).

Bar food (12-9(8 Sun)) ~ (0115) 925 4049 ~ Children in eating area of bar till 8pm ~ Open 11-11; 12-10.30 Sun

BEETHAM Map 3 B2
Wheatsheaf

Village (and inn) signposted just off A6 S of Milnthorpe

A new licensee has taken over this 16th-c coaching inn, but it remains a friendly place for an enjoyable meal. The opened-up front lounge bar has lots of exposed beams and joists and is decorated in warm ochre shades and gingham fabrics; the main bar is behind on the right, with well kept Jennings Bitter and Cumberland and a changing guest beer on handpump, and a fine choice of New World wines by the glass; there's also a cosy and relaxing smaller room for drinkers, and a roaring log fire. Imaginative, popular food includes good soups such as mushroom and tarragon (£2.95), interesting lunchtime sandwiches (from £3.95), deep-fried herb-crusted camembert on a toasted citrus salad (£4.85), warm salad of confit of duck with a blackcurrant relish (£5.50), crispy filo basket filled with a stir-fry of mushrooms, sweet potatoes and feta cheese (£8.25), chargrilled Barnsley lamb chop with garlic and thyme mash and redcurrant and tomato gravy or Caribbean chicken with lime and coconut (£9.95), and puddings such as sticky fudge and walnut pudding with butterscotch sauce (£4.75); they also offer a two-course lunch (£7.95). Daily newspapers and magazines to read. The upstairs no-smoking dining room is candlelit at night.

Bar food (standard food times) ~ Restaurant ~ (015395) 62123 ~ Children in eating area of bar ~ Open 11-3, 6-11; 12-3, 7-10.30 Sun ~ Bedrooms: £45S/£60B

BERWICK ST JAMES Map 1 C6
Boot

B3083, between A36 and A303 NW of Salisbury

There's a contented cosy atmosphere, a huge winter log fire in the inglenook fireplace at one end, sporting prints over a smaller brick fireplace at the other, and houseplants on the wide window sills in the bar at this attractive flint and stone pub. The flagstoned bar, which has well kept Bass and Wadworths IPA and 6X on handpump, a few well chosen house wines, half a dozen malts and farm cider, is partly carpeted, with a mix of tables, cushioned wheelback chairs, and a few bar stools by the counter. A charming small back no-smoking dining room has a nice mix of dining chairs around the three tables on its blue Chinese carpet, and deep pink walls with an attractively mounted collection of boots. It's a pity we don't get more reports about the very good bar food here, as they use as much local produce as possible, vegetables may come from the garden in season, and there is a good imaginative menu: soup (£3.95), fried camembert with raspberry coulis, seafood salad with lemon and dill mayonnaise or breaded butterfly prawns with sweet chilli sauce (£5.50), fresh fish of the day, twice baked goats cheese soufflé with creamy cheese sauce, chilli or lasagne (£7.95), fried lambs kidneys on apple rösti with cider jus or beef in stilton stew (£8.95), chicken in a white wine, tomato, garlic and black olive sauce with linguini (£10.25), warm salad of smoked pigeon breasts and sautéed potatoes with rémoulade sauce (£10.50) and 10oz sirloin steak (£12.95). Service is very friendly and helpful; maybe unobtrusive piped jazz. The sheltered side lawn, very neatly kept with pretty flowerbeds, has some well spaced picnic-sets.

Bar food (12-2.30, 6.30-9.30(7-9 Sun)) ~ Restaurant ~ (01722) 790243 ~ Children welcome ~ Open 12-3, 6-11(7-10.30 Sun); closed Mon lunchtime, 25, 26 Dec evening

BERWICK ST JOHN Map 1 C6
Talbot

Village signposted from A30 E of Shaftesbury

Harvey the cat has featured in most of the last 10 editions of the *Good Pub Guide*, but this is his first time at this lovely old village pub, just taken over by the former owners of the Cott at Dartington and other Devon institutions. This is a smaller place than their previous pubs, and they are loving the much more hands-on approach they can take here. Very enjoyable freshly prepared bar food from a daily changing blackboard menu might include vegetable and pearl barley broth (£3.50), grilled goats cheese (£4.75), mixed mushroom risotto (£5.95), moussaka and feta cheese salad or sausage and mash (£6.50), rabbit casserole on grainy mustard mash (£6.75), steak and kidney pudding (£6.95), with more substantial evening dishes such as Thai crab cakes with coriander and sweet tomato dressing or wild mushroom tartlet with beetroot and apple salsa (£4.75), duck casserole with black pudding, juniper and orange (£9.95), halibut steamed on a prawn risotto with asparagus and lemon butter (£12.50), fillet steak with roasted onions and red wine sauce (£15.50), and puddings such as apple and almond pudding, chocolate brandy mousse and rhubarb and ginger fool (£3.75). Well kept Bass, Butcombe and Wadworths 6X on handpump, farm cider, fresh juices, and a fine choice of wines. The single long, heavily beamed bar is simply furnished with cushioned solid wall and window seats, spindleback chairs, a high-backed built-in settle at one end, and tables that are candlelit in the evenings. There's a huge inglenook fireplace with a good iron fireback and bread ovens, and nicely shaped heavy black beams and cross-beams with bevelled corners.

Bar food (standard food times) ~ Restaurant ~ (01747) 828222 ~ Children welcome ~ Open 12-2.30, 6.30-11; 12-4 Sun; closed Sun evening, and Mon except bank holidays

BETCHWORTH Map 2 D4
Red Lion

Turn off A25 W of Reigate opp B2032 at roundabout, then after 0.3 miles bear left
into Old Road, towards Buckland

Much changed in the last three years or so, this is now a civilised dining
pub – indeed, almost more restaurant-with-rooms than pub. The light and
airy bar, with a log-effect gas fire and pictures above its panelled dado, has
plenty of tables, with steps down to a stylish new long flagstoned room,
and a dining room, candlelit at night, which strikes some readers as Tuscan
in mood. The good food, served generously, includes sandwiches (from
£3.85), home-made soup (£3.95), deep-fried camembert with cumberland
sauce (£4.75), pâté with chutney (£4.95), ploughman's (£5.25), good steak
and kidney pudding or roast vegetable risotto (£7.95), minted shoulder of
lamb (£9.50), steaks (from £10.95), and daily specials such as parma ham
and mascarpone tartlet with an exotic citrus dressing (£5.95) or salmon
with a cajun crust and mint yoghurt (£10.95). There's particular praise for
puddings (£4.25), like sticky toffee pudding or raspberry cream tartlet;
Sunday lunch is particularly popular. The dining room is no smoking. Well
kept Adnams, Fullers London Pride and Greene King Old Speckled Hen or
Ringwood Best on handpump, good house wines, and charmingly
enthusiastic and helpful waitress service. There may be piped pop music.
Outside are plenty of picnic-sets on a lawn with a play area, and in good
weather tables set for dining on a rose-trellised terrace. The garden backs
on to the village cricket green, and you don't notice the road at the front,
as it's set well below the pub in a tree-lined cutting. We have not yet had
reports from readers on the bedrooms, in a separate new block.

Bar food (all day wkdys; 12-4, 5.30-10(8.45 Sun) Sat) ~ Restaurant ~
(01737) 843336 ~ Children welcome ~ Open 11-11; 12-10.30 Sun; closed
31 Dec-2 Jan ~ Bedrooms: £75S/£85S

BICKLEY MOSS Map 3 D2
Cholmondeley Arms

Cholmondeley; A49 5½ miles N of Whitchurch; the owners would like us to list them under Cholmondeley village, but as this is rarely located on maps we have mentioned the nearest village which appears more often

Very popular with readers for its enjoyable food, this imaginatively converted Victorian building, with a steeply pitched roof, gothic windows and huge old radiators, was the local school until 1982. There's a relaxing informal atmosphere in the cross-shaped high-ceilinged bar, which is filled with eye-catching objects such as old school desks above the bar on a gantry, masses of Victorian pictures (especially portraits and military subjects), and a great stag's head over one of the side arches. There's a mix of seats from cane and bentwood to pews and carved oak settles, and the patterned paper on the shutters matches the curtains. You'll have to book at weekends for the bar food; the menu changes daily but might include home-made courgette soup (£3.25), sandwiches (from £3.95), green mussels grilled with a lobster butter or duck and brandy pâté with cumberland jelly (£4.75), game pie with a puff pastry crust or leek and cheddar soufflé grilled with cheese (£7.95), bass fillets on buttered samphire with a light velouté sauce, rack of lamb with a garlic and thyme sauce or pheasant in an apple and calvados sauce (£9.95), chicken breast with mushroom, Dijon mustard and cream (£9.25), and puddings such as syrup tart and cream or spotted dick and custard (£4.25). Well kept Adnams Bitter, Banks's Mild, Marstons Pedigree, Weetwood Old Dog and a guest such as Timothy Taylors Landlord on handpump. An old blackboard lists 10 or so interesting and often uncommon wines by the glass; big (4-cup) pot of cafetière coffee, teas, and hot chocolate. Comfortable and clean bedrooms are across the old playground in the headmaster's house; there are seats out on a sizeable lawn. Cholmondeley Castle and gardens are close by.

Bar food (12-2.30, 6.30-9.30) ~ Restaurant ~ (01829) 720300 ~ Children in eating area of bar and restaurant ~ Open 11-3, 6.30-11; 12-3, 6.30-10.30 Sun ~ Bedrooms: £45B/£60B

BLACKBROOK Map 2 D4
Plough

On byroad E of A24, parallel to it, between Dorking and Newdigate, just N of the turn E to Leigh

In summer, the white frontage of this neatly kept, comfortable pub is quite a sight with its pretty hanging baskets and window boxes; there are new tables and chairs on the terrace, and a children's Swiss playhouse furnished with little tables and chairs in the secluded garden. Inside, the partly no-smoking red saloon bar has fresh flowers on its tables and on the window sills of its large linen-curtained windows, and down some steps, the public bar has brass-topped treadle tables, a formidable collection of ties, old saws on the ceiling, and bottles and flat irons; piped music, shove-ha'penny, and cribbage. As well as reasonably priced and enjoyable lunchtime bar snacks such as taramasalata or hummus with pitta bread (£3.25), local sausages (£3.95), filled baked potatoes (from £3.95), ploughman's (£4.75), and toasted bagels (from £4.95), there are daily specials such as spinach, mushroom and sweetcorn chowder (£2.75), tartlet of ratatouille and gruyère (£3.75), terrine of game with cranberry sauce (£3.95), vegetable paella (£5.95), deep-fried fillets of cod or lasagne (£6.95), roast bacon-wrapped breast of guinea fowl on couscous with orange and lemon sauce (£9.45), and steaks (from £11.95), and puddings such as apple and cranberry pie, spiced bread and butter pudding or strawberry meringue sundae (£3.45); they hold four popular curry evenings a year. Well kept Badger Best, Old Ale, and Tanglefoot, Gribble Inn Fursty Ferret, and Badger K & B Sussex on handpump, 16 wines by the glass, and several ports; friendly and efficient service from smartly dressed staff. The countryside around here is particularly good for colourful spring and summer walks through the oak woods. The pub usually hosts an atmospheric carol concert the Sunday before Christmas. More reports please.

Bar food (standard food times; not Mon evening) ~ (01306) 886603 ~ Children welcome till 9pm ~ Open 11-2.30(3 Sat), 6-11; 12-3, 7-10.30 Sun; closed 25 and 26 Dec, 1 Jan

BOUGH BEECH Map 2 D4
Wheatsheaf
B2027, S of reservoir

There's a lovely bustling and friendly atmosphere in this fine old pub, and the landlady and her staff make both visitors and locals most welcome; there are also thoughtful touches like piles of smart magazines to read, nice nibbles, chestnuts to roast in winter, summer Pimms and mulled wine in winter. The neat central bar and the long bar (with an attractive old settle carved with wheatsheaves, shove-ha'penny, dominoes, and board games) have unusually high ceilings with lofty oak timbers, a screen of standing timbers and a revealed king post. Divided from the central bar by two more rows of standing timbers – one formerly an outside wall to the building – is the snug, and another bar. Other similarly aged features include a piece of 1607 graffiti, 'Foxy Galumpy', thought to have been a whimsical local squire. There are quite a few horns and heads, as well as a sword from Fiji, crocodiles, stuffed birds, swordfish spears, and the only matapee in the south of England on the walls and above the massive stone fireplaces. The menu includes mozzarella and tomato crostini with rocket pesto, spiced chicken and plum sauce crostini, macaroni cheese and ploughman's (all £5.95), three cheese pasta with garlic bread or vegetable lasagne (£6.95), fillet of smoked haddock with spinach, mash and citrus sauce (£7.95), Thai or Indian curry, cold smoked chicken with grapefruit salad with citrus mayonnaise or lambs liver with bacon, black pudding and mash (all £8.95), and puddings like ginger pudding with brandy and ginger wine sauce, chocolate pecan tart or blackberry and apple pie. Well kept Butcombe Bitter, Fullers London Pride, Greene King Old Speckled Hen, Harveys Sussex, and Shepherd Neame Master Brew on handpump, good wines including local wine, and several malt whiskies. There's a rustic cottage, plenty of seats, and flowerbeds and fruit trees in the sheltered side and back gardens. The pub is thought to have started life as a hunting lodge belonging to Henry V.

Bar food (12-10) ~ (01732) 700254 ~ Children in eating area of bar ~ Folk and country Weds 8.30 ~ Open 11-11; 12-10.30 Sun

BRAMFIELD Map 2 A6

Queens Head

The Street; A144 S of Halesworth

Over half the dishes on the menu at this deservedly popular old pub have received an organic authentification. Although much emphasis is placed on the imaginative food, there are plenty of drinking locals, and friendly, helpful licensees to create a relaxed, bustling atmosphere. The high-raftered lounge bar has scrubbed pine tables, a good log fire in its impressive fireplace, and a sprinkling of farm tools on the walls; a separate no-smoking side bar has light wood furnishings. Delicious dishes might include sandwiches, potato and fresh lovage or celery soup (£3.25), dates wrapped in bacon on a mild mustard sauce (£4.15), ceviche of fresh mackerel and sardine fillets (£4.25), mushroom and fresh herb omelette with exotic leaf, bean and apple salad (£5.50), chicken, leek and bacon crumble or steak, kidney and mushroom in ale pie (£7.25), local venison and wild boar sausages with onion gravy (£7.95), lamb shank in red wine with garlic mash (£13.95), daily specials such as grilled goats cheese on a roast beetroot and walnut salad (£4.50) and whole fresh red snapper baked in a parcel with orange and garlic (£9.95), and home-made puddings like rhubarb crumble ice cream, wild strawberry sorbet, chocolate and Cointreau pot or sticky toffee pudding (from £2.95). They keep a good English cheeseboard (£3.75), and good bread comes with nice unsalted butter. Good, polite service (real linen napkins), well kept Adnams Bitter and Broadside, half a dozen good wines by the glass, home-made elderflower cordial, and local apple juices and organic wines and cider.

Bar food (12-2, 6.30-10(7-9 Sun)) ~ (01986) 784214 ~ Children in eating area of bar ~ Open 11.45-2.30, 6.30-11; 12-3, 7-10.30 Sun; closed 25 Dec evening, 26 Dec

BRANCASTER STAITHE Map 3 D5
White Horse
A149 E of Hunstanton

The mussels, samphire, cockles and oysters they serve at this seaside pub are all collected from the bottom of the garden, which gives on to saltings and a sea channel. Given the unassuming exterior of this place you'd never guess what was in store for you inside, let alone the lovely views. It's an airy open-plan bistro-style inn with big windows, solid stripped tables with country chairs and pews on the mainly stripped wood floors, and cream walls packed with interesting local black and white photographs. Stools line a handsome counter manned by friendly young staff, and there's a particularly easy-going relaxed atmosphere here. You get the lovely views of the Norfolk Coastal Path, tidal marsh and Scolt Head Island beyond from tables (laid for eating) by great picture windows round to the side and back of the bar. The airy dining conservatory with sun deck and terrace enjoys the same view. One dining area is no smoking. Well kept Adnams, Greene King IPA and Abbot, Woodfordes Wherry and a guest such as Black Sheep on handpump, 20 malt whiskies and about a dozen wines by the glass from an extensive and thoughtful wine list; bar billiards. The menu changes twice a day and is extremely good. At lunchtime it might include home-made soup (from £2.50), moules marinières (£4.65/£8.50), toasted goats cheese with oven roasted plum tomatoes and pesto dressing (£4.95), seared scallops with wilted red chard and caper oil (£7.75), pork and leek sausages (£7.95), battered whiting (£8.15), braised ling with chick-pea and red chard cream (£9.50) and fried chicken breast with wild mushroom cream (£9.75). Evening dishes may be a touch more expensive: grilled bass with roasted plum tomato or rib-eye steak with warm tomato and onion salad (£12.95) and grilled halibut with house-made squid ink linguini, spinach and tomatoes (£13.25). Very well designed bedrooms each have their own outside terrace and view.

Bar food (standard food times; not Sat evening) ~ Restaurant ~ (01485) 210262 ~ Children welcome ~ Live folk or Irish Fri evening ~ Open 11-11; 12-10.30 Sun; closed 25 Dec evening ~ Bedrooms: £60B/£90B

BRANSCOMBE Map 1 D4
Masons Arms

Main Street; signposted off A3052 Sidmouth—Seaton

As well as comfortable bedrooms in this very popular inn, they now have three cottages across the road which can be let with full hotel facilities or as self-catering units. There's a hundred-year-old photograph up on the wall featuring the inn and these cottages and one proudly bears a sign 'Devon Constabulary' – so no after-hours drinking in those days. The rambling low-beamed main bar has a massive central hearth in front of the roaring log fire (spit roasts on Tuesday and Sunday lunch and Friday evenings), windsor chairs and settles, and a good bustling atmosphere. The no-smoking Old Worthies bar has a slate floor, a fireplace with a two-sided woodburning stove, and woodwork that has been stripped back to the original pine. The no-smoking restaurant (warmed by one side of the woodburning stove) is stripped back to dressed stone in parts, and is used as bar space on busy lunchtimes. Under the new head chef, they now bake much of their bread and make their own jams, chutneys, and pickles. Good bar food includes soups such as roasted tomato and fennel (£2.95), a terrine of pasta and spinach wrapped in prosciutto ham (£4.25), moules marinières (£5.25), their own oak smoked salmon with horseradish cream (£6.50), deep-fried cod in beer batter (£7.95), grilled cumberland sausage with spring onion mash and a redcurrant reduction (£8.75), well liked steak and kidney pudding (£9.25), sautéed local crab cakes with lemon mayonnaise (£9.50), crispy roasted duckling on a potato and celeriac rösti and caramelised parsnips with an orange sauce and spiced plum chutney (£13.75), and daily specials such as smoked haddock terrine (£4.75), grilled herrings (£7.25), fillet of pork with oriental-style vegetables (£10.50), and whole grilled bass stuffed with baby spinach and garlic (£12.95); puddings like sherry trifle, crème brûlée or apple crumble. Well kept Bass, Otter Ale and Bitter, and two guest beers on handpump; they hold a beer festival in July and keep 30 malt whiskies, 12 wines by the glass, and farm cider; polite, attentive staff. Darts, shove-ha'penny, dominoes, and skittle alley. Outside, the quiet flower-filled front terrace has tables with little thatched roofs, extending into a side garden.

Bar food (standard food times) ~ Restaurant ~ (01297) 680300 ~ Children welcome but must be well behaved ~ Open 11-11; 12-10.30 Sun; 11-3, 6-11 in winter ~ Bedrooms: £22/£44(£72S)(£60B)

BRANSFORD Map 1 A5

Bear & Ragged Staff

Off A4103 SW of Worcester; Station Road

It's probably best to book a table if you want to eat at this stylish but welcoming place; there's quite an emphasis on the dining side, with proper tablecloths, linen napkins, and fresh flowers on the tables. Changing bar food might include soup (£3.25), lunchtime filled rolls (from £3.95), five-cheese tortellini baked in tomato sauce (£5.65), cajun spiced salmon fillet or grilled chicken breast with potato scones (£6.50), duck confit with creamy mash and red wine sauce (£6.75) and specials such as avocado, crab and tomato pancake (£5.50), roast shallot and woodland mushroom tart (£8.95) and roast monkfish in parma ham (£12.95) with puddings such as Thai spiced poached pear with caramelised pineapple or rhubarb tart with crunchy hazelnut topping (£3.75). There are fine views over rolling country from the cheerful interconnecting rooms (one room in the restaurant is no smoking) as well as some seats by an open fire, and well kept Bass and Highgate Special on handpump; a good range of wines (mainly New World ones), lots of malt whiskies, and quite a few brandies and liqueurs; cribbage, dominoes, and piped music.

Bar food (standard food times) ~ Restaurant ~ (01886) 833399 ~ Children welcome in eating area of bar and restaurant till 9pm ~ Jazz first Sun evening of month ~ Open 12-2.30, 6-11; 12-2.30, 7-10.30 Sun

BREARTON Map 3 B3
Malt Shovel

Village signposted off A61 N of Harrogate

As they don't take bookings (but there is a waiting list system) in this especially popular, 16th-c village pub, you do have to arrive at opening time to be sure of a seat. Several heavily-beamed rooms radiate from the attractive linenfold oak bar counter with plush-cushioned seats and a mix of tables, an ancient oak partition wall, tankards and horsebrasses, both real and gas fires, and paintings by local artists (for sale) and lively hunting prints on the walls. Quite a choice of decent, reasonably priced bar food might include sandwiches, mussels in white wine, garlic and herbs (£3.95), good ham and blue wensleydale tart, nut roast with pesto cream sauce or ploughman's (£5.25), steak in ale pie (£6.25), sausages and mash or pheasant, rabbit and hare pie (£6.50), seafood au gratin, liver, bacon and black pudding or warm chicken salad with lemon dressing (£6.95), tuna with warm potato salad and lemon and caper dressing (£7.95), chargrilled steaks (from £8.50), and puddings such as apple and bramble crumble or sticky toffee pudding (£2.75). Well kept Black Sheep Bitter, Daleside Nightjar, and Durham Magus, and two guests such as Goose Eye Brontë or Rudgate Ruby Mild on handpump, real cider, 30 malt whiskies, and a small but interesting and reasonably priced wine list (they will serve any wine by the glass); they serve their house coffee (and a guest coffee) in cafetières. Darts, shove-ha'penny, cribbage, and dominoes. You can eat outside on the small terrace on all but the coldest of days as they have outdoor heaters; there are more tables on the grass. This is an attractive spot off the beaten track, yet handy for Harrogate and Knaresborough.

Bar food (standard food times; not Sun evening, not Mon) ~ No credit cards ~ (01423) 862929 ~ Children welcome ~ Open 12-2.30, 6.45-11; 6.30-10.30 Sun; closed Mon

BRIDGNORTH Map 3 E3
Bear
Northgate (B4373)

At lunchtime, a good crowd of locals and visitors gathers to enjoy the interesting daily specials in this attractive cream-painted former coaching inn: chive and wild mushroom risotto with fresh parmesan topping (£5), blue cheese soufflé with sautéed potatoes (£5.20), mushroom and chicken crêpes with cream sauce (£5.80), seared tuna steak on Thai-style salad with ginger dressing or exotic stir-fried pineapple chicken with toasted cashews (£6), and salmon and ginger fishcakes on creamed spinach with tomato coulis (£6.20); they also offer sandwiches (from £1.60), soup (£2.50), ploughman's or ham and egg (£4.25), and rump steak (£5.75), and Thursday evening gourmet dinners when the lounge is transformed into a restaurant with table service. Booking is essential for this; juke box, dogs welcome. There are two unpretentious carpeted bars: on the left of the wide entrance hall, brocaded wall banquettes, small cushioned wheelback chairs, whisky-water jugs hanging from the low joists, gas-type wall lamps; on the right, rather similar furnishings, with the addition of a nice old oak settle and one or two more modern ones, more elbow chairs, a few brasses, and local memorabilia from antique sale and tax notices to small but interesting photographs of the town. From here, french windows open on to a small sheltered lawn with picnic-sets. There's a comfortable and friendly bustle, helped along by well kept ales on handpump from the central servery, including Bathams Best, Boddingtons, Hobsons, Holdens, and a guest such as Salopian Golden Thread or Timothy Taylors Landlord, and several wines by the glass.

Bar food (lunchtime only (except Thurs evening); not Sun) ~ No credit cards ~ (01746) 763250 ~ Children in eating area of bar ~ Open 11(10.30 Sat)-2.30(3 Sat), 5-11; 12-3, 7-10.30 Sun ~ Bedrooms: £35S/£52B

BRIG O' TURK Map 4 D2
Byre

A821 Callander—Trossachs, just outside village

Set in a lovely secluded spot on the edge of a network of forest and lochside tracks in the Queen Elizabeth Forest Park, this carefully converted pub (its name means cowshed) is ideally situated for walking, cycling, and fishing. Inside, the beamed bar is cosy and spotless, with paintings and old photographs of the area, some decorative plates, comfortable brass-studded black dining chairs, an open fire, and rugs on the stone and composition floor. Good, enjoyable, interesting bar food includes french onion soup with thyme, garlic and parmesan shavings (£2.95; cullen skink £3.25), coarse game terrine on warm brioche and orange chutney (£3.25), steamed Shetland mussels with parsley, shallots, garlic and white wine (£4.25), Toulouse sausages on spring onion mash and red wine jus (£7.95), chicken marinated with spices and fried with peppers, tomatoes and oregano on tagliatelle (£8.50), cod fillet with a mint and chilli crust on couscous (£8.95), game pie or slow roasted pork hock on pinto beans, grilled chorizo and plum tomato sauce (£9.50), and puddings such as pear and ginger strudel or pecan pie (from £2.95); friendly, helpful service. The more elaborate menu in the no-smoking restaurant is popular in the evenings – it's worth booking then. Well kept Heather Fraoch Heather Ale on handpump, and several malt whiskies; traditional Scottish piped music. There are tables under parasols outside.

Bar food (12-2, 6-9) ~ Restaurant ~ (01877) 376292 ~ Children in eating area of bar and restaurant ~ Open 12-3, 6-11(12 Fri and Sat); 12-11 Sun; closed Mon

BROADHEMBURY Map 1 D4
Drewe Arms

Signposted off A373 Cullompton—Honiton

One of the things that makes this marvellous place so special – apart
from the delicious fish dishes – is the way the hard-working licensees
have managed to create a friendly, chatty atmosphere in which anyone
walking in for just a drink would not feel remotely awkward. The bar has
a proper pubby feel, neatly carved beams in its high ceiling, and
handsome stone-mullioned windows (one with a small carved
roundabout horse), and on the left, a high-backed stripped settle
separates off a little room with flowers on the three sturdy country tables,
plank-panelled walls painted brown below and yellow above with
attractive engravings and prints, and a big black-painted fireplace with
bric-a-brac on a high mantelpiece; some wood carvings, walking sticks,
and framed watercolours for sale. The flagstone entry has a narrow
corridor of a room by the servery with a couple of tables, and the cellar
bar has simple pews on the stone floor; the dining room is no smoking.
Most people do come to enjoy the unfailingly good food: open
sandwiches (from £5.25; gravadlax £5.75; sirloin steak and melted
stilton £6.95), daily specials such as spicy tomato soup (£5), griddled
sardines (£7 small helping, £9 large helping), smoked haddock and stilton
rarebit (£7 small helping, £10.50 large helping), wing of skate with black
butter and capers (£11), fillet of brill with horseradish hollandaise
(£11.50), sea bream with orange and chilli (£12.50), fillet of beef with
pesto (£16), whole lobster (£18.50), and puddings such as spiced pears
with stem ginger ice cream or rhubarb compote with vanilla ice cream
(£4.50); they also offer a three-course meal (£25.25) with choices such as
marinated herring with a glass of aquavit, fillet of turbot, and St-Emilion
chocolate pudding. Best to book to be sure of a table. Well kept Otter
Bitter, Ale, Bright and Head tapped from the cask, and a very good wine
list laid out extremely helpfully – including 12 by the glass; shove-
ha'penny, dominoes and cribbage. There are picnic-sets in the lovely
garden, which has a lawn stretching back under the shadow of chestnut
trees towards a church with its singularly melodious hour-bell. Thatched
and very pretty, the 15th-c pub is in a charming village of similar cream-
coloured cottages.

Bar food (standard food times; not Sun evening) ~ Restaurant ~ (01404)
841267 ~ Well behaved children in eating area of bar and in restaurant ~
Open 11-3, 6-11; 12-3 Sun; closed Sun evening, 31 Dec

BUNBURY Map 3 D3
Dysart Arms

Bowes Gate Road; village signposted off A51 NW of Nantwich; and from A49 S of
Tarporley – coming this way, coming in on northernmost village access road, bear
left in village centre

Although this friendly, cheerful pub is popular for its good food, it's a nice
place to come just for a drink. The tables on the terrace and in the
immaculately kept, slightly elevated garden are very pleasant in summer,
with views of the splendid church at the end of the picturesque village, and
the distant Peckforton Hills beyond. Inside, nicely laid out airy spaces
ramble around a pleasantly lit central bar. Under deep Venetian-red
ceilings, the knocked-through cream-walled rooms have red and black tiles,
some stripped boards and some carpet, a comfortable variety of well
spaced big sturdy wooden tables and chairs, a couple of tall bookcases,
some carefully chosen bric-a-brac, properly lit pictures and warming fires
in winter. One area is no smoking, and they have dominoes. They've
lowered the ceiling in the more restauranty end room (with its book-lined
back wall), and there are lots of plants on the window sills. Interesting food
from a changing menu might include home-made soup (£3.25), sandwiches
(from £3.75), grilled bruschetta of goats cheese topped with walnut
crumble on a beetroot and chive salad (£4.95), sautéed tiger prawns with
tomato salsa and ciabatta bread (£5.95), local sausages with mash and
onion gravy (£7.95), salmon fillet teriyaki on roasted asparagus (£10.95),
turkey escalope dusted with paprika on linguini with creamy mustard
sauce, shoulder of lamb with a red wine and rosemary sauce (£10.95) and
well liked puddings such as baked vanilla cheesecake, apple pie or
raspberry crème brûlée with shortbread biscuits (£3.75) as well as a good,
changing selection of cheeses. Well kept Boddingtons and Timothy Taylors
Landlord, and a couple of guests such as Weetwood Eastgate and Yorks
Yorkshire Terrier on handpump, good interesting wines by the glass. The
staff are friendly and efficient; it's part of the small pub group which
includes the Grosvenor Arms at Aldford.

*Bar food (12-2.15, 6-9.30; 12-9.30(9 Sun)Sat) ~ (01829) 260183 ~ Under
10s in eating area of bar, and only till 6pm ~ Open 11-11; 12-10.30 Sun*

BURFORD Map 1 B6
Lamb

Sheep Street; A40 W of Oxford

This consistently popular, classic 15th-c Cotswold stone inn impresses readers with its courteous service, well cooked food and timeless atmosphere – one reader writes that it's still as good as when he visited it fifty years ago. The roomy beamed main lounge is charmingly traditional, with distinguished old seats including a chintzy high-winged settle, ancient cushioned wooden armchairs, and seats built into its stone-mullioned windows, bunches of flowers on polished oak and elm tables, oriental rugs on the wide flagstones and polished oak floorboards, and a winter log fire under its fine mantelpiece. Also, a writing desk and grandfather clock, and eye-catching pictures, shelves of plates and other antique decorations. The public bar has high-backed settles and old chairs on flagstones in front of its fire. It's best to get there early if you want a table in the bar where enjoyable (though not cheap) daily changing bar food includes sandwiches or filled baguettes (from £3.50), home-made soup (£3.75), ploughman's (£5.75), coarse veal and quail pâté (£5.95), sautéed chicken livers with bacon and caramelised onions (£7.50), fresh grilled sardine fillets with creamed spinach sauce or wild mushroom risotto (£7.95) and lamb and mint sausages (£9); on Sundays there are proper roasts but no bar meals. They stick quite rigidly to food service times; the peaceful formal restaurant is no smoking. Well kept Hook Norton Best, Wadworths 6X and a guest such as Badger IPA are dispensed from an antique handpump beer engine in a glassed-in cubicle (you'll be given the choice between straight glass or handle when you order); good wines. A pretty terrace leads down to small neatly kept lawns surrounded by flowers, flowering shrubs and small trees, and the garden itself is a real suntrap enclosed as it is by the warm stone of the surrounding buildings.

Bar food (lunchtime only; not Sun) ~ Restaurant (evenings; Sun lunch) ~ (01993) 823155 ~ Children welcome ~ Open 11-2.30, 6-11; 12-3, 7-10.30 Sun; closed 25 and 26 Dec ~ Bedrooms: £70B/£115B

BURLTON Map 3 D2
Burlton Inn
A528 Shrewsbury—Ellesmere, near junction with B4397

This is a smashing place, very well run by the particularly friendly and helpful licensees, and with super new bedrooms and popular, imaginative food. Everything in the three fresh-feeling cottagey connecting rooms seems meticulously arranged and cared for, from the flower displays in the brick fireplace or beside the neatly curtained windows, to the piles of *Country Living* and interior design magazines left seemingly casually in the corner. There are a few racing prints, spurs and brasses on the walls, and open fires in winter; dominoes and cribbage. Good bar food such as home-made soup (£3.25), chicken liver and mushroom pâté with a red onion and apple marmalade (£5.25), a trio of Italian cold meats with sharp apricot chutney (£5.50), hot prawn pot with a cream and wine sauce topped with parmesan and gruyère (£5.95), steak and kidney in ale pie (£7.50), ricotta, feta and vine leaf tart with a tomato and basil relish (£8.75), Thai salmon topped with crème fraîche and sesame-dressed leaves (£9.50), fettuccine with scallops and smoked salmon in a cream and white wine sauce (£12.50), and steaks (from £12.50), with daily specials like grilled halloumi cheese with tomato on a ciabatta croûte and Mediterranean salad (£8.50), fresh dressed crab with cucumber and dill mayonnaise (£8.95), supreme of chicken stuffed with goats cheese and honey glazed or fresh fillet of grilled plaice topped with anchovy butter (£9.50). They have up to a dozen home-made puddings such as white chocolate cheesecake with a sharp raspberry coulis, sticky toffee pudding, crème caramel or apricot egg custard tart (£3.75); cheerful service. Well kept Banks's and three guests such as Batemans XXXB, Jennings Cocker Hoop, and Woods Shropshire Lad on handpump. There are tables on a small lawn behind, with more on a strip of grass beyond the car park, and smart wooden furniture on the pleasant terrace. The pub sign is a reminder of the days when this was known as the Cross Keys; dogs welcome.

Bar food (12-2, 6.30-9.45(7-9.30 Sun); limited menu Mon lunchtime) ~ (01939) 270284 ~ Well behaved children in eating area of bar ~ Open 11-3, 6-11; 12-3.30, 7-10.30 Sun; closed bank hol Mon lunchtimes; evening 25 Dec, 26 Dec ~ Bedrooms: £45B/£70B

BURNHAM MARKET Map 3 D5

Hoste Arms

The Green (B1155)

This civilised but informally smart 17th-c hotel is a fine example of how good food, accommodation and a little town local can be offered in one place. The boldly decorated bars are nice and pubby with massive log fires and are enjoyed by a friendly muddle of gentry, farmers, fishermen and shoppers. The panelled bar on the right has a series of watercolours showing scenes from local walks, there's a bow-windowed bar on the left, a nice sitting room, a little art gallery in the staircase area, and well kept Greene King IPA and Abbot and Woodfordes Wherry and Nelson's Revenge on handpump, a good wine list with plenty of big names including champagne by the glass, a decent choice of malt whiskies, and freshly squeezed orange juice. Imaginative, highly enjoyable food includes sandwiches, soup (£3.25), sticky pork salad with mango and Namm Jim dressing (£4.95), tempura black pudding with poached egg and devilled sauce (£5.25), dressed Cromer crab with chicory and french bean salad (£5.95), fried lambs liver with mustard mash or grilled red mullet with pasta tossed in a herb cream (£6.95), seared tuna with oriental vegetables and hoi sin sauce (£9.95), whole lemon sole with crushed potatoes and soft herb butter emulsion (£11.75), honey glazed duck breast, celeriac purée and provençale sauce (£12.25), and crisp fried bass on fennel, wild rice and sweet pea dressing (£13.75). A pleasant walled garden at the back has tables on a terrace.

Bar food (standard food times) ~ Restaurant ~ (01328) 738777 ~ Children welcome away from bar area ~ Open 11-11; 12-10.30 Sun ~ Bedrooms: £66S/£90B

CAMBRIDGE Map 2 A4
Cambridge Blue

85 Gwydir Street

Totally no smoking and completely free of piped music, this quiet backstreet pub is run in the attractively distinctive and friendly style of the couple who made a runaway success of the Free Press in Cambridge a couple of years ago. Its two simple uncluttered rooms have simple, old-fashioned bare-boards-style furnishings with candles on the tables, a big collection of oars and so many rowing photographs that you feel you're browsing through someone's private family album. Beers are picked from interesting, mostly East Anglian but sometimes distantly located small breweries such as Iceni, Hobsons, Milton and Potton with a few from more usual brewers such as Adnams, Nethergate, Woodfordes. There's a decent choice of wines and malt whiskies. Good value, generous home-made food is served in the attractive little conservatory dining area, and might include filled ciabattas (from £2.50), two home-made soups (£2.95), a cold table with game or picnic pies, nut roast, various quiches, and so forth (from £4.25), chilli (£4.75), chicken or vegetable burritos (£5), daily specials such as navarin of lamb or cod and lime leaf pie (£4.75), and puddings such as treacle tart or apricot crumble (£1.95). The surprisingly large back garden is home to a couple of rabbits and a boules pitch.

Bar food (12-2.30, 6-9.30) ~ (01223) 361382 ~ Children welcome in conservatory till 9pm ~ Open 12-2.30(3 Sat), 6-11; 12-3, 6-10.30 Sun; closed evening 25 Dec

CARTHORPE Map 3 B3
Fox & Hounds

Village signposted from A1 N of Ripon, via B6285

With friendly, attentive staff, a fine wine list, and particularly good, enjoyable food, it is not surprising that this neatly kept, extended dining pub is doing so well; to be sure of a table it's best to book (particularly at weekends). Served by well trained staff, the interesting dishes might include a choice of home-made soups (£2.65), black pudding with caramelised apple and onion marmalade (£3.95), smoked trout fillets with horseradish sauce (£4.45), chicken breast filled with coverdale cheese in a creamy sauce (£8.95), poached Scottish salmon with hollandaise sauce (£9.25), roast rack of lamb on a blackcurrant croûton with redcurrant gravy (£11.95), and half a roasted Gressingham duckling with orange sauce, parsley and thyme stuffing and apple sauce (£12.95), with daily specials like fresh salmon fishcakes (£3.95), duck-filled filo pastry parcels with plum sauce (£4.95), steak and kidney pie (£7.95), prawn curry (£8.95), baked haddock with a crispy crumb crust (£9.25), and braised lamb shank with root vegetable purée or whole dressed fresh Whitby crab (£9.95), and puddings such as white chocolate cheesecake with a dark chocolate ice cream or sticky ginger sponge pudding with ginger wine and brandy sauce (£3.75). They do offer sandwiches, and three-course Sunday lunch (£11.95; children £6.95). There are some theatrical memorabilia in the corridors, and the cosy L-shaped bar has quite a few mistily evocative Victorian photographs of Whitby, a couple of nice seats by the larger of its two log fires, plush button-back built-in wall banquettes and chairs, plates on stripped beams, and some limed panelling; piped light classical music. An attractive high-raftered no-smoking restaurant leads off with lots of neatly black-painted farm and smithy tools. Well kept John Smiths Bitter on handpump, and from their extensive list they will open any wine for you just to have a glass.

Bar food (standard food times; not Mon) ~ Restaurant ~ (01845) 567433 ~ Children welcome ~ Open 12-2.30, 7-11(10.30 Sun); closed Mon; first full week of New Year

CASTERTON Map 3 B3
Pheasant

A683 about a mile N of junction with A65, by Kirkby Lonsdale; OS sheet 97 map
reference 633796

The licensees of this civilised inn work very hard to ensure that – despite
the fact that it is a pleasant place to stay overnight and the food is good
and imaginative – they remain a proper pub with a relaxed, chatty
atmosphere and a warm welcome for both the friendly crowd of locals and
for the many visitors. The neatly kept and attractively modernised beamed
rooms of the main bar have padded wheelback chairs, plush wall settles,
newspapers and magazines to read, a woodburning stove surrounded by
brass ornaments in a nicely arched bare stone fireplace with polished brass
hood, and well kept Theakstons Bitter and Old Peculier and guests such as
Black Sheep Bitter, Dent Bitter or Wye Valley Bitter on handpump; over 30
malt whiskies, and a good wine list offering 12 by the glass. There's a
further room (which is no smoking) across the passage with a piano. Good
bar food includes home-made soup (£2.50), lunchtime sandwiches (from
£2.75) and smoked salmon and scrambled eggs or ploughman's (£5.95),
home-made Chinese vegetable spring rolls with a mild chilli dip (£4.95),
local cumberland sausage with apple and sultana chutney (£6.75), beef in
ale pie or spinach, feta cheese and mushroom strudel with salsa sauce
(£6.95), Aberdeen Angus steaks (from £12.95), and daily specials such as
creamed mushrooms with chives topped with herbed crumbs and oven
baked (£4.25), dressed crab with mango mayonnaise (£4.95), roast leg of
lamb with minted gravy and roasted vegetables (£7.95), guinea fowl with a
rich red wine and mushroom sauce (£8.95), and seafood mixed grill
(salmon, tuna, halibut, swordfish and crevettes £13.95); hearty breakfasts.
The restaurant is no smoking. Darts, dominoes, chess, cards, draughts,
piped music, and weekly winter quiz evenings. There are some tables with
cocktail parasols outside by the road, with more in the pleasant garden.
The nearby church (built for the girls' school of Brontë fame here) has
some attractive Pre-Raphaelite stained glass and paintings. Dogs welcome.

*Bar food (standard food times) ~ Restaurant ~ (015242) 71230 ~ Children
welcome ~ Open 11-3, 6-11(10.30 Sun) ~ Bedrooms: £40B/£72B*

CASTLE BYTHAM Map 3 D4
Castle Inn

Village signposted off A1 Stamford—Grantham, or off B1176 N of Stamford; High
Street

The thriving village atmosphere and cheerfully welcoming service
(everyone's 'dearie', 'sweetie', 'my darling') put a smile on your face almost
as soon as you step through the door here. The bar, cosily lit with table
lamps and soft wall lights, has some small dark brown plush button-back
banquettes and a mix of other seats, lots of brass and copper toasting
forks, tongs, candlesticks, jugs and pots gleaming around the log fire,
horsebrasses on the black beams and joists, and a few farm tools, antlers
and heavy horse tack on the stripped stone walls. Bow windows look down
over the village (which is attractive) to rolling countryside beyond. Robust
home cooking is a high point. The menu includes soup (£2.95), sandwiches
(from £3.25), hot smoked mackerel with horseradish sauce (£3.95), crispy
Thai-style prawns (£4.25), chicken curry or steak and kidney pie with suet
crust (£6.25), ham and mushroom tagliatelle (£6.50), grilled lamb cutlets
(£7.50), salmon in asparagus and lobster sauce (£8.25), and puddings
(£3.50). Main dishes come with six or seven carefully cooked vegetables –
their sauté potatoes are particularly good. Well kept real ales such as
Adnams Best, Boddingtons, Oakham JHB and Shepherd Neame Bishops
Finger on handpump; efficient cheerful service even on very busy nights;
may be piped pop music. A back dining area on the left, with Regency-
striped pink wallpaper and a collection of china and other pigs, is no
smoking, and their Christmas decorations can be rather special. There are
metal tables on a little back terrace, and they have CCTV for parked cars.

*Bar food (12-2, 6.30-10) ~ Restaurant ~ (01780) 410504 ~ Children in
restaurant ~ Open 12-2, 6.30-11(10.30 Sun); closed Mon*

CASTOR Map 3 E5
Fitzwilliam Arms

Village signposted off A47 just W of Peterborough

Recently taken over by the Cheesemans this thatched stone building has been very attractively reworked as a rather unusual dining pub. The most striking feature is towards the far end, where the foody heart of the pub consists of a smart free-standing green-enamelled cooker, a cabinet of choice meats and fish waiting for the chef-manager's deft chopping and griddling, a shellfish bar with several types of Iranian caviar as well as oysters and so forth, and even a lobster tank. Beyond here, a no-smoking room has a striking combination of finely detailed and interesting Mogul-style Indian pictures with elegant spindly black metal furniture, and this somewhat esoteric note echoes elsewhere in the pub's long pleasantly divided bar: Indonesian-style heavy metal and hardwood tables among more orthodox pub ones, some silvery alloy café tables and chairs alongside conventional seats. Well kept Adnams, Brewsters Marquis and Marstons Pedigree on handpump, and a good choice of wines – with shelves of sparkling wine glasses. It's a very well run place, with good quick service, but maybe piped music. The village, now peacefully bypassed, is a pretty one.

Bar food (12-2, 6.30-10(7-9.30 Sun)) ~ Restaurant ~ (01733) 380251 ~ Children welcome if eating ~ Open 11-3, 6-11; 12-3, 7-10.30 Sun

CAWDOR Map 4 C2
Cawdor Tavern

Just off B9090 in Cawdor village; follow signs for Post Office and village centre

Those of you who enjoy the odd dram of whisky will be spoilt for choice at this welcoming Highland village pub, with over 100 to pick from – including some rare brands. The rather modern frontage hides some surprisingly elegant fittings inside, including some beautiful oak panelling in the substantial rather clubby lounge, gifted to the tavern by a former Lord Cawdor and salvaged from the nearby castle; more recent panelling is incorporated into an impressive ceiling. The public bar on the right has a brick fireplace housing an old cast-iron stove, as well as elaborate wrought-iron wall lamps, and an imposing pillared serving counter. Enjoyable bar food at lunchtime includes soup (£2.30), sandwiches (from £2.65), warm crab tart (£3.95), Thai chicken strips or grilled goats cheese and fennel salad (£4.25), filled baked potatoes (£4.50), ploughman's (£4.75), venison sausage and mash (£5.95), haddock in beer batter with home-made tartare sauce (£6.95), and grilled gammon with an orange and madeira glaze (£7.40), with evening dishes such as crab and salmon with white wine and cream in a choux bun (£4.95), mini seafood platter (£4.85), chicken breast filled with haggis and a Drambuie and mushroom cream sauce (£9.25), fillet of Shetland salmon on wilted spinach with a tomato and garlic cream sauce (£9.45), and roast breast of guinea fowl with black pudding and a mushroom and whisky sauce (£10.25), and daily specials such as crab and prawn risotto with pesto marie rose or pigeon breast on puy lentils with port jus (£3.95), half a pot roast pheasant with onions and shallot reduction (£9.95), and duck breast on home-made rhubarb chutney with claret gravy (£10.75); puddings such as home-made cheesecake, home-made apple pie or chilled lemon posset with orange shortbread (from £3.15). The restaurant is partly no smoking. Well kept Aviemore Stag and Worthingtons, and a guest from Black Isle, Isle of Skye or Orkney on handpump; darts, pool, cribbage, dominoes, Jenga, board games, cards, fruit machine, juke box, TV, and piped music. There are tables on the front terrace, with tubs of flowers, roses, and creepers.

Bar food (12-2, 5.30-9) ~ Restaurant ~ (01667) 404777 ~ Children welcome away from public bar ~ Open 11-11(12.30 Sat); 12.30-11 Sun; 11-3, 5-11 in winter

CAWSTON Map 3 D6
Ratcatchers

Eastgate, S of village – on B1149 from Norwich turn left towards Haveringland at crossroads ½ mile before the B1145 Cawston turn

The name of this warmly welcoming dining pub is supposed to have originated at the turn of the century when the building was first converted to an inn, and the local ratcatcher was the first person to stay here. These days the very atmospheric cosy L-shaped beamed bar has an open fire, nice old chairs and a fine mix of walnut, beech, elm and oak tables, a quieter and cosier candlelit dining room on the right, and a conservatory. There are no-smoking areas throughout the pub. The very good food is probably some of the best in the area, so it's as well to book to be sure of a table. The menu includes smoked mackerel (£4.45), fried whitebait (£4.90), shell-on prawns (£4.95), ploughman's (£5.85), sausage and mash (£5.95), cottage pie (£6.75), Indonesian stir-fry (£7.75), beef and ale or fish pie (£8.20), peppered chicken (£9.85), and daily specials such as lemon sole or wild salmon with Thai prawns (£11.95) and roast guinea fowl with fresh herbs and wild mushrooms, bacon and juniper sauce (£8.95). Well kept Adnams Best, Greene King IPA and a beer named for the pub (brewed for them by Hancocks) on handpump, a good wine list with half a dozen by the glass; dominoes, cribbage, and piped music. There are tables on the terrace by special outside heaters for dining in cooler weather.

Bar food (12-2, 6.15-9.45) ~ Restaurant ~ (01603) 871430 ~ Children welcome ~ Open 11.45-3, 5.45(6.30 Sun)-11

CHALGROVE Map 2 C3
Red Lion

High Sreet (B480 Watlington—Stadhampton)

The local church has owned this traditional pub since it first appeared in written records in 1637, and probably a good bit longer as some of the timbers date back to the 11th c. The picnic-sets in front are attractively floodlit at night and inside there's a smartly contemporary twist to its décor. All the walls are painted a crisp white, which contrasts strikingly with the simple dark furnishings, the windows have neatly chequered green curtains and fresh flowers, and there's an old woodburner and a log fire. Across from the fireplace is a painting of the landlady's aunt, and there are a few carefully collected prints and period cartoons. There's quite an emphasis on the food, and changing menus might include soup (from £3.25), filled baguettes (from £3.50), goats cheese tartlet with shallot purée or grilled asparagus with bacon and balsamic vinegar (£4.50), spicy meatballs with tomato sauce and linguini (£5.95) and warm tuna niçoise salad (£6.95) with more elaborate evening dishes such as roasted poussin spatchcock with lime and ginger and hot potato salad (£8.50); puddings such as dark chocolate soufflé with home-made shortbread (£3.50); restricted menu Monday and Tuesday lunchtime; children's menu (£3.50) or they can have smaller portions of main meals. Well kept Brakspears, and Fullers London Pride and one of their seasonal ales on handpump, and a decent wine list (they will generally open a bottle of wine and buy back the remainder if you don't finish it); pleasant service. The back dining room (sometimes used for functions) is no smoking; piped music, cribbage, dominoes, shove-ha'penny and darts in the tiled public bar. They play aunt sally in the good big garden behind, which has a pergola and play equipment. There are some notable medieval wall paintings in the church; the partly thatched main street of the village is pretty.

Bar food (standard food times; not Sun and Mon evening) ~ Restaurant ~ (01865) 890625 ~ Children in eating area of bar ~ Open 12-3, 6-11; 12-3, 7-10.30 Sun; closed a few days between 25 Dec and 1 Jan

CHAPEL AMBLE Map 1 D2
Maltsters Arms

Village signposted from A39 NE of Wadebridge, and from B3314

Especially warm and welcoming, this bustling pub is well worth the drive down the little high-hedged roads. The attractively knocked-together rooms have black oak joists in the white ceiling, partly panelled stripped stone walls, heavy wooden tables on the partly carpeted big flagstones, a large stone fireplace, and a pleasant, relaxed atmosphere; the bar extension is hung with ship pictures, a large collection of keyrings, and a growing collection of seafaring memorabilia. There's also a side room and upstairs family room, and the eating areas are all no smoking. Popular bar food at lunchtime includes open sandwiches and ploughman's, home-made soup (£3.15), curry of the day or pork stroganoff (£5.50), chicken liver parfait with orange and red onion marmalade or steak and kidney pie (£5.95), langoustines with whisky and horseradish cream sauce (£6.25), and Cornish sirloin steak (£9.95); in the evening, it is more elaborate with dishes such as chargrilled vegetable salad (£5.25), oven baked sardines (£5.50), asparagus tart with chargrilled baby fennel and carrots with a béarnaise sauce (£9.95), roasted duck breast on braised red cabbage with chilli, spring onion, ginger and sesame, served with a Chinese-style sherry, orange and vanilla jus (£13.25), whole megrim sole baked with local crab, white wine and cream, topped with gingered breadcrumbs (£13.95), and puddings like lemon brûlée or chocolate cheesecake. Well kept Bass, Greene King Abbot, Sharps Coaster, Maltsters Special (brewed specially for the pub by Sharps), and maybe a couple of guests like Fullers London Pride or Sharps Will's Resolve on handpump kept under light blanket pressure; 22 wines by the glass, a growing collection of malt whiskies, a good range of brandies and armagnacs, and even milk shakes. Cribbage, dominoes, backgammon, and piped music. Benches outside in a sheltered sunny corner, and pretty hanging baskets and tubs.

Bar food (12-2(1.45 in winter), 6.15-9.30) ~ Restaurant ~ (01208) 812473 ~ No children in the bar and must be over 8 in restaurant ~ Open 11-2.30, 6-11; 12-2.30, 7-10.30 Sun; closed evening 25 Dec

CHEADLE Map 3 D3
Queens at Freehay

A mile SE of Cheadle; take Rakeway Road off A522 (via Park Avenue or Mills Road), then after a mile turn into Counslow Road

This pub seemed to us a bit smaller than the Yates's last one (the Izaak Walton at Cresswell) – but that could easily be because most of their old customers seem to have followed them here, and been topped up by a whole lot of new ones. Certainly, the thriving atmosphere goes well with the surroundings: the comfortable lounge bar is attractively decorated with small country pictures, its pretty curtains matching the cushions. It opens through an arch into a light and airy dining area, with neatly spaced tables. It's the food that is the main thing here: mainly familiar sorts of dishes, nothing too far out, but all cooked carefully with good flavours, and nicely presented. The menu might include lunchtime snacks such as filled baked potatoes (from £2.50), crusty rolls (from £3.25), local black pudding with crispy bacon and cheddar or duck and noodle stir-fry (£3.95) with other dishes such as spinach and ricotta cannellini, fisherman's bake or fish and chips (£7.95), chicken filled with stilton and bacon in mild mustard sauce or mini lamb joint with mash and red wine gravy (£8.95), with blackboard specials such as home-made game pie or fresh local rainbow trout with lemon and butter (£8.95), roast duck with port and cranberry sauce (£9.95) or poached halibut with white wine, cream and grapes (£10.95); puddings such as hot chocolate fudge cake and treacle and walnut tart (from £2.95). Well kept Marstons Pedigree on handpump; quick attentive service.

Bar food (12-2(2.30 Sun), 6(6.30 Sun)-9.30) ~ Restaurant ~ (01538) 722383 ~ Well behaved children in eating area of bar and restaurant ~ Open 12-2.30, 6-11; 12-3, 6.30-10 Sun; closed 25 and 26 Dec, evening 1 Jan

CHESTER Map 3 D2
Albion

Park Street

The landlord of this old-fashioned corner pub is devoted to his striking collection of World War I memorabilia: throughout, you'll find big engravings of men leaving for war, similarly moving prints of wounded veterans, and other more expected aspects – flags, advertisements and so on. Free from piped music, noisy machines and children, its separate rooms are an oasis of calm, tucked away in a quiet part of town just below the Roman Wall. The attractively muted post-Edwardian décor includes floral wallpaper, appropriate lamps, leatherette and hoop-backed chairs, a period piano, and cast-iron-framed tables, with an attractive side dining room. Appealing to a good mix of ages, it's friendly and chatty; it can get quite smoky. Well kept Cains, Greenalls, Timothy Taylors Landlord and maybe a couple of weekly guests such as Batemans XXXB and Caledonian Deuchars IPA on handpump, up to 30 malt whiskies and fresh orange juice; the wines are non-French. Service is very friendly (though they don't like people rushing in just before closing time – and won't serve crisps or nuts). Home-cooked food in huge helpings includes Staffordshire oatcakes filled with black pudding, honey-roast gammon with cumberland sauce, roast turkey, vegetarian haggis, and Lincolnshire sausages in red wine and shallot sauce (all £5.95); they are used to being asked for one dish with two sets of cutlery. Puddings might include cold melted chocolate pudding, home-made brandy and apricot ice cream and fresh lemon and lime cheesecake (£2.95); they also do great doorstep sandwiches. The landlord still has plans for a couple of bedrooms with bathrooms, maybe by early 2002.

Bar food (12-2, 5.30(7 Sun)-8, 6-8.30 Sat) ~ (01244) 340345 ~ Open 11.30-3, 5(6 Sat)-11; 12-3, 7-10.30 Sun

CHESTER Map 3 D2
Old Harkers Arms

1 Russell Street, down steps off City Road where it crosses canal – under Mike
Melody antiques

From inside this well converted Victorian canalside warehouse you can
watch the canal boats drift past. The lofty ceiling and tall windows give a
feeling of space and light, yet the tables are carefully arranged to create a
sense of privacy. The nicely decorated bar has attractive lamps, interesting
old prints on the walls, and newspapers and books to read from a well
stocked library at one end. The menu changes frequently, and popular tasty
bar food might include sandwiches (from £3.25), toasted ciabattas and
baguettes (£3.95), soup (£3.25), ploughman's (£5.25), grilled salmon
marinated in sherry and soya sauce with mange tout and crispy ginger
(£7.50), baked avocado filled with stilton and mixed nuts or penne pasta
with gammon, apricots, mushrooms, chicory and cream sauce (£6.95), and
rib-eye steak (£12.95), with puddings such as Belgian chocolate, biscuit and
nut slice or passion fruit sorbet (£3.25); Sunday roast; on Monday evening
two courses and half a bottle of wine are £12.95. The bar counter,
apparently constructed from salvaged doors, serves well kept real ales on
handpump including Boddingtons, Lees and Weetwood Best and up to five
guests such as Caledonian 80/-, Fullers London Pride, Greene King Old
Speckled Hen and Roosters Yankee; around 50 malt whiskies, and decent
well described wines. Popular with a young crowd on Saturday evening.
The pub is part of the same small group that owns the Grosvenor Arms at
Aldford and the Dysart Arms at Bunbury (see entries).

*Bar food (12-2.30(2 Fri), 5.30-9.30; 12-9.30 Sat(9 Sun); not Fri evening) ~
Restaurant ~ (01244) 344525 ~ Children welcome till 7pm ~ Open
11.30-11; 12-10.30 Sun*

CHICKSGROVE Map 1 C6
Compasses

From A30 5½ miles W of B3089 junction, take lane on N side signposted Sutton Mandeville, Sutton Row, then first left fork (small signs point the way to the pub, in Lower Chicksgrove; look out for the car park)

While the reliably good food at this pleasantly relaxed old thatched house may be snappily modern, the welcoming atmosphere in the bar remains reassuringly traditional, with old bottles and jugs hanging from beams above the roughly timbered counter, farm tools and traps on the partly stripped stone walls, and high-backed wooden settles forming snug booths around tables on the mainly flagstone floor. As well as soup (£3.95) and sandwiches (from £3.45), enjoyable meals from an imaginative changing menu might include popular goats cheese and pesto rustic loaf or bacon and onion tartlet (£4.95), scallops with mustard, cream and sun-dried tomato (£7.50), steak and kidney pie (£7.95), fried wild mushrooms with apple cream sauce and noodles (£8.95), braised leg of lamb with garlic, tomato and rosemary, sausage and mash or fried shark steak with fruit salad (£9.95), venison fillet with sweet cream sauce (£10.95), pigeon breast with wild mushrooms (£13.95), braised crocodile in cajun spices (£15.45), and puddings such as lemon cheesecake and pineapple in gin and Pimms (£3.75); all meals are served with a good choice of vegetables. Welcoming bar staff serve well kept Bass, Chicksgrove Churl (brewed for the pub by Wadworths), Wadworths 6X and maybe a guest such as Tisbury Stonehenge or Adnams Best on handpump, and six wines by the glass; cribbage, dominoes, bagatelle and shove-ha'penny. The quiet garden and flagstoned farm courtyard are very pleasant places to sit, and there's a nice walk to Sutton Mandeville church and back via Nadder Valley. Be warned, they close on Tuesdays after bank holiday Mondays.

Bar food (standard food times; not Sun evenings) ~ Restaurant ~ (01722) 714318 ~ Well behaved children welcome ~ Open 12-3, 6-11; 12-3, 7-10.30 Sun; closed Mon except bank holidays, then cl Tues ~ Bedrooms: £40S/£55S

CILGERRAN Map 1 A3
Pendre

High Street, off A478 2¼ miles S of Cardigan

The price of the well presented home-made bar food at this very friendly, ancient pub (said to be one of the oldest in west Wales) continues to amaze readers. All main courses are £4 and might include trout with apple and marmalade cream, mushroom stroganoff, pork with spiced cabbage and onions in mild mustard sauce or roasted chicken in honey and pink peppercorn sauce. Starters range from £1.50 for pâté with whisky mango chutney to £2.50 for soup with cheese and toast or poached prawns with sesame toast. Puddings might include bread and butter pudding or apple, banana and marmalade crumble (£1.75) as well as unusual home-made ice creams such as chocolate digestive, turkish delight and mince pie and brandy (from £1.75). The original bar area has massive stripped 14th-c medieval stone walls above a panelled dado, with elbow chairs and settles, and some beautifully polished slate flooring. Besides the comfortable lounge bar, there's a restaurant area. Well kept Tomos Watkins OSB and Whoosh on handpump and possibly a guest in summer; prompt welcoming service; shove-ha'penny, cribbage, fruit machine and darts in the public bar. A small terrace has sturdy tables, and there are more and an enclosed play area in the garden. The other end of the town leads down to the River Teifi, with a romantic ruined castle on a crag nearby, where coracle races are held on the Saturday before the August bank holiday. The local wildlife park nearby is well worth a visit, and this is a good area for fishing.

Bar food (12-2, 6-8.30; Sun 7-8.30, not lunchtime) ~ Restaurant ~ No credit cards ~ (01239) 614223 ~ Children in eating area of bar and restaurant ~ Open 12.30-3, 6-11; 12-3, 7-11 Sun; if it's quiet 12-2, 6-9.30 in winter ~ Bedrooms: £15(£25S)/£30S

CLYST HYDON Map 1 D4
Five Bells

West of the village and just off B3176 not far from M5 junction 28

'What a nice pub' is a comment many readers make about this most attractive, thatched place, and the licensees are extremely friendly and welcoming. The bar is spotlessly kept and divided at one end into different seating areas by brick and timber pillars; china jugs hang from big horsebrass-studded beams, there are many plates lining the shelves, lots of sparkling copper and brass, and a nice mix of dining chairs around small tables (fresh flowers and evening candles in bottles), with some comfortable pink plush banquettes on a little raised area; the pretty no-smoking restaurant is up some steps to the left and has been redecorated this year in blue and gold. Past the inglenook fireplace is another big (but narrower) room they call the Long Barn with a pine dresser at one end and similar furnishings. Good, popular home-made daily specials might include garlic mushrooms (£3.95), crispy bacon and stilton salad (£4.25), avocado baked with Somerset brie and pepperoni (£4.25), mussels in cider and cream or kiln-roasted hickory-smoked salmon fillet (£4.95), home-made steak and kidney pudding (£8.25), lamb shank roasted with honey and rosemary (£10.25), smoked fish platter (£10.95), pink sea bream (£11.50), and T-bone steaks (£14.45); also, sandwiches (from £3), home-made soup (£2.95), courgettes provençale (£5.25), platters (from £5.50), cold home-cooked ham (£7.25), steaks (from £10.45), and children's menu (£2.25). Well kept Cotleigh Tawny, O'Hanlon's Blakeley's Best, and Otter Bitter on handpump, a thoughtful wine list, and several malt whiskies. The cottagey front garden is a fine sight with its thousands of spring and summer flowers, big window boxes and pretty hanging baskets; up some steps is a sizeable flat lawn with picnic-sets, a play frame, and pleasant country views.

Bar food (standard food times) ~ Restaurant ~ (01884) 277288 ~ Well behaved children in eating area of bar ~ Open 11.30-2.30, 6.30-11(10.30 Sun); evening opening 7 (6.30 Sat) in winter

COCKWOOD Map 1 D4
Anchor

Off, but visible from, A379 Exeter—Torbay

Immensely popular, this is a very well run place with obliging, speedy service, and particularly good fish dishes. From a large menu, there are 30 different ways of serving mussels (£5.95 normal size helping, £9.95 for a large one), 12 ways of serving scallops (from £5.25 for a starter, from £12.95 for a main course), 10 ways of serving oysters (from £6.95 for starter, from £13.95 for main course), and 5 'cakes' such as crab cakes or mussel cakes (£5.95 for starter, £9.95 for main course), as well as tuna steak in tomato and garlic (£5.95), locally caught cod (£6.25), whole grilled plaice (£6.50), and a shellfish selection (£14.95), and lots of daily specials. Non-fishy dishes feature as well, such as home-made soup (£2.50), sandwiches (from £2.65), home-made chicken liver pâté (£3.85), cheese and potato pie (£4.50), home-made steak and kidney pudding (£5.50), rump steak (£8.95), and children's dishes (£2.50). But despite the emphasis on food, there's still a pubby atmosphere, and they keep six real ales on handpump or tapped from the cask: Bass, Flowers Original, Fullers London Pride, Greene King Old Speckled Hen, Otter Ale and Wadworths 6X. Also, a rather good wine list (10 by the glass – they do monthly wine tasting evenings September–June), 25 brandies, 70 malt whiskies, and west country cider. The small, low-ceilinged, rambling rooms have black panelling, good-sized tables in various alcoves, and a cheerful winter coal fire in the snug; the cosy restaurant is no smoking. Darts, dominoes, cribbage, table skittles, fruit machine, and piped music. From the tables on the sheltered verandah you can look across the road to the bobbing yachts and crabbing boats in the harbour. Nearby parking is difficult when the pub is busy – which it usually is.

Bar food (12-3(2.30 Sun), 6.30-10(9.30 Sun)) ~ Restaurant ~ (01626) 890203 ~ Children in eating area of bar and in restaurant ~ Open 11-11; 12-10.30 Sun; closed evening 25 Dec

COLEFORD Map 1 D4
New Inn

Just off A377 Crediton—Barnstaple

The garden of this 600-year-old inn has been landscaped, and new chairs, tables and umbrellas placed on the new decking under the willow tree along the stream; there are more seats on the terrace. Inside, there are several interestingly furnished areas that spiral around the central servery, with ancient and modern settles, spindleback chairs, plush-cushioned stone wall seats, some character tables – a pheasant worked into the grain of one – and carved dressers and chests; also, paraffin lamps, antique prints and old guns on the white walls, and landscape plates on one of the beams, with pewter tankards on another; the resident parrot Captain is chatty and entertaining. The servery itself has settles forming stalls around tables on the russet carpet, and there's a winter log fire. Using good local produce, the highly enjoyable bar food might include soup (£3.50), filled baguettes (from £3.95), omelettes or smoked fish platter (£4.95), ploughman's or Mediterranean vegetables and pasta bake (£5.95), creamy fish pie, chicken and mushroom stroganoff or liver and bacon (all £6.95), steaks (from £6.95), Italian beef (£7.95), confit of duck with caramelised onions (£8.95), fillet of beef with green peppercorn sauce and roasted cherry tomatoes (£15.95), and puddings such as treacle and lemon tart with clotted cream, fruit crumble or sticky date pudding (from £3.50); the restaurant is no smoking. Well kept Badger Best, Everards Beacon Ale, Exmoor Gold, and Otter Ale on handpump, and quite a range of malt whiskies, ports and cognacs. Fruit machine (out of the way up by the door), darts, and piped music. This is one of the oldest 'new' inns in the country.

Bar food (till 10(9.30 Sun)) ~ Restaurant ~ (01363) 84242 ~ Children in eating area of bar and in restaurant ~ Open 12-2.30, 6-11; 12-2.30, 7-10.30 Sun; closed 25 and 26 Dec ~ Bedrooms: £55B/£65B

COMBE HAY Map 1 C5
Wheatsheaf

Village signposted from A367 or B3110 S of Bath

Particularly in good weather, this is a smashing place to be. There are three dovecotes built into the walls, tables on a spacious terraced lawn overlooking the lovely valley, church, and ancient manor stables, and award-winning flowers; plenty of good nearby walks, too. Inside, the pleasantly old-fashioned rooms have low ceilings, warm burgundy walls, brown-painted settles, pews and rustic tables, a very high-backed winged settle facing one big log fire, old sporting and other prints, and quite a few earthenware jugs. Popular bar food includes home-made soup (£3.50), ploughman's (from £5.25), glazed ham (£5.90), smoked chicken and ham terrine or home-made lasagne (£6.50), home-made vegetarian nut roast with madeira sauce, venison sausages and pork and wild mushroom sausages with an onion and cranberry sauce, home-made steak and kidney pie or sautéed tiger prawns in garlic butter and dill (all £8.50), and breast of wood pigeon and mushroom tossed in a madeira jus on a crisp vegetable rösti (£11.50); the restaurant is no smoking. Well kept Bath Gem, Courage Best and Greene King Old Speckled Hen tapped from the cask, several malt whiskies, and decent wines; shove-ha'penny, dominoes and cribbage.

Bar food (12-2, 6.15-9.30) ~ (01225) 833504 ~ Children welcome ~ Open 11-3, 6-11; 12-4, 7-10.30 Sun; closed 25 and 26 Dec and 1 Jan ~ Bedrooms: £50S/£75S

CONSTABLE BURTON Map 3 B3
Wyvill Arms

A684 E of Leyburn

The gardens behind this creeper-covered ex-farmhouse have been landscaped, and there is now a herb and vegetable garden, and several large wooden benches with large white parasols for outdoor dining. Inside, the bar is decorated with teak and brass, with mirrors along the back of the bar, wine racks, and ornate shelving, and a bar counter which came from a bank 30 years ago. There's a mix of seating (including a 1695 mop-hair engraved-back chair won by the licensee's grandfather in a boxing match), a finely worked plaster ceiling with the Wyvill family's coat of arms, and an elaborate stone fireplace. The second bar, where food is served, has semi-circled, upholstered alcoves, a seventies juke box with music for all ages, and old oak tables; the reception area of this room includes a huge chesterfield which can seat up to eight people, another carved stone fireplace, and an old leaded church stained-glass window partition. Both rooms are hung with pictures of local scenes, most of which are prints done by the local artist, Peter Alice. Using locally supplied produce, the enjoyable home-made food includes light lunches such as soup (£2.45), scrambled egg and smoked salmon (£3.75), Mediterranean risotto (£5.45), duck leg with a pear and ginger sauce (£5.75), omelettes (from £5.95), and steak and mushroom pie or gammon and eggs (£7.45), as well as marinated charred ribs with barbecue sweet and sour sauce (£4.25), spicy meatballs (£4.45), salmon and crab fishcake with a poached egg and a tangy sauce (£5.25), Thai-style vegetable stir-fry (£6.95), steak and onion pie (£7.95), grilled breast of chicken with leek, bacon and stilton sauce or lemon sole with chilli and red pepper butter (£8.95), fillet of pork with an apple and mint sauce and juniper butter (£9.95), braised knuckle of pork with sauerkraut, roasted garlic potatoes and a pork jus or monkfish tails wrapped in parma ham on a bed of spinach with a shi-itake red wine emulsion (£10.95), and steaks (from £12.95). Well kept Black Sheep, Boddingtons, John Smiths Bitter, and Theakstons Best on handpump, and a thoughtful wine list; cribbage and dominoes. The white bull terrier is called Tricky.

Bar food (standard food times) ~ Restaurant ~ (01677) 450581 ~ Children welcome ~ Open 11-3, 6-11; 12-3, 7-10.30 Sun; closed Mon Jan-Mar unless bookings or B&B ~ Bedrooms: £34B/£56B

CONSTANTINE Map 1 E2
Trengilly Wartha

Constantine signposted from Penryn—Gweek Road (former B3291); in village turn
right just before Minimarket (towards Gweek); in nearly a mile pub signposted left;
at Nancenoy, OS Sheet 204 map reference 731282

Cleverly, the licensees have managed to make this tucked-away inn appeal
to a wide range of customers – not an easy thing to do. Families are made
welcome, but for those in search of a good pint, a proper pub meal and a
glance at a newspaper, this is also a smashing place to visit (quieter during
the week). Food in both the bar and restaurant has had consistent praise
this year, the wine list is especially good and thoughtful, and it's a super
place to stay, with tasty breakfasts. The long low-beamed main bar has a
woodburning stove and attractive built-in high-backed settles boxing in
polished heavy wooden tables, and at one end, shelves of interesting wines
with drink-in and take-out price labels (they run their own retail wine
business, Cochonnet Wines). There's a bright no-smoking family
conservatory with an area leading off that houses pool, darts, shove-
ha'penny, dominoes, cribbage, and shut the box; they run their own cricket
team. Popular bar food includes soup (£2.40), local feta cheese, bean and
tomato salad (£3.90), Cornish meaty or vegetarian pasties (£4), devon blue
cheese and walnut pâté (£4.80), sausages with mustard mash and onion
gravy (£5.20), ploughman's and salads (from £5.30), leek and cheese
soufflé (£7.80), Thai pork (£8.20), crab cakes (£10.50), specials like half a
dozen Helford oysters (£8), duck tagine with preserved lemon, tomato and
spiced couscous (£10.40) or monkfish and king prawns in a green Thai
curry sauce (£10.50), and proper food for children (from £3.50). Well kept
Skinner's Knocker, Sharps Cornish, and maybe a local guest on handpump
or tapped from the cask. Over 50 malt whiskies (including several extinct
ones), 20 wines by the glass (from a fine list of 250), and around 10
armagnacs. The pretty landscaped garden has some tables under large
parasols, an international sized piste for boules, and a lake; lots of
surrounding walks.

*Bar food (12-2.15(2 Sun), 6.30(7 Sun)-9.30) ~ Restaurant ~ (01326) 340332
~ Children welcome ~ Open 11-3, 6.30-11; 12-3, 7-10.30 Sun ~ Bedrooms:
£40(£48B)/£60(£72B)*

CORSCOMBE Map 1 C5
Fox

On outskirts, towards Halstock

The menu at this picturesque old thatched pub is absolutely spot on. They source supplies carefully, and use the best local produce, free range and organic where possible. Dishes are traditionally imaginative combining well matched English and continental ingredients. There might be wild garlic soup (£4.50), tomato and basil risotto (£4.95), warm pigeon breast and bacon salad (£5.50), chicken in a creamy sauce with celery and red pepper sauce (£7.95), braised venison with juniper berries and red wine (£9.50), lamb shank with mustard mash (£13.25), halibut steak with tapenade crust or roast john dory with thyme and sea salt (£14.95), seared scallops with orange braised fennel (£16.50). They stick to the good old favourite puddings such as treacle tart, bread and butter pudding and meringues with clotted cream and make their own ice cream and sorbets (£3.25). It's in a lovely country spot with roses over the door, a friendly golden retriever, Bramble (who loves a bit of attention), his friend Cracker and his son called Rayburn (no other dogs are allowed), ducks and chickens. A flagstoned room on the right has lots of beautifully polished copper pots, pans and teapots, harness hanging from the beams, small Leech hunting prints and Snaffles prints, Spy cartoons of fox hunting gentlemen, a long scrubbed pine table (a highly polished smaller one is tucked behind the door), and an open fire. In the left-hand room (partly no smoking) there are built-in settles, candles on the blue-and-white gingham tablecloths or barrel tables, an assortment of chairs, lots of horse prints, antlers on the beams, two glass cabinets with a couple of stuffed owls in each, and an L-shaped wall settle by the inglenook fireplace; darts, dominoes and backgammon. The no-smoking dining room which is open at weekends and for winter breakfast has an Aga, pine cupboards, a Welsh dresser, and lots of personal memorabilia. In summer, breakfast is taken in the conservatory with its maturing vine, orchids, and huge oak table. Well kept Exmoor Ale and Fullers London Pride and a summer guest like Exmoor Fox on handpump, a very good thoughtful wine list, local cider and home-made elderflower cordial, damson vodka, and sloe gin. There are seats across the quiet village lane on a lawn by the little stream, and this is a nice area for walks.

Bar food (till 9.30 Fri, Sat) ~ Restaurant ~ (01935) 891330 ~ Well behaved children welcome ~ Open 12-3(3.30 Sat), 7-11; 12-4, 7-10.30 Sun; closed 25 Dec ~ Bedrooms: £60B/£65(£70B)

COTTESMORE Map 3 E4
Sun

B668 NE of Oakham

The emphasis at this 17th-c stone-built thatched village pub is on the good imaginative food, which might include soup (£2.75), feta salad (£2.95), king prawns in garlic butter (£4.75), steak baguette (£5.95), grilled sardines or lasagne (£6.25), seared salmon fillet with lemon butter (£7.50), seafood tagliatelle (£7.95), roast duck (£10.95), and puddings such as chocolate sponge or apple crumble (£3.25). There are not many tables in the rooms off the bar, so it pays to get there early, or even book. As well as stripped pine furnishings, there's a winter fire in the stone inglenook, and pictures on the sunny yellow walls; piped music. Besides Adnams and Everards Tiger they have a guest beer such as Jennings Sneck Lifter on handpump, and also decent wines. Service is friendly and helpful. There are tables out in the garden; boules.

Bar food (standard food times; not Sun evening, Mon) ~ Restaurant ~ (01572) 812321 ~ Open 11.30-2.30, 6.30-11; closed 25, 26 Dec

COTTON Map 2 A5
Trowel & Hammer

Mill Road; take B1113 N of Stowmarket, then turn right into Blacksmiths Lane just N of Bacton

The spreading series of quiet rooms at this civilised wisteria-covered pub have fresh flowers, lots of beamery and timber baulks, a big log fire (as well as an ornate woodburning stove at the back), and plenty of wheelbacks and one or two older chairs and settles around a variety of tables. Much emphasis is placed on the highly enjoyable, fairly priced food, and it's probably best to book. The menu changes daily but might include tomato and basil soup (£2.50), assiette of squid, goujons of cod and whitebait with tartare sauce (£3.95), sweet cured herrings in honey and mustard mayonnaise (£4.25), smoked salmon with chive crème fraîche (£4.75), walnut and gorgonzola filled pasta with smoked cheddar shavings or fish pie (£6.95), medallions of salmon with Thai-style noodles and spicy tomato sauce (£7.55), pork steak with stilton and walnut sauce (£7.95), fried king scallops with creamy basil sauce and pasta or grilled monkfish with spinach and creamy chive and saffron sauce (£8.95), duck breast with wild cherry and orange sauce (£9.75); polite, helpful staff. Well kept Adnams, Greene King IPA and Abbot, and a guest from a brewer like Mauldons and Nethergate Bitter on handpump or tapped from the cask, an interesting wine list and lots of unusual spirits; pool, fruit machine and piped music. A pretty back garden has lots of roses and hollyhocks, neat climbers on trellises, picnic-sets and a recently renovated swimming pool.

Bar food (12-2, 6-9(10 Fri, Sat)) ~ Restaurant ~ (01449) 781234 ~ Well behaved children in eating area of bar ~ Open 12-3, 6-11; 12-11 Sat; 12-10.30 Sun

CRANMORE Map 1 C5
Strode Arms

West Cranmore; signposted with pub off A361 Frome—Shepton Mallet

This old former farmhouse is run by people who care about their customers whether they are regulars or visitors – and there are plenty of each. The rooms have charming country furnishings, fresh flowers (and pretty dried ones), pot plants, a grandfather clock on the flagstones, remarkable old locomotive engineering drawings and big black and white steam train murals in a central lobby, good bird prints, newspapers to read, and lovely log fires in handsome fireplaces. The same menu for the popular food is used in both the bar and restaurant, though sandwiches (from £2.75), ploughman's (from £4.75), and baked potatoes (£4.95) are only served in the bar. Daily specials include smoked trout, prawn and spinach terrine (£4.75), cheese, potato and onion pasties (£6.25), cottage pie (£6.85), fresh fish (from £8), sugar-baked ham with parsley sauce (£8.25), and puddings such as lime and ginger crunch flan, raspberry, pear and almond crumble or fresh strawberry roulade (from £3); there's also soup (£3), scallops and bacon (£6.25), ham and eggs (£6.75), spaghetti with a fresh tomato and basil sauce (£7.25), home-made pies (£7.50), smoked haddock and cod fishcakes (£8.25), wild boar steak grilled with an apple and honey crust (£8.75), and steaks (from £9.85). Half the restaurant and half the bar area are no smoking; friendly service. Well kept Oakhill Best, Wadworths 6X and IPA, and a guest from Hook Norton, Skinners or Wychwood on handpump, an interesting choice of wines by the glass from a thoughtful list, and lots more by the bottle, and quite a few liqueurs and ports. The pub is an attractive sight in summer with its neat stonework, cartwheels on the walls, pretty tubs and hanging baskets, and seats under umbrellas on the front terrace; more seats in the back garden. On the first Tuesday of each month, there's a vintage car meeting, and the East Somerset Light Railway (which we hope is still open by the time this book is published) is not far away.

Bar food (till 10pm Fri and Sat) ~ Restaurant ~ (01749) 880450 ~ Children in restaurant ~ Open 11.30-2.30, 6.30-11; 12-3, 7-10.30 Sun; closed Sun evening Oct-Mar

CRAWLEY Map 2 D2
Fox & Hounds

Village signposted from A272 and B3420 NW of Winchester

This solidly constructed mock Tudor building is one of the most striking in a village of fine old houses. Each timbered upper storey successively juts further out, with lots of pegged structural timbers in the neat brickwork, and elaborately carved steep gable-ends. Restored recently and re-opened as a village pub, the beamed rooms are warmed by three log fires, there's a relaxed atmosphere, evening candlelight, a mix of attractive wooden tables and chairs, helpful and friendly staff, well kept Adnams, Butcombe, and Wadworths IPA, 6X, and seasonal ales on handpump, and interesting wines. Using fresh local produce, the very good bar food might include sandwiches, watercress soup (£3.95), chicken liver parfait with spicy chutney (£5), wild mushroom and sun-dried tomato risotto (£5.25), pork and leek sausages with bubble and squeak (£6.95), liver and bacon (£7.50), rabbit and partridge stew or chicken and coconut curry (£8.50), gateau of aubergine, courgette and dorset blue vinney cheese (£8.95), tuna niçoise or loin of pork with bean sprouts and spicy sauce (£9.95), grilled marlin with citrus marmalade (£12.75), rack of lamb with olive mash and black pudding or venison with a gooseberry sauce (£12.95), and chargrilled sirloin with caramelised onion and blue cheese (£13.50). Summer barbecues in the garden.

Bar food (12-2, 6-9(9.30 Fri, Sat)) ~ Restaurant ~ (01962) 776006 ~ Children welcome away from bar ~ Open 11-3, 6-11; 12-3, 6-10.30 Sun

CRAYKE Map 3 D4
Durham Ox

Off B1363 at Brandsby, towards Easingwold; West Way

The Fosse Way passes through this village, but this pub is quite a stumbling-block; once sat down to such an enjoyable lunch, you may decide that's the end of your walk. The old-fashioned lounge bar has venerable tables and antique seats and settles on the flagstones, pictures and photographs on the dark red walls, interesting satirical carvings in its panelling (which are Victorian copies of medieval pew ends), polished copper and brass, and an enormous inglenook fireplace with winter log fires (flowers in summer). In the bottom bar is a framed illustrated account of the local history (some of it gruesome) dating back to the 12th c, and a large framed print of the original famous Durham Ox, which weighed 171 stones. Some of the panelling here divides off a bustling public area, which has a good lively atmosphere and more traditional furnishings. Consistently good food includes home-made soups with home-made bread (£3.95), sandwiches (from £4.95; with chips and salad), duck leg confit or Yorkshire black pudding terrine with a port reduction and pickled walnuts (£4.95), main courses such as seared calves liver, beetroot mash, grilled pancetta, shallot and red wine jus or seared fillet of bass with warm spring onion, new potato and caper salad and balsamic vinegar (£12.95), sautéed loin of venison, haggis mashed potato, swede fondant and whisky sauce (£14.95), daily specials, a cheeseboard with home-made fruit cake, chutneys and local cheeses (£3.95 for two choices, £5.95 for the full cheeseboard), and delicious puddings such as coffee bean scented crème brûlée with a white chocolate water ice (£4.95). Well kept John Smiths, Tetleys, and Theakstons XB on handpump, with maybe a guest such as Charles Wells Bombardier; piped music (some feel it unnecessary), fruit machine, and dominoes. There are seats outside on a terrace and in the courtyard, and the comfortable bedrooms are in converted farm buildings (we'd be grateful for any reports on these); disabled access. The tale is that this is the hill which the Grand Old Duke of York marched his men up; the view from the hill opposite is wonderful.

Bar food (standard food times) ~ Restaurant ~ (01347) 821506 ~ Children in eating area of bar till 9pm ~ Open 12-3, 6-11; 11-11 Sat; 12-10.30 Sun; 12-3, 6-11 Sat in winter; closed 31 Dec ~ Bedrooms: £70B/£80B

CRAZIES HILL Map 2 C3
Horns

From A4, take Warren Row Road at Cockpole Green signpost just E of Knowl Hill,
then past Warren Row follow Crazies Hill signposts

The gentrified country atmosphere and friendly welcome in this tiled
whitewashed cottage are much enjoyed by its many customers – plus the
fact that there is no juke box, fruit machine or piped music. The
comfortable welcoming bars have rugby mementoes on the walls, exposed
beams, open fires and stripped wooden tables and chairs. The no-smoking
barn room is opened up to the roof like a medieval hall, and terracotta
walls give it a cosy feel. Popular bar food includes lunchtime baguettes,
soup (£4.25), Thai crab cakes or breaded butterfly prawns with chilli and
garlic mayonnaise (£5.95), tagliatelle with a creamy feta cheese, smoked
salmon and coriander sauce (£7.75), beef, mushroom and Guinness pie
(£7.95), roast chicken supreme with a sherry and tarragon sauce on a bed
of roasted courgettes (£9.95), and daily specials like green shell mussels in
white wine, coriander and chilli butter (£5.25), spinach and mushroom
lasagne (£6.95), and cod fillet with English mustard and breadcrumbs with
lemon butter (£12.95). Fish comes daily from Billingsgate, and it is
essential to book a table at weekends (it does get particularly busy on
Sunday lunchtimes). Well kept Brakspears Bitter, Special, and seasonal ales
on handpump, a thoughtful wine list, several malt whiskies – and they
make a good bloody mary. There's plenty of space in the very large garden.

*Bar food (standard food times; not Sun evening) ~ Restaurant ~ (0118) 940
1416 ~ Children in restaurant lunchtimes only ~ Open 11.30-2.30(3 Sat),
6-11; 12-10.30 Sun*

CRICKHOWELL Map 1 B4

Bear

Brecon Road; A40

It's worth making a detour to visit this perfectly run old coaching inn with readers continuing to praise the excellent food, service and atmosphere here. Beautifully made using plenty of local ingredients, regularly changing bar meals might include soup (£2.95), sandwiches (from £3.25), Welsh rarebit with grilled smoked bacon (£4.25), chestnut mushrooms stuffed with garlic butter, coated in herb breadcrumbs (£4.95), mussels in leek, saffron and garlic cream sauce (£5), ploughman's (from £5.75), faggots in onion gravy (£5.95), goats cheese and fried onion pie with baked ratatouille (£7.75), braised lambs hearts in red wine and black pudding sauce (£7.95), baked fresh salmon fillet with basil leaves in filo pastry with pesto cream sauce (£8.50) and delicious puddings such as treacle sponge pudding or plum terrine wrapped in marzipan (£3.50) or home-made ice creams (£2.95); they've a good range of Welsh cheeses. Their Sunday lunch is very popular. There's a calmly civilised atmosphere in the comfortably decorated, heavily beamed lounge, which has lots of little plush-seated bentwood armchairs and handsome cushioned antique settles, and a window seat looking down on the market square. Up by the great roaring log fire, a big sofa and leather easy chairs are spread among the rugs on the oak parquet floor; antiques include a fine oak dresser filled with pewter and brass, a longcase clock and interesting prints. The family bar is partly no smoking. Well kept Bass, Hancocks HB, Greene King Old Speckled Hen and a guest on handpump; malt whiskies, vintage and late-bottled ports, and unusual wines (with about a dozen by the glass) and liqueurs, with some hops tucked in among the bottles. Their apple juice comes from a mountainside orchard a few miles away. Service is swift and friendly even at really busy times. The back bedrooms – particularly in the quieter new block – are the most highly recommended, though there are three more bedrooms in the pretty cottage at the end of the garden. Lovely window boxes, and you can eat in the garden in summer; disabled lavatories.

Bar food (12-2, 6-10) ~ Restaurant ~ (01873) 810408 ~ Children in eating area of bar and must be over 5 in restaurant ~ Open 10.30-3, 6-11; 11.30-3, 7-10.30 Sun ~ Bedrooms: £52B/£68B

CROOK Map 3 B2

Sun

B5284 Kendal—Bowness

Although much emphasis is placed on the consistently good, interesting food here, there's still something of the atmosphere of a village local, and the staff are very friendly. The two rooms are opened together so that the dining area now dominates, and one area is no smoking. The food is highly enjoyable and includes lunchtime sandwiches and baked potatoes, and moules marinières or garlic mushrooms and smoked bacon salad (£4.50), honey and orange roasted duck breast with a citrus crème fraîche dressing or smoked shell-on prawns with aïoli (£4.95), Italian seafood salad (£5.50), home-made steak in ale pie (£7.50), garlic and herb tagliatelle or seared tuna with fresh fruit (£9.50), venison and red wine casserole (£9.95), warm smoked salmon steak with hollandaise and dauphinoise potatoes or fried lemon sole fillets with shallots, lemon, thyme and capers (£9.95), roast guinea fowl with grapes in a white wine and tarragon sauce or roast duck with fresh ginger and Grand Marnier (£10.50), and proper puddings such as spotted dick, damson fool or chocolate and hazelnut roulade (£3.85). Well kept Boddingtons, Courage Directors, Greene King Old Speckled Hen, and Theakstons on handpump, an interesting choice of good value wines, and a welcoming fire; darts and dominoes. The pub is set away from the Windermere bustle and looks over rolling hills.

Bar food (standard food times) ~ Restaurant ~ (01539) 821351 ~ Children in eating area of bar and restaurant ~ Open 11-3, 5-11; 11-11 Sat; 12-10.30 Sun

CROSTHWAITE Map 3 B2
Punch Bowl

Village signposted off A5074 SE of Windermere

While people do just drop into this idyllically placed 16th-c inn for a drink, it would seem a shame to miss out on the excellent, imaginative food. Readers very much enjoy staying here as well. There are several separate areas carefully reworked to give a lot of space, and a high-raftered central part by the serving counter with an upper minstrel's gallery on either side; the bar and snug area are no smoking. Steps lead down into a couple of small dimly lit rooms on the right, and there's a doorway through into two more airy rooms on the left. It's all spick and span, with lots of tables and chairs, beams, pictures by local artist Derek Farman, and an open fire. As well as a set-price lunch (two courses £8, three courses £10.95), the imaginative food might include sandwiches, home-made tomato and basil soup with pesto (£2.70), crispy duck leg confit salad with provençale mixed leaf salad (£5.25), baked goats cheese salad on oven-baked beetroot with button onions, watercress and a walnut oil dressing (£5.50), layered white crab meat salad with a sweet chilli, red pepper and lime sauce (£6.25), grilled aubergine, courgette and polenta topped with melted lancashire cheese and a tomato sauce (£8.25), chargrilled tuna steak on crushed potatoes with braised ginger, leeks and five spice sauce or grilled chicken with a spicy tomato, red and green pepper sauce (£10.95), chargrilled fillet of lamb with a creamy Thai curry sauce (£11.25), escalope of calves liver with sage leaves (£12.25), and puddings such as honey and Drambuie crème brûlée, sticky Tunisian-style orange and lemon cake, and chocolate brownie with home-made chocolate chip ice cream and a chocolate sauce (from £3.75); popular Sunday lunch. Well kept Barngates Tag Lag, Black Sheep, and Wells Bombardier on handpump, a carefully chosen wine list, and several malt whiskies. There are some tables on a terrace stepped into the hillside.

Restaurant ~ (015395) 68237 ~ Children welcome ~ Open 11-11; 12-3 Sun; closed Sun evening, all day Mon (open bank hols and all through Easter) ~ Bedrooms: £37.50B/£55B

CROWLE Map 1 A6
Old Chequers

2.6 miles from M5 junction 6; A4538 towards Evesham, then left after 0.6 miles; Crowle Green

Handy for the motorway, this smoothly run much-modernised dining pub rambles extensively around an island bar, with plush-seated mate's chairs around a mix of pub tables on the patterned carpet, some brass and copper on the swirly-plastered walls, lots of pictures for sale at the back, and a coal-effect gas fire at one end (there's central heating too). A big square extension on the right, with shinily varnished rustic timbering and beamery, has more tables. Popular generous food (all home-made) includes good value imaginative light lunches such as soup (£2.25), grilled black pudding topped with bacon, tomato and cheese, chicken liver in cream and brandy, smoked haddock and prawns in cheese sauce or grilled goats cheese with roasted vegetables (£5.75) with other dishes such as mushroom stroganoff or sweet potato pancakes (£5.95), Thai chicken curry or chicken boursin (£9.75), lamb cutlets with redcurrant, mint and orange sauce (£11) and fresh fish such as grilled lemon sole with lemon butter, bass with olive and parmesan mash or monkfish wrapped in parma ham with curried mayonnaise (£11); puddings such as crème brûlée (from £3.25). Service is prompt and friendly; well kept real ales such as Archers, Banks's and Camerons on handpump, good value house wines. There are picnic-sets out on the grass behind, among shrubs and small fruit trees – a pleasant spot, with pasture beyond. Disabled access.

Bar food (12-1.45, 7-9.45; not Sun evening) ~ Restaurant ~ (01905) 381275 ~ Children in eating area of bar at lunchtime ~ Open 12-2.30, 7(10.30 Sun)-11; closed 25 and 26 Dec

DANEHILL Map 2 D4
Coach & Horses

From A275 in Danehill (S of Forest Row), take School Lane towards Chelwood Common

Set in attractive countryside, this cottagey pub has a relaxed, friendly atmosphere, and a mix of chatty customers. There's a little public bar to the right with half-panelled walls, simple furniture on highly polished wooden floorboards, a small woodburning stove in the brick fireplace, and a big hatch to the bar; darts. The main bar is on the left with plenty of locals crowding around the wooden bar counter or sitting at the high wooden bar stools enjoying the well kept Harveys Best, and a couple of guests such as Adnams Best or Badger Best on handpump. Drinks are stacked in a nice old-fashioned way on shelves behind the bar, and there's just one table on the stripped wood floor here. A couple of steps lead down to a half-panelled area with a mix of wheelbacks and old dining chairs around several characterful wooden tables on the fine brick floor, a large lantern in the tiny brick fireplace, and some large Victorian prints; candles and flowers on the tables. Down another step to the dining area with stone walls, a beamed vaulted ceiling, baskets and hops hanging from other beams, and a woodburning stove; through a lovely arched doorway is a small room with just a couple of tables; piped jazz. Served by friendly staff, the enjoyable bar food includes snacks such as sandwiches (from £3.75; steak with tomato and lettuce £4.95), filled baked potatoes (from £4.50), and grilled focaccia with onion, anchovy, olive and emmenthal cheese or grilled ciabattas with pesto, mozzarella and tomato (£4.95), plus home-made soup (£3.95), seared squid with pancetta (£4.95), citrus-marinated black tiger prawns (£5.95), lamb and mint sausages with colcannon mash and mustard sauce or a proper fish pie (£7.95), leek and gruyère tart (£8.50), rack of lamb with tomato and coriander tabouleh (£9.95), daily specials such as Thai green vegetable curry with coconut relish (£8.50) or chicken breast filled with mascarpone and thyme cream (£9.95), and puddings such as summer fruit and white chocolate strudel, chocolate and orange tart or apple and calvados pancakes (£3.95); a good wine list. There's a big attractive garden with plenty of seats, and fine views of the South Downs. More reports please.

Bar food (till 9.30pm Fri and Sat; not Sun evening exc bank hol wknds) ~ Restaurant ~ (01825) 740369 ~ Well behaved children welcome ~ Open 11.30-3, 6-11; 12-4, 7-10.30 Sun; closed evenings 25 and 26 Dec and 1 Jan

DODDISCOMBSLEIGH Map 1 D4
Nobody Inn

Village signposted off B3193, opposite northernmost Christow turn-off

For many, a visit to this immensely popular inn is a yearly pilgrimage. Mr Borst-Smith is very much a hands-on licensee, working hard with his staff to ensure that whether you are coming in for a light lunch and a pint, an evening meal, or an overnight stay, you will be warmly welcomed. The two rooms of the lounge bar have handsomely carved antique settles, windsor and wheelback chairs, benches, carriage lanterns hanging from the beams, and guns and hunting prints in a snug area by one of the big inglenook fireplaces. They keep perhaps the best pub wine cellar in the country – 800 well cellared wines by the bottle and 20 by the glass kept oxidation-free; there's also properly mulled wine and twice-monthly tutored tastings (they also sell wine retail, and the good tasting-notes in their detailed list are worth the £3.50 it costs – anyway refunded if you buy more than £30-worth); also, a choice of 240 whiskies, local farm ciders, and well kept Bass, Nobody's (brewed by Branscombe), Otter Ale, and a guest such as RCH East Street Cream on handpump. Good bar food includes good home-made soups (£3.50) and daily specials such as guinea fowl and chestnut terrine with tomato and apple chutney, wild mushroom risotto with garlic and cream dressing, and Thai prawn fishcakes with salsa (£3.90), sausage and mash with onion gravy (£5.50), hot lentil and walnut cakes with red onion marmalade and yoghurt or creamy salmon, green peppercorn, and white wine tagliatelle (£5.80), beef in ale, lamb casseroled with honey, mint, pine nuts and apricots, and breast of chicken in an apple, celery and calvados sauce (£7.90), and herb-crumbed butterfish on sweet potato mash with coriander sauce (£8.50); puddings like treacle and house malt whisky tart, raspberry and passion fruit mousse with hazelnut biscotti or plum pudding with toffee sauce (all £3.90). They keep an incredible choice of around 50 west country cheeses (half a dozen £5; you can buy them to take away as well). The restaurant is no smoking. There are picnic-sets on the terrace with views of the surrounding wooded hill pastures. The medieval stained glass in the local church is some of the best in the west country. No children are allowed inside the pub.

Bar food (till 10pm) ~ Restaurant ~ (01647) 252394 ~ Open 12-2.30, 6-11; 12-3, 7-10.30 Sun; closed 25 and 26 Dec ~ Bedrooms: £23(£38B)/£66(£70B)

DOWNHAM Map 3 C3
Assheton Arms

From A59 NE of Clitheroe turn off into Chatburn (signposted); in Chatburn follow
Downham signpost

This delightfully set dining pub takes its name from the family of Lord
Clitheroe, who bought this stone-built village in 1558 and have preserved it
in a traditional style ever since. A massive stone fireplace helps divide the
separate areas of the rambling beamed bar, which is cosiest in winter, and
is furnished with olive plush-cushioned winged settles around attractive
grainy oak tables, some cushioned window seats, and two grenadier busts
on the mantelpiece. Window seats, and picnic-sets outside, look across to
the church; part of the bar is no smoking. Bar food includes home-made
ham and vegetable broth (£2.95), sandwiches (from £3.75; not Saturday
evening or Sunday lunchtime), ploughman's (£4.50), chicken liver pâté
(£4.75), courgettes with tomato, garlic, pesto and mozzarella (£6.75),
chicken and mushroom pie (£6.95), venison, bacon and cranberry casserole
(£7.95), grilled plaice with parsley butter (£8.95), and seafood specials such
as grilled scallops with garlic butter and gruyère cheese (£6.50), half a
dozen oysters (£6.95), grilled bream (£8.95) and monkfish with brandy,
cream and peppercorns (£9.50); puddings and children's meals (£3.50);
speedy service. Boddingtons or Castle Eden under light blanket pressure;
decent wines by the glass or bottle; piped music.

*Bar food (12-2, 7-10) ~ (01200) 441227 ~ Children welcome ~ Open 12-3,
7-11(10.30 Sun)*

EASINGTON Map 2 B3
Mole & Chicken

From B4011 in Long Crendon follow Chearsley, Waddesdon signpost into Carters
Lane opposite the Chandos Arms, then turn left into Chilton Road

To be sure of getting a table in this friendly dining pub – set in rolling open
countryside – it's best to book beforehand. This is very much the place for a
special meal out (they don't offer bar snacks), and from the changing
restaurant menu you might find enjoyable starters such as home-made
soup (£3.50), grilled crostini of smoked fish and cream cheese or roasted
large field mushrooms with spinach and cheese (£5.95), and sautéed king
prawns with garlic and chilli (£6.95), with main courses like pasta tossed
with roasted vegetables and parmesan or much liked duck and bacon salad
with a warm plum sauce (£8.95), chargrilled salmon fillet with a lemon and
parsley butter (£9.95), roasted guinea fowl thighs stuffed with pork and
garlic and served with wild rice and a red wine and mushroom sauce
(£11.50), and Gressingham duck with orange sauce or chargrilled English
steak (£12.95); several daily changing fish choices, too. Decent French
house wines (and a good choice by the bottle), over 40 malt whiskies, and
well kept Greene King IPA and Morlands Old Speckled Hen on handpump.
The open-plan layout is very well done, so that all the different parts seem
quite snug and self-contained without being cut off from what's going on,
and the atmosphere is chatty and relaxed. The beamed bar curves around
the serving counter in a sort of S-shape, and there are pink walls with lots
of big antique prints, and (even at lunchtime) lit candles on the medley of
tables to go with the nice mix of old chairs; good winter log fires. The
garden, where they sometimes hold summer barbecues and pig and lamb
roasts, has quite a few tables and chairs.

*Restaurant (12-2, 7-10; 12-9.30 Sun) ~ (01844) 208387 ~ Children welcome
~ Open 12-3, 6-11; 12-10.30 Sun*

EAST LINTON Map 4 D3
Drovers

5 Bridge Street (B1407), just off A1, Haddington—Dunbar

Well run by two sisters, this comfortable old inn stands out for its enjoyable bar food, good choice of well kept real ales and genuinely pubby atmosphere. The main bar feels a bit like a welcoming living room as you enter from the pretty village street, with faded rugs on the wooden floor, a basket of logs in front of the woodburning stove, and comfortable armchairs and nostalgic piped jazz lending a very relaxed feel. There's a goat's head on a pillar in the middle of the room, plenty of hops around the bar counter, fresh flowers and newspapers, and a mix of prints and pictures (most of which are for sale) on the half-panelled, half-red-painted walls. A similar room leads off, and a door opens out onto a walled lawn with tables and maybe summer barbecues. Changing every week, up to six real ales might include Adnams Broadside, Belhaven Best, Deuchars IPA, Orkney Dark Island, and Shepherd Neame Spitfire; smartly dressed staff provide particularly helpful service. Relying on fresh local ingredients delivered daily (their local meats are excellent), the very good food might include soups such as smoked haddock and potato or creamed carrot and tarragon (from £2.50), home-made chicken liver pâté (£4.50), griddled black pudding and bacon in a creamy pepper sauce (£6), braised sausages in onion gravy and spicy mash (£6.50), steak, mushroom and Guinness pie (£7), Thai-style curry of vegetables or salmon fillet on a bed of spinach and mornay sauce (£7.50), roast rib of beef with Yorkshire pudding (£8), roast duckling breast in a sweet berry sauce or saddle of rabbit with caramelised carrots and shallots (£13), and puddings such as mango cheesecake with a pomegranate and passion fruit syrup or rich chocolate swiss flan (from £3). Part of the upstairs restaurant is no smoking; dominoes. The gents' has a copy of the day's *Scotsman* newspaper on the wall.

Bar food (12-2, 6.30-10; not Sat evening) ~ Restaurant ~ (01620) 860298 ~ Children welcome ~ Folk and other music Weds evening ~ Open 11.30-2.30, 5-11 Mon; all day till 11pm Tues, till 12.30am Weds-Thurs, till 1am Fri-Sat; 12.30-12 Sun; closed 25 Dec, 1 Jan

EAST MORDEN Map 1 D6
Cock & Bottle

B3075 between A35 and A31 W of Poole

You do need to book to be sure of a table at this popular dining pub. As well as lunchtime ploughman's (£5.50), changing bar food might include home-made pâté (£4.95), bouillabaisse (£4.95), brie and pancetta tartlet (£5.65), spicy crab cakes with a Thai dipping sauce (£5.75), spinach and feta cheese filo parcels with spicy tomato coulis (£7.25), red Thai chicken curry (£8.95), whole local plaice (£8.95), very good steak and kidney pudding or pigeon pie (£9.25), beef wellington (£15.25), puddings such as rum and raisin white chocolate tart or spotted dick (from £3.75), and children's dishes (£3.50). Most of the restaurant is no smoking. Well kept Badger Best, Tanglefoot and King and Barnes Sussex on handpump, and a good choice of decent house wines including half a dozen by the glass; cordial service (though when it's busy food can take a time to come). The refurbished interior is divided into several communicating areas (mostly laid out for dining) with heavy rough beams, some stripped ceiling boards, squared panelling, a mix of old furnishings in various sizes and degrees of antiquity, small Victorian prints and some engaging bric-a-brac. There's a good log fire, intimate corners each with just a couple of tables. Although the emphasis is on dining, there is a pubby wood floored public bar (with piped music, fruit machine and a sensibly placed darts alcove). This in turn leads on to yet another characterful dining room. They have some disabled facilities. There are a few picnic-sets outside, a garden area, and an adjoining field with a nice pastoral outlook.

Bar food (12-2, 6(7 Sun)-9) ~ Restaurant ~ (01929) 459238 ~ Children in restaurant ~ Open 11-3, 6-11; 12-3, 7-10.30 Sun

EAST TYTHERLEY Map 1 C6

Star

Off B3084 N of Romsey, via Lockerley – turn off by railway crossing nr Mottisfont Abbey

The bar in this 16th-c dining pub has a mix of comfortable furnishings, log fires in attractive fireplaces, and horsebrasses and saddlery; there's a lower lounge bar, and a cosy and pretty no-smoking restaurant. Good, interesting bar food (they tell us prices and choices have not changed since last year) includes open sandwiches or baguettes (£3.25), steak and kidney pie or chilli (£5.95), and daily specials such as fried duck liver on rye and caraway toast (£3.95), double baked goats cheese (£4.75), tiger prawn and scallop risotto (£4.95), pumpkin ravioli and bok choi (£7.90), liver and bacon (£7.95), monkfish and roasted carrot with chicken and black pudding (£12), and puddings like dark Belgian chocolate mousse or caramelised apple tart (from £3.50). You can eat the same menu in the bar or restaurant. Well kept Gales HSB, Ringwood Best, and a guest beer, several malt whiskies, and a thoughtful wine list with 10 by the glass. Chess, and a skittle alley for private functions. There are seats on the smartly furnished terrace, and a children's play area. The comfortable cottage-style bedrooms overlook the village cricket pitch.

Bar food (standard food times) ~ Restaurant ~ (01794) 340225 ~ Children welcome ~ Open 11-2.30, 6-11; 11-11 Sat; 12-10.30 Sun; 11-2.30, 6-11 Sat in winter; closed evening 25 Dec and 26 Dec ~ Bedrooms: £45S/£60S

EAST WITTON Map 3 B3
Blue Lion
A6108 Leyburn—Ripon

This is a consistently first-class inn, deservedly popular, and there's always a good mix of customers keen to enjoy the top quality drinks, imaginative food, and courteous, friendly welcome – many customers choose to stay overnight. The big squarish bar has high-backed antique settles and old windsor chairs and round tables on the turkey rugs and flagstones, ham-hooks in the high ceiling decorated with dried wheat, teazles and so forth, a Delft shelf filled with appropriate bric-a-brac, several prints, sporting caricatures and other pictures on the walls, a log fire, and daily papers; the friendly labrador is called Archie. Changing regularly, the excellent food might include sandwiches, home-made soup (£3.40), caesar salad with pancetta and chargrilled chicken (£4.95), Thai-style crab fishcake with chilli jam (£5), corned beef hash with a fried egg (£5.25), fresh mussels baked with white wine, garlic and aromatics topped with a herb crust (£5.50), smoked wild boar sausage with bubble and squeak and red wine sauce (£5.75), fresh tagliatelle tossed with cep sauce and finished with parmesan (£8.50), steak and kidney pudding or sautéed escalope of guinea fowl with a tomato and spinach compote (£10.95), braised leg of lamb with flageolet beans and herb mash (£11.75), and poached fillet of smoked haddock on new potatoes, topped with a poached egg and toasted with gruyère (£12.25); lovely puddings and good breakfasts; no snacks on Sunday lunchtime. Well kept Black Sheep Bitter and Riggwelter, and Theakstons Best and Old Peculier, and decent wines with quite a few by the glass. Picnic-sets on the gravel outside look beyond the stone houses on the far side of the village green to Witton Fell, and there's a big, pretty back garden.

Bar food (standard food times) ~ Restaurant ~ (01969) 624273 ~ Children in eating area of bar and restaurant ~ Open 11-11; 12-10.30 Sun ~ Bedrooms: £53.50S/£69S(£79B)

EDINBURGH Map 4 D3
Starbank

67 Laverockbank Road, off Starbank Road; on main road Granton—Leith

There are great views over the Firth of Forth from the windows in the neat and airy bar of this comfortably elegant welcoming pub. It's not just the views that make this pub popular though – they serve around eight well kept real ales from all around Britain on handpump which change continually but might include Bass, Belhaven 80/-, IPA, St Andrews and Sandy Hunters, Broughton Greenmantle, Orkney Dark Island, Timothy Taylors Landlord and Wadworths 6X. There's a good choice of wines too (all 23 are served by the glass), and as many malt whiskies; TV. Served by friendly, helpful staff, the good value tasty bar food is all home-made. Nicely presented dishes include soup (£1.50), chicken liver pâté (£2.50), a daily vegetarian dish (£4.25), ploughman's or steak mince and potatoes (£5), roast leg of lamb with mint sauce or supreme of chicken with tarragon cream sauce (£5.50), halibut steak with orange sauce or minute steak with pepper cream sauce (£6.50), and puddings (£2.50). The conservatory restaurant is no smoking; sheltered back terrace.

Bar food (12-2.30, 6-9; 12.30-9 wknds) ~ Restaurant ~ (0131) 552 4141 ~ Children welcome ~ Jazz second Sun and folk last Sun in month ~ Open 11-11(12 Thurs-Sat); 12.30-11 Sun

EVERSLEY Map 2 C3
Golden Pot

Eversley Centre; B3272

The Monday evening rösti menu is as popular as ever at this little brick building – as is the other enjoyable food. There's a comfortable, easy-going atmosphere in the different spreading areas, bowls of lilies, candles in bottles on the tables, and one particularly snug part by the log-effect gas fire, with two armchairs and a sofa; piped music. The rösti have toppings such as melted cheese and two fried eggs (£6.50) or bratwurst and onion sauce (£6.75), and other dishes may include gnocchi tossed in olive oil with sage and parmesan or potted prawns (£4.50), smoked chicken salad with fresh mango and cajun croûtons (£4.75), crab gravadlax or hot smoked salmon (£6.25), seared fresh tuna with coriander and a chilli dressing (£5.95), herby ratatouille (£8.95), red wine risotto with dolcelatte and rocket (£9.50), roast pork wrapped in parma ham with sage and a madeira sauce (£11.95), fishy main courses such as skate in black butter or monkfish with tomato sauce (from £11 to £14), and puddings like pear tartlet with clotted cream or white and dark chocolate pyramid with a rich Belgian truffle mousse (from £3.95). Well kept Badger Tanglefoot, Greene King IPA and Ruddles Best, Wadworths 6X, and maybe Wychwood Hobgoblin on handpump, and 12 wines by the glass; piped music. The pretty restaurant is no smoking. There are some picnic-sets in front by the car park with masses of colourful flowering pots, tubs, and window boxes.

Bar food (12-2.15, 6.30-9.15(9.30 Fri, Sat)) ~ Restaurant ~ (0118) 973 2104 ~ Pianist/vocalist/guitarist Mon evening ~ Open 11-3(3.30 Sat), 6(5 Fri)-11; 12-3.30, 7-10.30 Sun

FIFIELD Map 1 B6
Merrymouth
A424 Burford—Stow

Readers are full of praise for the interesting food and well trained staff at this isolated family-run 13th-c stone pub. It has a civilised but warmly welcoming atmosphere in the simple but comfortably furnished L-shaped bar, with nice bay-window seats, flagstones, horsebrasses and antique bottles hanging from low beams, some walls stripped back to the old masonry, and an open fire in winter; backgammon, dominoes and piped classical music. The freshly made bar food might include sandwiches (from £2.50; beef baguette £5.25), soup (£2.95), mushrooms cooked in whisky (£3.95), braden rösti (£4.75), spicy chickpea casserole (£6.95), steak and kidney pie (£7.50), chicken in celery, mushroom, onion and yoghurt sauce (£7.95), chargrilled steaks (from £7.95), and daily specials such as stilton and walnut pâté (£4.25), butterbean and mushroom bake (£6.95), tasty guinea fowl (£8.95), barbary duck breast (£9.75) and lemon sole (£10.50), with home-made puddings such as raspberry and marshmallow meringue and bread pudding with whisky sauce (from £3.50). Well kept Hook Norton Best, Wychwood Hobgoblin and maybe a guest such as Wadworths 6X on handpump, good wines including three by the glass; except for six tables in the bar the pub is no smoking. There are tables on a terrace and in the back garden (there may be a little noise from fast traffic on the road); dogs on leads welcome. The bedrooms are well cared for and quaint. The Domesday Book mentions an inn on this site and its name comes from the Murimuth family, who once owned the village in which it is set.

Bar food (standard food times) ~ Restaurant ~ (01993) 831652 ~ Well behaved children welcome in eating area of bar ~ Open 12-3, 6-10.30 (11 Sat); 12-3, 7-10 Sun; closed Sun evening in winter ~ Bedrooms: £45S/£65B

FLETCHING Map 2 D4
Griffin
Village signposted off A272 W of Uckfield

In a pretty spot on the edge of Sheffield Park, this civilised old inn has
tables in the lovely back garden with fine rolling Sussex views, and more
seats on a sheltered gravel terrace where they may have spit roasts; plenty
of space for children. Inside, the beamed and quaintly panelled bar rooms
have a good bustling atmosphere, blazing log fires, old photographs and
hunting prints, straightforward furniture including some captain's chairs,
china on a Delft shelf, and a small bare-boarded serving area off to one
side. A snug separate bar, now called the Club Room, has sofas, pool, a
juke box, and TV. Popular, imaginative bar menu (using as much local
organic produce as possible) includes pumpkin, honey and ginger soup
(£4.50), local ewes cheese and parsley mousse terrine with sun-dried
tomato dressing (£5.50), hot ciabatta sandwiches (Thai marinated breast of
chicken £5.50, tuna niçoise £5.95), spicy lamb meatballs with minted
yoghurt on tagliatelle or leek, gruyère and goats cheese tart (£6.95), steak
and kidney pudding with parsley mash or slow-cooked lamb shanks
(£8.50), fried marinated salmon on noodles with bok choi (£9.50), pot-
roasted local pheasant with bacon and puy lentils (£9.95), confit of duck
with honey and cloves on a potato and celeriac rösti (£10.50), and
puddings such as rhubarb and ginger crumble, chocolate and cognac flan,
and seasonal fruit brûlée (£4.95). There's a more elaborate (and expensive)
restaurant menu. At busy times you can expect a long wait for food. Well
kept Badger Tanglefoot and K&B, Hardy Country, Harveys Best, and
Rother Valley Level Best on handpump, and a fine wine list with several
(including champagne) by the glass. Some of the bedrooms in the converted
coach house have four-poster beds and a fireplace.

*Bar food (standard food times) ~ Restaurant ~ (01825) 722890 ~ Children
in eating area of bar and restaurant ~ Live music Fri evening and Sun
lunchtime ~ Open 12-3, 6-11; 12-11 Sat; 12-3, 7-10.30 Sun; 12-3, 6-11 Sat
in winter; closed 25 Dec ~ Bedrooms: /£75S(£85B)*

FORD Map 1 B5
White Hart

A420 Chippenham—Bristol; follow Colerne sign at E side of village to find pub

Unfaltering over the years, the continuing popularity of this fine stone country inn apparently stems from its ability to be all things to all people. Ideal for a weekend country break for those who want to treat themselves to good food and a comfortable night's sleep, the cosy bar also draws a younger crowd of locals in the evening, who make the most of the good range of beer and other drinks on offer. Set in stunning countryside, the grounds are wonderful in summer, when peacocks strut around the garden and you can sit on the terrace by the trout stream that babbles under a little stone bridge; there are good walks in the hills beyond the pub, too. There are heavy black beams supporting the white-painted boards of the ceiling, tub armchairs around polished wooden tables, small pictures and a few advertising mirrors on the walls, and an ancient fireplace (inscribed 1553); pool on a circular table, dominoes, TV, board games and piped music. They keep fine wines (including about eight by the glass), farm cider, a dozen malt whiskies, and up to eight well kept (if not cheap) real ales on handpump or tapped from the cask such as Bybrook White Hart, Courage Directors, Theakstons, Wadworths 6X and a couple of guests such as Burton Bridge Bitter and Thomas Hardy Royal Oak; friendly and helpful service. You will need to book for the very enjoyable, interesting food, which might include lunchtime bar snacks such as good soups like celery or lentil, mushroom and tarragon (£2.95), filled baguettes (from £3.95), ploughman's (from £4.75), provençale vegetables and polenta (£5.25), smoked duck breast with potato salad, hazelnut dressing and crispy vegetables or lambs liver and bacon with mash and onion gravy (£6.25), Thai chicken curry (£6.50) and grilled salmon with lemon butter (£6.95), and a more elaborate evening menu with dishes ranging from duck confit with caramelised pineapple and fried pak choi (£5.95) to roast soy marinated chicken breast with noodles and stir-fried vegetables in oyster sauce (£11.95) and grilled turbot fillet on buttered spinach with scallop, asparagus and saffron risotto and chive cream sauce (£17.50); three-course set lunch menu (£13.95). All bedrooms are spacious and well equipped; excellent breakfasts, and a secluded swimming pool for residents (the peacocks can make for an unusual dawn chorus).

Bar food (12-2, 7-9.30(10 Fri, Sat; 9 Sun)) ~ Restaurant ~ (01249) 782213 ~ Children in pool room and buttery ~ Open 11-3, 5-11; 12-3, 7-10.30 Sun; closed 25 Dec evening ~ Bedrooms: £64B/£84B

FRESHWATER Map 1 D6
Red Lion

Church Place; from A3055 at E end of village by Freshwater Garage mini-roundabout follow Yarmouth signpost, then take first real right turn signposted to Parish Church

Although this dining pub is tucked well enough out of the way to have kept a genuinely local atmosphere, the food is so popular that if you want to eat here it's a good idea to book ahead. Well cooked imaginative daily specials are listed on a big blackboard behind the bar, and might include clam chowder or bacon and lentil soup (£3), spicy coated sardines or crab and stilton stuffed mushrooms (£5.25), vegetable stir-fry (£6.95), home-made fishcakes with parsley sauce or leek and chicken pie (£7.25), moules marinières (£7.95), pork steak with brandy and mushrooms (£8.75), rack of lamb with redcurrant gravy (£13.95) or whole lobster thermidor (£18.95); puddings might include chocolate and orange cheesecake, treacle sponge and whisky and walnut trifle (£3). Service can be a bit slow. The comfortably furnished open-plan bar has open fires, low grey sofas and sturdy country-kitchen-style furnishings on mainly flagstoned floors, with bare boards at one end, and lots of local pictures and photographs and china platters on the walls. Well kept Flowers Original, Fullers London Pride, Goddards Special and Shepherd Neame Spitfire on handpump, and there's a good choice of wines including 16 by the glass; fruit machine and piped classical music. There are tables on a grassy area at the back (some under cover), behind which is the kitchen's herb garden, and a couple of picnic-sets in a quiet tucked-away square at the front, near the church; nearby good walks, especially around the River Yar.

Bar food (12-2, 6.30-9) ~ (01983) 754925 ~ Children over 10 ~ Open 11.30-3, 5.30-11; 11-4, 6-11 Sat; 12-3, 7-10.30 Sun; closed 25 Dec evening

FROGGATT EDGE Map 3 D3

Chequers

B6054, off A623 N of Bakewell; OS Sheet 119 map reference 247761

Froggatt Edge is just up through the woods behind this beautifully situated busy country inn, flourishing under its new licensees. The fairly smart bar has library chairs or small high-backed winged settles on the well waxed floorboards, an attractive richly varnished beam-and-board ceiling, antique prints on the white walls, partly stripped back to big dark stone blocks, and a big solid-fuel stove; one corner has a nicely carved oak cupboard. One of the main draws here is the tasty unusual bar food in the partly no-smoking dining area. The menu changes all the time but there might be soup (£2.25), very enjoyable hearty sandwiches (from £3.25, smoked salmon £5.50), smoked duck with kumquat chutney or bresaola with truffle oil and parmesan (£3.95), walnut and seared sweet pepper penne (£5.50), sausage of the day, mushroom and red pepper stroganoff (£5.95), chicken on pasta with ratatouille (£7.25), baked salmon and leeks (£7.95), minted lamb chops with sweet pepper cracked wheat (£8.95), whole baked grey mullet with vegetable pilau rice (£9.95), pork fillet with poached pear and mustard sauce (£10.20), 8oz sirloin (£10.95) and puddings such as chocolate and chestnut mousse and rhubarb puff pastry tart with Greek yoghurt (£2.50-£4.95); pleasant efficient service. Well kept Marstons Pedigree, Theakstons and a guest such as Black Sheep on handpump, a good range of malt whiskies and a changing wine board; piped music. There are seats in the peaceful back garden; six nicely furnished comfortable bedrooms.

Bar food (12-3, 5.30-9.30) ~ (01433) 630231 ~ Children in no-smoking section ~ Jazz last Weds of month ~ Open 12-3, 5.30-11; 12-11 Sat; 12-10.30 Sun ~ Bedrooms: £48B/£64B

GLASGOW Map 4 D2
Babbity Bowster
16-18 Blackfriars Street

This lively but stylish 18th-c town house is welcoming and cosmopolitan, with something of the feel of a continental café bar. The simply decorated light interior has fine tall windows, well lit photographs and big pen-and-wash drawings in modern frames of Glasgow and its people and musicians, dark grey stools and wall seats around dark grey tables on the stripped wooden boards, and an open peat fire. A big ceramic of a kilted dancer and piper in the bar illustrates the 18th-c folk song ('Bab at the Bowster') from which the pub takes its name. The bar opens on to a terrace with tables under cocktail parasols, trellised vines and shrubs, and adjacent boules; there may be barbecues out here in summer. Popular, well presented bar food includes several hearty home-made soups in two sizes (from £1.75), toasted sandwiches (from £3.50), haggis, neeps and tatties (£4.50; they also do a vegetarian version), stovies (£4.95), cauliflower moussaka (£5.95), good daily specials such as rabbit and red wine casserole (£6.50), and evening tapas (from £2.50). There are more elaborate meals in the airy upstairs restaurant. Well kept Caledonian Deuchars IPA and Belhaven IPA alongside well chosen guests such as Church End Cuthberts and Durham Magus on air pressure tall fount, a remarkably sound collection of wines, malt whiskies, cask conditioned cider, and good tea and coffee. Enthusiastic service is consistently efficient and friendly, taking its example from the vivacious landlord. They have live Celtic music on Saturday; dominoes. The bedrooms aren't huge and could do with being freshened up.

Bar food (12-11) ~ Restaurant ~ (0141) 552 5055 ~ Well behaved children away from main bar ~ Folk sessions Sat afternoon ~ Open 11(12.30 Sun)-12; closed 25 Dec ~ Bedrooms: £50S/£70B

GLASTONBURY Map 1 C5
Who'd A Thought It
Northload Street (off A39/B3151 roundabout)

Attractively reworked a few years ago, this makes nice use of mellow reclaimed brick, relaid flagstones and pine panelling. Above an old-fashioned range are hung fly-fishing rods and a gun, and the walls (and even the ceiling of the no-smoking eating area) are profusely decorated with blue and white china, lots of photographs including aerial ones of old Glastonbury, and bygones from a shelf of earthenware flagons and another of old bottles to venerable enamel advertising signs. There are several linked areas, friendly, light and airy, with black beams and joists, coal fires, and a mix of furnishings from built-in pews to stripped country tables and chairs; one room shows a well uncovered in the 1980s. A good range of freshly prepared and nicely presented honest food includes soup (£2.65), sandwiches (from £2.95), filled baguettes (from £3.25), goats cheese on roasted vegetables (£3.75/£5.95), beef or spinach and stilton lasagne (£6.25), pie and roast of the day (£6.50), fried tuna or swordfish (£6.95) and puddings (£2.95). Well kept Palmers IPA, Gold and 2000 on handpump, good value wines, pleasant staff and daily papers. The lavatories are worth a look (the gents' has all you don't need to know, from what to do in a gas attack to a history of England from the Zulu Wars to World War II; the ladies' is more Beryl Cook). The outside of the pub is attractive.

Bar food (12-2, 6-10; 12-2.30, 6-9.30 Sun) ~ (01458) 834460 ~ Children in the well room ~ Open 11-2.30, 5-11(11-11 Fri, Sat); 12-2.30, 6-10.30 Sun; closed 25 Dec evening ~ Bedrooms: £40B/£58B

GOSFIELD Map 2 B5
Green Man

3 miles N of Braintree

This smart dining pub is especially popular for its help-yourself lunchtime cold table, where you can choose from a tempting selection of home-cooked ham and pork, turkey, tongue, beef and poached or smoked salmon, as well as game pie, salads and home-made pickles (from £6.95). There's a good choice of generous, mostly traditional English bar food including soups such as game with sherry (from £2.85), sandwiches (from £2.40), filled baked potatoes (from £2.60), soft roe on toast (£3.75), mixed grill (£7.25), calves liver and bacon or pork chops marinated in oil and mustard (£7.95), and chicken breast filled with crab, cream cheese and prawns (£8.95), as well as a decent selection of fresh fish such as trout baked with almonds (£7.50) or swordfish steak (£8.25); vegetarian dishes such as deep-fried vegetable platter are available on request (£6.25). Mouth-watering home-made puddings include fruit pies, pavlovas and treacle tart (£3), vegetables are fresh and the chips home-made. The landlady is welcoming and you can expect friendly, efficient service. There's a laid-back sociable atmosphere in the two little bars, which have well kept Greene King IPA and Abbot on handpump. Many of the decent nicely priced wines are by the glass; darts, pool, fruit machine and juke box. Booking is advisable even midweek if you want to eat here.

Bar food (12-2, 6.45-9; not Sun evening) ~ Restaurant ~ (01787) 472746 ~ Well behaved children in restaurant and eating area of bar ~ Open 11-3, 6-11; 12-3, 7-10.30 Sun

GREAT HAMPDEN Map 2 B3
Hampden Arms

Village signposted off A4010 N and S of Princes Risborough

In a lovely quiet spot opposite the village cricket pitch, this friendly pub is popular for its good, interesting food. There might be home-made soup (£3.50), good value light lunches such as cottage pie, chicken and ham bake or cannelloni (all £4.95), vegetarian lasagne (£5.95), steak and mushroom pie, ham and egg, butterfly prawns, various omelettes or coquilles St-Jacques (all £6.95), giant cod or rib-eye steak (£8.95), orange pork (£10.95), chicken maryland (£11.95), and puddings such as sticky toffee pudding or banana pancake (£3.50). A small corner bar has well kept Adnams, Brakspears, and Fullers London Pride on handpump, and winter mulled wine; service is quietly obliging. The green-walled front room has broad dark tables, with a few aeroplane pictures and country prints; the back room has a slightly more rustic feel, with its cushioned wall benches and big woodburning stove; one room is no smoking. There are tables out in the tree-sheltered garden; on the edge of Hampden Common, the pub has good walks nearby.

Bar food (12-2, 6.30-9.30) ~ (01494) 488255 ~ Children welcome ~ Open 12-3, 6.30-11; 12-3, 6.30-10.30 Sun; may close some Sun or Mon evenings

GREAT WHITTINGTON Map 3 A3
Queens Head

Village signposted off A68 and B6018 just N of Corbridge

The two beamed rooms at this simple but civilised stone inn are comfortably furnished and neatly decorated with some handsome carved oak settles among other more modern furnishings, a mural over the fireplace near the bar counter, old prints and a collection of keys, and log fires. A fairly wide-ranging menu served by courteous helpful staff includes lunchtime sandwiches (£3.50) and ploughman's (£4.50), as well as more elaborate dishes such as smoked chicken and hazelnut salad (£4.95), home-made seafood ravioli with cheese sauce or smoked salmon and tiger prawn mille feuille with lime and fennel salsa (£5.95), honey-roast gammon with dijon mustard mash and peppercorn sauce (£8.95), honey-fried chicken on noodles with ginger and lemon marmalade or cod fillet with spinach and herb crust (£10.95), roast duck breast on spiced cabbage with ginger and balsamic glaze (£12.95), two or three daily specials such as trout fillet with roasted fennel (£9.95) and puddings such as nougat ice cream on fruit coulis or chocolate mousse with coffee anglaise (£3.50); the restaurant is no smoking. Well kept Black Sheep Best, Hambleton Bitter and Queens Head Bitter (brewed for them by Hambleton) on handpump, 30 malt whiskies, and decent wines; maybe unobtrusive piped music. There are six picnic-sets on the small front lawn, and the surrounding partly wooded countryside is pretty.

Bar food (standard food times) ~ Restaurant ~ (01434) 672267 ~ Children in eating area of bar and restaurant ~ Open 12-2.30, 6-11; 12-3, 7-10.30 Sun; closed Mon except bank holidays

GREAT WOLFORD Map 1 A6
Fox & Hounds

Village signposted on right on A3400 3 miles S of Shipston on Stour

New licensees at this inviting 16th-c stone pub are running it along the same successful lines as the previous owners, which means that although its main draw is still the imaginative bar food there's also a very good range of real ales and a welcoming pubby atmosphere. The cosy low-beamed old-fashioned bar has a nice collection of chairs and candlelit old tables on spotless flagstones, old hunting prints on the walls, and a roaring log fire in the inglenook fireplace with its fine old bread oven. A small tap room serves well kept Hook Norton and around five changing beers, which might include Adnams Broadside, Cottage Champflower and Great Western and Timothy Taylors Landlord on handpump, and over 200 malt whiskies. Alongside straightforward meals such as sandwiches (from £3.75), soup (£2.95) and ploughman's (from £6.95), imaginative daily specials might include fresh sardines stuffed with onions and basil with provençale sauce (£3.75), roasted Mediterranean vegetable salad (£5.25), caesar salad (£5.75/£8.95), salmon fillet poached on local asparagus with hollandaise (£9.95), Cornish lemon sole topped with prawns, garlic and mascarpone (£11.50), fried guinea fowl on bacon and lyonnaise potatoes with a plum and herb compote (£10.95), baked potato skins filled with tomato and cream cheese and puréed potatoes topped with mozzarella with tomato coulis (£8.25), and puddings such as lavender crème brûlée or elderflower and rhubarb fool (from £4.50). There's a well on the terrace outside. They don't serve breakfast if you stay here.

Bar food (12-2.30, 7-9) ~ Restaurant ~ No credit cards ~ (01608) 674220 ~ Well behaved children welcome ~ Jazz Sun evening ~ Open 12-3, 6-11; closed Mon ~ Bedrooms: £35B/£55B

HADDENHAM Map 2 B3
Green Dragon

Village signposted off A418 and A4129, E/NE of Thame; then follow Church End signs

The interesting choice of food still remains the main reason for coming to this popular dining pub. As well as sandwiches (from £3.25), there might be home-made soup (£3.50), baked courgette and goats cheese cake served with roast vegetables (£4.95), crab and salmon fishcakes with mango salsa (£5), special steak sandwich on garlic bread with home-made chips (£6.95), a trio of pork sausages on mash with onion gravy and crisp fried onions (£7.50), home-made pie of the day (£8.50), Cornish fillets of bass on braised fennel with juniper berries (£11), sautéed Gressingham duck breast with wild mushroom and thyme jus or fillet steak encased in cashel blue cheese with a port sauce (£11.50), and puddings like lemon tart with raspberry sorbet or sticky toffee pudding with toffee sauce (£3.95); they offer a set price menu on Tuesday and Thursday evenings which they call Simply a Tenner, which is very popular and best to book in advance. Well kept Fullers London Pride and Vale Wychert on handpump, and sensibly priced, well chosen wines including a few by the glass. The main area is divided into two high-ceilinged communicating rooms, decorated with attractive still lifes and country pictures; piped music. For those just wanting a drink, there is still a respectable corner set aside. A big sheltered gravel terrace behind the pub has white tables and picnic-sets under cocktail parasols, with more on the grass, and a good variety of plants. This part of the village is very pretty, with a duckpond unusually close to the church.

Bar food (not Sun evening) ~ Restaurant ~ (01844) 291403 ~ Well behaved children in restaurant (must be over 7 in the evenings) ~ Open 11.30-2.30, 6.30-11; 12-2 Sun; closed Sun evening

HARE HATCH Map 2 C3
Queen Victoria
Blakes Lane; just N of A4 Reading—Maidenhead

As well as being a friendly local where you can enjoy the consistently well kept real ales, this is also a pub with good, interesting food and a welcome for visitors. The two chatty, low-beamed bars are nicely furnished with flowers on tables, strong spindleback chairs, wall benches and window seats, and decorations such as a stuffed sparrowhawk and a Delft shelf lined with beaujolais bottles; the tables on the right are no smoking. Changing daily, popular bar food might include sandwiches (from £2.20), olive and stilton pâté (£2.95), sautéed chicken livers with brandy and cream (£3.95), steak and oyster pie (£5.80), sizzling Thai pork, Chinese chicken, pepper and onion kebab, smoked fish medley, and cheese and chilli beef tortillas (all £5.95), and barbary duck breast in rosemary and garlic (£9.95); vegetables are fresh. Well kept Brakspears Bitter, Special, Old and a seasonal beer on handpump, a fair choice of wines by the glass, and obliging service. Dominoes, cribbage, fruit machine, and three-dimensional noughts and crosses. There's a flower-filled no-smoking conservatory, and a robust table or two in front by the car park.

Bar food (12-2.30, 6.30-10.30; 12-10 Sun) ~ Restaurant ~ (0118) 940 2477 ~ Children welcome ~ Open 11-3, 5.30-11; 12-10.30 Sun

HAROME Map 3 B4

Star

Village signposted S of A170, E of Helmsley

For those not wanting to drive home after a delicious meal in this pretty 14th-c thatched inn, you can now stay in one of the two bedrooms in their nearby thatched 15th-c cottage. The interior of the pub is charming, with a dark bowed beam-and-plank ceiling, well polished tiled kitchen range, plenty of bric-a-brac, interesting furniture (this was the first pub that 'Mousey Thompson' ever populated with his famous dark wood furniture), two wonderful log fires, daily papers and magazines, and a no-smoking dining room; the coffee loft in the eaves is popular. For the excellent, inventive food, fish is delivered daily from Hartlepool, they grow their own herbs and some vegetables, use local hen, duck, and guinea fowl eggs, and three types of honey from the village; they also offer 15 British cheeses. Changing daily, the dishes might include sandwiches, spring green soup with smoked bacon dumplings (£2.95), terrine of boiled gammon with a fried quail egg, spiced pineapple pickle, and mustard seed dressing (£4.95), shallow-fried kipper croquettes with tartare velouté, flat parsley, and anchovy salad (£5.50; main course £9.95), a plate of marinated spring vegetables with cauliflower purée and roast almond cream (£5.95), grilled queen scallops with avocado fritters and smoked bacon (£7.95; main course £12.95), breast of corn-fed guinea fowl with celeriac purée, fairy ring mushrooms, tarragon and dry sherry (£10.95), warm salad of locally reared duck with wild turnip rösti and raisin stuffing (£12.50), roast loin of suckling pig with cider potato, sage, and black pudding stuffing, and cider brandy sauce (£13.50), fillet of brill with a deep-fried scampi fritter, pea purée, and cherry tomato ketchup (£13.95), and puddings like baked ginger parkin with rhubarb ripple ice cream and hot spiced syrup, sticky plum pudding with cognac custard and apple brandy compote or caramelised fresh lemon tart with a sauce of raspberries (from £4.50); good, helpful service. Well kept Black Sheep, John Smiths, Theakstons Best, and a guest like Black Sheep Riggwelter on handpump, farm ciders, freshly squeezed juices, home-made rhubarb schnapps or bramble vodka, and quite a few wines by the glass from a fairly extensive wine list. There are some seats and tables on a sheltered front terrace with more in the garden with fruit trees and a big ash behind. They have a village cricket team.

Bar food (11.30-2, 6.30-9.30; 12-6 Sun; not Sun evening, not Mon) ~ Restaurant ~ (01439) 770397 ~ Children welcome ~ Open 11.30-3, 6.15(6 Sat)-11; 12-10.30 Sun; closed Mon; 1 wk Nov; 3 wks Jan ~ Bedrooms: £45B/£90B

HARRINGWORTH Map 3 E4
White Swan

Seaton Road; village SE of Uppingham, signposted from A6003, A47 and A43

Set in a pretty village with a famous 82-arch railway viaduct, this limestone Tudor inn still shows signs of its coaching days in the blocked-in traces of its carriage-entry arch. There's a pleasantly calming atmosphere and the staff are friendly and efficient. The neatly kept central bar area has good solid tables, a hand-crafted oak bar counter with a mirror base and an attractive swan carving on its front, an open fire, and pictures relating to the World War II airfield at nearby Spanhoe among a collection of old village photographs (in which many of the present buildings are still recognisable). The roomy and welcoming lounge/eating area has comfortable settles, while a quieter no-smoking dining room has a collection of old jugs, craft tools, dried flower arrangements and locally painted watercolours. Cooked by a Spanish chef, good, varied bar food includes sandwiches (from £2.50), soup (£2.95), hot baguettes (from £3), home-made chicken liver pâté or grilled goats cheese with sun-dried tomatoes and black olives (£3.95), asparagus, mushroom and brie pancakes or grilled chicken stuffed with onion and mushrooms and topped with stilton, (£6.95), venison sausages, bubble and squeak and onion gravy (£7), braised lamb knuckle with rosemary, orange and redcurrant sauce (£8.95) and steaks (from £8.95) with puddings such as strawberry jam sponge pudding and hot chocolate brownies (£2.95). Well kept Greene King IPA and Ruddles County and maybe a guest such as Wadworths 6X on handpump. Darts and piped music; tables outside on a little terrace.

Bar food (12-2, 7-10(9 Sun)) ~ Restaurant ~ (01572) 747543 ~ Children in eating area of bar and restaurant ~ Fri music night twice a month ~ Open 11.30-2.30, 6.30-11; 12-3, 7-10.30 Sun ~ Bedrooms: £40S/£55S

HATTON Map 1 A6
Falcon

4.6 miles from M40 junction 15; A46 towards Warwick, then left on A4177, and keep on past Hatton; Birmingham Road, Haseley

Very handy for Warwick, this well reworked old pub has five calm and relaxing open-plan rooms working their way around a central island bar. Lots of stripped brickwork, low beams, tiled and oak-planked floors tell of the building's internal age, with a couple of dark blue walls, nice prints and old photographs, arrangements of pretty fresh flowers, big turkey rugs and a nice mix of stripped and waxed country tables and various chairs adding a smart touch. A big barn-style back dining area is no smoking. A wide choice of interesting food includes lunchtime sandwiches (from £2.95), soup (£3.50), pâté with beetroot and mango chutney (£4.50), crispy duck salad with hoisin (£4.95), wild mushroom stroganoff (£6.95), calves liver on potato and onion rösti with port sauce (£7.50), beef, garlic and black peppercorn stew with roasted root vegetables (£8.50) and duck breast with orange sauce (£9.25). Well kept Banks's Bitter and Original, Hook Norton Best, M&B Brew XI, Marstons Pedigree and a guest such as Otter on handpump. A well separated games room has darts, fruit machine and a TV, and there are picnic-sets out on lawns at the side and behind.

Bar food (12-3, 7-9(6-9.30 Sat); 12-3 Sun; not Sun evening) ~ Restaurant ~ (01926) 484737 ~ Children welcome in the no-smoking area ~ Open 11.30-11; 12-10.30 Sun

HEDLEY ON THE HILL Map 10
Feathers

Village signposted from New Ridley, which is signposted from B6309 N of Consett;
OS Sheet 88 map reference 078592

The landlady's interest in vegetarian food is reflected in five or so tempting
vegetarian dishes at this delightful old stone pub. The menu changes twice
a week and given the standard of the imaginative cooking is very good
value. There might be lettuce, mange tout and mint soup (£3.25), caesar
salad (£3.95), goats cheese and red onion tart or spiced chick-pea, sweet
potato and vegetable tortilla (£6.25), salmon steak with lemon and parsley
butter or pork casserole with apricots and spices (£6.50), lamb casserole
with fresh pesto and tomatoes or sun-dried tomato, olive and roast pepper
risotto (£7.50) and puddings such as pear and ginger pudding or whisky
and honey ice cream (£3.25). There's still a good pubby atmosphere in the
three well kept turkey-carpeted traditional bars, with beams, open fires,
stripped stonework, solid brown leatherette settles and old black and white
photographs of local places and country folk working the land. Well kept
Boddingtons, Mordue Workie Ticket and two guest beers from brewers
such as Big Lamp and Black Sheep on handpump; they hold a mini beer
festival around Easter with over two dozen real ales which ends with a
barrel race on Easter Monday; decent wines, and around 30 malt whiskies.
Darts, shove-ha'penny, table skittles, cribbage, and dominoes. From picnic-
sets in front you can watch the world drift by.

*Bar food (not lunchtimes or Mon except bank holidays) ~ No credit cards ~
(01661) 843607 ~ Children in eating area of bar and family room till 9pm ~
Open 6-11; 12-3, 6-11 Sat; 12-3, 7-11 Sun; closed wkday lunchtimes except
bank holidays and 25 Dec*

HELSTON Map 1 E2
Halzephron

Gunwalloe, village about 4 miles S but not marked on many road maps; look for
brown sign on A3083 alongside perimeter fence of RNAS Culdrose

Even at their busiest, the hard-working licensee and her staff at this former
smugglers' haunt are unfailingly welcoming and helpful – and the
imaginative food continues to delight readers. The bustling and pleasant bar
is spotlessly clean with comfortable seating, copper on the walls and
mantelpiece, and a warm winter fire in the big hearth; there's also quite a
small no-smoking family room. At lunchtime, bar snacks include
sandwiches (from £2.90; super crab £7.50), home-made soup (£3.80),
freshly made pâté or mushrooms sautéed with herbs in a cream sauce with
garlic bread (£5), ploughman's (from £5), and platters such as crab, prawn
or smoked salmon (from £10.50), with evening choices like breast of
chicken marinated in herbs and dijon mustard, breadcrumbed and deep
fried (£9.50), and chargrilled sirloin steak (£11.90); evening specials might
include smoked salmon pâté (£5), duck leg confit on oriental cabbage with
sweet and sour sauce (£6.10), pasta with Mediterranean vegetables,
artichokes, olives and sun-dried tomatoes with olive oil and basil, topped
with parmesan (£8.30), sweet and sour pork with egg fried rice (£9.90),
roast saddle of lamb with an apricot and rosemary stuffing on garlic pomme
purée, with a date compote and red wine sauce (£10.90), wild boar, juniper
and borlotti bean casserole (£11.80), caramelised Gressingham duck on
butternut squash purée with redcurrant juniper jus (£13), and home-made
puddings like lemon mousse, hot chocolate fudge cake or caramel cream
pots (from £3.20); all the eating areas are no smoking. Well kept Sharps
Cornish Coaster, Own and Doom Bar, and St Austell Daylight Robbery on
handpump, a good wine list, 40 malt whiskies, and around 25 liqueurs;
dominoes and cribbage. There are lots of lovely surrounding unspoilt walks
with fine views of Mount's Bay, Gunwalloe fishing cove is just 300 yards
away, and there's a sandy beach one mile away at Church Cove.

*Bar food (standard food times; not 25 Dec) ~ Restaurant ~ (01326) 240406
~ Children in family room ~ Open 11-2.30, 6(6.30 winter)-11; 12-2.30,
6.30-10.30 Sun; closed 25 Dec ~ Bedrooms: £38B/£68B*

HETTON Map 3 B3
Angel

Just off B6265 Skipton—Grassington

This particularly well run place remains a firm favourite with many of our readers. The car park is usually full by 11.45, but despite its popularity, the bar staff greet everyone on arrival and remain efficient and welcoming throughout; they now take bookings and use a blackboard to chalk up a waiting list. The first-class, imaginative food is what customers have come to enjoy (though the range of drinks is excellent, too): home-made black pudding with crisp pancetta and braised puy lentils (£4.95), grilled goats cheese on toasted ciabatta with a black olive and tomato salsa (£5.25), little moneybags (seafood baked in a crisp pastry bag with lobster sauce, £5.50), home-cured and air-dried beef with rocket, parmesan and virgin oil (£6.50), local cornfed chicken breast wrapped in air-dried ham on a bed of celeriac and tarragon chicken jus (£11.95), roast breast of Goosnargh duckling with corn syrup and ginger, garnished with spring onions and shi-itake mushrooms or seared fillet of bass on a crisp tomato tart, rocket salad, drizzled with pesto (£13.95), roast loin of Yorkshire Dales lamb and seared kidneys with creamed spinach and roast garlic (£14.50), daily specials such as cream of roast butternut squash soup (£3.50), queen scallops baked in garlic butter and gruyère (£4.95; main course £7.50), award-winning pork sausage with rich onion gravy (£7.95), poached fillet of smoked haddock, spinach, slow roast tomatoes, and hollandaise sauce (£8.25), Italian antipasti (£9.25), and puddings like chocolate brownie cheesecake, crème brûlée or warm bread and butter pudding (from £4.50). Well kept Black Sheep Bitter, Tetleys, and Timothy Taylors Landlord and Golden Best on handpump, 300 wines (with 25 by the glass, including champagne), and a good range of malt whiskies. The four timbered and panelled rambling rooms have lots of cosy alcoves, comfortable country-kitchen chairs or button-back green plush seats, Ronald Searle wine snob cartoons and older engravings and photographs, log fires, and in the main bar, a Victorian farmhouse range in the big stone fireplace; the snug and bar lounge are no smoking (as is the main restaurant). Wooden seats and tables under colourful sunshades on the terrace.

Bar food (12-2.15, 6-9) ~ Restaurant ~ (01756) 730263 ~ Well behaved children welcome ~ Open 12-3, 6-10.30(11 Sat); closed 1 week Jan

HEYDON Map 2 B4
King William IV
Off A505 W of M11 junction 10

For years the licensee here, Elizabeth Nicholls, has led the way forward in vegetarian cooking in pubs, showing others what can easily be done with a little extra thought and effort. Last year this immaculately run place won our National Vegetarian Pub of the Year award. It isn't just that they offer around a dozen vegetarian dishes, it's the fact that they are genuinely interesting, too: asparagus, broccoli and roquefort lattice puff with a cheese fondue, cashew and pine kernel stir-fry with noodles and crackers, baked field mushrooms with Mediterranean fruits and emmenthal crust, ricotta, leek and sweet chestnut crumble, nutty and date curry, and nutmeg, spinach and cream cheese crispy pancakes with a tomato and chive sauce (from £7.95). Meat lovers are by no means left out though, with other enjoyable bar food including lunchtime sandwiches (from £3.15), filled baguettes (from £4), bangers and mash (£6.95), steak and kidney shortcrust pie (£7.95), confit of duck or beef and mushrooms in stout with herb dumplings (£9.25), braised lamb shank with redcurrant jus or grilled swordfish steak with avocado and mango salsa (£10.95), with puddings like bread and butter pudding and fresh cream mousse or dark chocolate torte with raspberry coulis (from £4.95). Part of the restaurant is no smoking. The nooks and crannies of the beamed rambling rooms, warmed in winter by a log fire, are crowded with a delightful jumble of rustic implements like ploughshares, yokes and iron tools as well as cowbells, beer steins, samovars, cut-glass, brass or black wrought-iron lamps, copper-bound casks and milk ewers, harness, horsebrasses, smith's bellows, and decorative plates and china ornaments. Half a dozen well kept real ales include Adnams, Fullers London Pride, Greene King IPA and Abbot and Ruddles County and a guest such as Morrells Graduate on handpump. They'll also do you a cocktail here; friendly, efficient staff. Fruit machine and piped music. A new wooden deck has teak furniture and outdoor heaters, and there are more seats in the pretty garden.

Bar food (till 10pm (9.30pm Sun)) ~ Restaurant ~ (01763) 838773 ~ Children welcome in snug ~ Open 12-2.30, 6(6.30 winter)-11; 12-3, 7-10.30 Sun; closed 25 Dec

HEYTESBURY Map 1 C6
Angel

High Sreet; just off A36 E of Warminster

This peacefully set 16th-c inn is situated in a quiet village street just below Salisbury Plain, and is a very pleasant place to stay, with imaginative bar food, well kept ales, and above all, impeccable service ensuring that customers are well looked after. The spacious homely lounge on the right, with well used overstuffed armchairs and sofas and a good fire, opens into a charming back dining room which is simple but smart with a blue carpet, blue-cushioned chairs and lots of prints on the white-painted brick walls. On the left, a long beamed bar has a convivial evening atmosphere, a woodburner, some attractive prints and old photographs on its terracotta-coloured walls, and straightforward tables and chairs. The dining room opens on to an attractive secluded courtyard garden. Good food includes home-made soup (£3.50), filo prawns with sweet chilli mayonnaise (£5.50), filo basket with oyster mushrooms, spinach, feta and pink peppercorns (£5.75), sausage and mash (£6.50), game and vegetable pie (£6.95), braised lamb shank (£9.75), butterfly pork loin on baby spinach and oyster mushrooms with puy lentils (£10.95), roast salmon fillet with parmesan risotto and crispy leeks (£11.75), roast saddle of venison on red cabbage braised in orange and mixed spice (£14.75), puddings such as sticky toffee pudding with butterscotch sauce and Devon cream, warm frangipane and raspberry tart (£3.50), and English cheeses (£3.75). A good choice of very well kept beers includes Marstons Pedigree, Ringwood Best and Timothy Taylors Landlord on handpump; also around a dozen wines by the glass. Bedrooms are either new or recently refurbished.

Bar food (12-2, 7-9.30) ~ Restaurant ~ (01985) 840330 ~ Children welcome ~ Open 11.30-3, 6.30-11; 12-3, 7-10.30 Sun ~ Bedrooms: £40B/£50B

HIGHMOOR Map 1 C6
Rising Sun

Witheridge Hill, signposted off B481; OS Sheet 175 map reference 697841

Recently reworked as a dining pub, this pretty black and white building has an airy, civilised feel. There are seats around a few simple tables in a smallish carpeted area on the right, by the bar, with some bar stools too, and a big log-effect stove in a big brick inglenook fireplace. The main area spreading back from here has shiny bare boards and a swath of red carpeting, with well spaced tables, attractive pictures on cream or dark salmon walls, and a side bit with a leather settee, low games table and shove-ha'penny, liar dice, chess and so forth. There's some emphasis on the food side, which might include jalapeño peppers with yoghurt and mint dip (£4.25), baguettes (£4.85), ploughman's (from £4.95), spicy sausages (£5.75), vegetable, chicken or prawn Thai stir-fry (£6.85), moules marinières or breaded lemon sole (£7.45) and steaks (from £10.45) with specials such as crab cakes with chilli sauce or chicken liver pâté (£4.25), roast pork knuckle and mash or penne pasta with creamy pesto sauce (£7.25) and roast lamb shoulder with redcurrant and rosemary sauce (£9.25); puddings such as blackberry pancakes (from £3.25). Well kept Brakspears PA and SB on handpump, good pleasant service; may be unobtrusive piped pop music. There are picnic-sets on a fairy-lit terrace and on grass among trees; it's a nice quiet spot, by a rough sloping green.

Bar food (12-2.30, 7-9.30; 12-2.30, 6.30-9.15 Sun) ~ Restaurant ~ (01491) 641455 ~ Children welcome ~ Open 11-3, 6-11; 12-3, 6.30-10.30 Sun

HINDON Map 1 C6
Grosvenor Arms

B3089 Wilton—Mere

New licensees have cosied up this 18th-c coaching inn by painting the
traditional pubby bar red, decorating it with Victorian prints and artefacts
and bringing in a nice mix of old tables and chairs. The candlelight, lovely
log fire and fresh flowers help, and there are flagstones. Off the entrance
hall is a civilised no-smoking lounge with grey panelling, armchairs, settees,
a cushioned antique settle and country magazines. The long dining room
has been smartened up with cream paint and big photographs of the
surrounding area, and a huge window lets you view the goings on in the
kitchen. There's some concentration on good freshly made well presented
food, which changes daily but might include gazpacho soup (£3.95), grilled
open sandwiches (£4.50), sausage and mash (£6.95), smoked haddock
fishcakes with fresh bean salad and red pepper coulis (£7.50), tagliatelle
with langoustine and scallops (£8), grilled pork cutlet with braised fennel
(£8.95), sirloin steak with rocket and parmesan salad and creamed celeriac;
vegetables (£1.95), and puddings such as praline parfait with raspberry
coulis or orange and rosemary cheesecake (£4.50). Well kept Bass and
Wadworths 6X and a guest such as Tisbury Stonehenge on handpump,
good house wines including about a dozen by the glass, daily papers. There
are good teak chairs around tables under cocktail parasols and big
flowering tubs in the back courtyard, which is very prettily lit at night.

*Bar food (standard food times) ~ Restaurant ~ (01747) 820696 ~ Children
in eating area of bar and family room ~ Open 11-11; 12-3 Sun; closed Sun
evening ~ Bedrooms: £45.50B/£60B*

HOGNASTON Map 3 D3
Red Lion

Village signposted off B5035 Ashbourne—Wirksworth

Although there is an emphasis on the enjoyable food at this friendly welcoming place, it's still very much a pub where locals drop in for a drink. The open-plan oak-beamed bar has a good relaxed atmosphere, with almost a bistro feel around the attractive mix of old tables (candlelit at night) on ancient flagstones, and copies of *Country Life* to read. There are old-fashioned settles among other seats, three open fires, and a growing collection of teddy bears among other bric-a-brac. Well cooked popular bar meals include home-made soup (£3.95), devilled kidneys (£4.25), warm goats cheese tart (£5.25), Thai green chicken curry (£10.50), seafood marinara (£10.95), asparagus, sun-dried tomato and black olive risotto (£12.50), braised shank of lamb on olive mash (£14.95), fried beef fillet on puy lentils and béarnaise sauce (£16.95), puddings (from £3.95); booking is recommended for weekends. Well kept Marstons Pedigree, Greene King Abbot, Greene King Old Speckled Hen and a guest such as Timothy Taylor Landlord on handpump; country wines. Service is friendly and attentive; piped music. Handy for Carsington Reservoir.

Bar food (standard food times; not Sun evening, not Mon) ~ (01335) 370396 ~ Open 12-3, 6-11(7-10.30 Sun); closed Mon lunchtime ~ Bedrooms: £45S/£75S

HORNDON-ON-THE-HILL Map 2 C5
Bell

M25 junction 30 into A13, then left into B1007 after 7 miles, village signposted from here

This medieval hall (a real sight in summer when it's covered with flowers) seems to be doing better than ever, with readers singling out for comment the pleasant atmosphere, beautifully presented food and obliging and knowledgeable staff. They stock more than 100 well chosen wines from all over the world, including over a dozen by the glass, and you can buy bottles off-sales. The heavily beamed bar has some antique high-backed settles and benches, rugs on the flagstones or highly polished oak floorboards, and a curious collection of hot cross buns hanging from a beam. The popular menu, which changes twice a day, is available in the bar and no-smoking restaurant, and well cooked dishes might include sandwiches (from £4.95), swede soup (£3.95), grilled asparagus with olives and lemon mayonnaise (£5.50), yoghurt marinated cod with smoked tomato salsa or pot roast chicken with peas and girolles (£11.95), grilled smoked rib-eye steak or cold red wine poached halibut (£12.95), and puddings such as bramley apple and date ice cream or poached rhubarb with ginger praline meringue (from £4 – readers recommend the lemon tart with brandy snap); two-course set meal £13.95, three courses £15.95. They stock a good range of well kept real ales, with changing guests such as Batemans XXXB, Cottage Golden Arrow and Crouch Vale Brewers Gold joining Bass and Greene King IPA on handpump; occasional beer festivals. On the last weekend in June, the High Road outside is closed (by Royal Charter) for period-costume festivities and a crafts fair. The beamed bedrooms are very attractive.

Bar food (12-1.45, 6.45-9.45; not bank hol Mon) ~ Restaurant ~ (01375) 642463 ~ Children in eating area of bar and restaurant ~ Open 11-2.30 (3 Sat), 5.30(6 Sat)-11; 12-4, 7-10.30 Sun; closed 25 and 26 Dec ~ Bedrooms: /£65B

ICKLESHAM Map 2 D5
Queens Head
Just off A259 Rye—Hastings

There's a fine choice of drinks at this well run handsome pub, with 16 wines by the glass (many in small or large sizes), well kept Daleside Shrimpers, Greene King IPA and Abbot, and guests such as Fullers ESB, Hampshire Pride of Romsey, and Harveys Old on handpump, and Biddenden cider. The open-plan areas work round a very big serving counter which stands under a vaulted beamed roof, the high beamed walls and ceiling of the easy-going bar are lined with shelves of bottles and covered with farming implements and animal traps, and there are well used pub tables and old pews on the brown patterned carpet. Other areas (two are no smoking) are popular with diners and have big inglenook fireplaces. Generously served, enjoyable bar food includes sandwiches (from £2.45), home-made soup such as lentil and bacon or sweet potato and watercress (£3.25), home-made pâté (£3.95), soft herring roes on toast (£4.25), ploughman's (£4.50), home-cooked ham and egg (£5.50), broccoli and cauliflower cheese (£5.95), curry of the day or steak and mushroom in ale pie (£6.95), steaks (from £9.95), and home-made daily specials such as wild mushroom risotto (£5.75), chicken breast in stilton and apricot sauce (£6.95), lots of fresh fish (£7-£10), scallops in wine, cream and bacon sauce (£9.95), and puddings such as fruit crumble or banoffi pie (from £2.75); prompt service from friendly efficient staff. Shove-ha'penny, dominoes, fruit machine, and piped music. Picnic-sets look out over the vast, gently sloping plain of the Brede valley from the little garden, and there's an outside children's play area, and boules. Good local walks.

Bar food (12-2.45, 6.15-9.45; all day Fri-Sun; not 25, 26 Dec) ~ (01424) 814552 ~ Well behaved children in eating area of bar till 8.30pm ~ Live jazz/blues/folk/classical Tues evenings ~ Open 11-11; 12-10.30 Sun; closed evening 25 Dec

ICKLINGHAM Map 2 A5

Red Lion

A1101 Mildenhall—Bury St Edmunds

This civilised 16th-c thatched dining pub is the perfect place for a pleasant drink at the bar followed by a relaxing Sunday lunch. Get there a bit earlier (or book) for a table in the nicer beamed open-plan bar, which has a big inglenook fireplace and is attractively furnished with a nice mixture of wooden chairs, big candlelit tables and turkey rugs on the polished wood floor. A simpler area behind a knocked-through fireplace has dark wood pub tables on carpets; piped classical music. There's quite an emphasis on the popular enjoyable bar food, which includes home-made soup (£3.55), home-made pâté (£3.65), local sausages with mash and onion gravy (£6.25), lambs liver and bacon (£7.95), pork chops with apple and cider sauce or warm fillet of chicken and crispy pasta salad (£8.95) and over a dozen changing fish dishes such as mackerel with caper butter (£9.95), ling fillet with tomato soup and cheese (£10.95), mixed grill (£11.85) and bass with chilli butter (£15.95). Well kept Greene King IPA and Abbot on handpump, lots of country wines and fruit presses, and winter mulled wine. In front (the pub is well set back from the road), picnic-sets with colourful parasols overlook the car park and lawn, and at the back more seats on a raised terrace face the fields – including an acre of the pub's running down to the River Lark, with Cavenham Heath nature reserve beyond; giant outside Jenga; handy for West Stow Country Park and the Anglo-Saxon Village.

Bar food (12-2.30, 6-10; 12-2, 7.15-9.30 Sun) ~ Restaurant ~ (01638) 717802 ~ Children welcome ~ Open 12-2.30, 6-11; 12-2, 7.15-10.30 Sun

INNERLEITHEN Map 4 D3
Traquair Arms

Traquair Road (B709, just off A72 Peebles—Galashiels; follow signs for Traquair House)

This pleasantly modernised inn is a hospitable place to visit especially since the good bar food is served almost all day. Using lots of fresh local ingredients, enjoyable meals might include home-made soup (£2.10), filled baked potatoes (from £2.95), king prawn and chilli kebab (£3.95), omelettes (from £4), haggis sausages (£5.95), steak and ale pie (£6.65), Finnan savoury (made with smoked haddock, onions, local cheddar and double cream, £6.75), grilled escolar with coriander butter (£6.95), salmon, tomatoes and limes in filo pastry (£8.95), duck with apricot and brandy sauce (£9.25), and steaks (from £11.95), specials such as Boston bean casserole (£5.25) and fresh salmon fishcakes (£5.85); puddings (from £2.10). Locals and visitors alike gather around the warm open fire in the simple little bar where they serve well kept Broughton Greenmantle and (from nearby Traquair House) Traquair Bear plus a guest from Broughton on handpump; several malt whiskies and draught cider; piped music. Even when they're busy service is friendly and efficient. A pleasant and spacious dining room has an open fire and high chairs for children if needed; all the dining areas are no smoking. Comfortable bedrooms.

Bar food (12-9) ~ Restaurant ~ (01896) 830229 ~ Children welcome ~ Open 11(12 Sun)-12; closed 25 and 26 Dec, 1-4 Jan ~ Bedrooms: £45S/£70B

ISLE ORNSAY Map 4 C1
Eilean Iarmain

Signposted off A851 Broadford—Armadale

Overlooking the sea in a picturesque part of Skye, this welcoming hotel
forms part of Fearann Eilean Iarmain, a traditional estate covering 23,000
acres. With their own oyster beds, their own blend of whisky, Te Bheag,
and friendly staff whose first language is predominantly Gaelic, this
attractively positioned place exudes a thoroughly Scottish charm. Every day
a diver is sent to collect fresh scallops. Changing daily, enjoyable bar food
might include lunchtime sandwiches, langoustine spiced consommé (£2),
local mussels in white wine and garlic cream (£4), cannelloni with mixed
vegetables and herby tomato sauce topped with mozzarella (£7.50), grilled
pork chop on apple and garlic mash with calvados sauce or local salmon
wrapped in banana leaf with red pimiento olive couscous and beurre blanc
(£8.50), pheasant breast with wild mushroom and garlic cream or snapper
with roast butternut squash (£9.50), rib-eye steak (£11.95), and puddings
such as strawberry meringue roulade and vanilla and caramel mousse
(from £3); children's menu. The bustling bar has a swooping stable-stall-
like wooden divider that gives a two-room feel: good tongue-and-groove
panelling on the walls and ceiling, leatherette wall seats, brass lamps, a
brass-mounted ceiling fan, and a huge mirror over the open fire. There are
about 34 local brands of blended and vatted malt whisky (including a
splendid vatted malt, Poit Dhubh Green Label, bottled for them but
available elsewhere), and an excellent wine list; darts, dominoes, cribbage,
and piped music. The pretty, no-smoking candlelit dining room has a
lovely sea view past the little island of Ornsay itself and the lighthouse on
Sionnach built by Robert Louis Stevenson's grandfather (you can walk over
the sands at low tide); new, very comfortable and well equipped bedrooms
in a converted stable block across the road have the same outlook. The
most popular room has a canopied bed from Armadale Castle.

*Bar food (standard food times) ~ Restaurant ~ (01471) 833332 ~ Children
in restaurant, eating area of bar and family room – must leave bar by 8 ~
Open 11-1(12.30 Sat, 11.30 Sun) ~ Bedrooms: £90B/£120B*

LANGTHWAITE Map 3 B3
Charles Bathurst

Arkengarthdale, a mile N towards Tan Hill; generally known as the CB Inn

To make the most of the very good, imaginative food here, you should stay overnight in comfortable and extra-pretty bedrooms. This is a lovely – if bleak – spot, with wonderful views over Langthwaite village and Arkengarthdale, and there are plenty of surrounding walks; walkers and their well behaved dogs are welcome. Appropriately stolid from the outside, but warmly welcoming inside, this converted cottage has been knocked through to make a long bar with clean and uplifting décor, light pine scrubbed tables, country chairs and benches on stripped floors, plenty of snug alcoves, and a roaring fire. The island bar counter has well kept Black Sheep Bitter and Riggwelter, John Smiths and a guest like Theakstons Best on handpump, and a short but interesting list of wines; piped music, darts, pool, TV, cribbage and dominoes. Using local ingredients and cooked by the licensee, the impressive food might include filled baguettes (from £3.25; hot tomato, mushroom and mozzarella £3.65), Tuscan bean soup or liver and orange pâté (£3.85), smoked herring and sweet pepper salad with avocado (£3.95), Thai spare ribs (£4.25), steak and kidney pie (£7), dry smoked loin of bacon with dijon glaze (£7.20), smoked cod fishcake with poached egg and hollandaise (£7.60), locally shot game pie (in season, £8.75), fresh dressed crab with minted new potatoes (£9.30), and shank of local lamb with lentil cake and juniper jus, grilled fillet of bass on baby leaf spinach and gruyère sauce or guinea fowl, boned and stuffed, with lime, ham and madeira jus (£10.50). At busy times of year you may need to book a table; the dining room is no smoking. Service is quick and attentive.

Bar food (standard food times) ~ Restaurant ~ (01748) 884567 ~ Children welcome ~ Open 11-11; 3-11 Mon-Thurs during Dec-Feb; 12-10.30 Sun ~ Bedrooms: /£60B

LANGTON GREEN Map 2 D4
Hare

A264 W of Tunbridge Wells

With its pubby but comfortable atmosphere, this big Edwardian place is somewhere women feel as equally at home as men. The good, interesting food is what most customers are after: home-made soup (£3.75), stilton, celery and pecan nut tart with a raspberry dressing (£3.95), sandwiches (from £4.25; cumberland sausage topped with sticky caramelised red onion relish £4.95), salmon and smoked haddock fishcakes with a tomato and spring onion salad or smoked ham, penne pasta and artichokes in a creamy pesto (£6.95), sardines with garlic and lemon butter (£7.25), meatloaf with parsley new potatoes and mushroom sauce (£7.95), cod fillet in a sesame crust with stir-fried vegetables and a sweet chilli and soy sauce or roast half shoulder of lamb with a rosemary and red wine sauce (£11.50), hare casserole with a leek and bacon mash (£12.95), and puddings like home-made apple pie, fruit crumble or sticky toffee pudding (from £3.95). There's a pleasant feeling of space throughout with lots of big windows and high ceilings in the knocked-through rooms, which have dark-painted dados below light walls, oak furniture and turkey carpets on stained wooden floors, old romantic pastels, and plenty of bric-a-brac (including a huge collection of chamber-pots). Old books, pictures and two big mahogany mirror-backed display cabinets crowd the walls of a big chatty room at the back, which has lots of large tables (one big enough for at least 12) on a light brown carpet. From here french windows open on to a sheltered terrace with picnic-sets looking out on to a tree-ringed green. Well kept Greene King IPA and Abbot, and a couple of guests like Everards Tiger or Flowers Original on handpump, lots of wines by the glass, and over 40 malt whiskies; piped pop music in the front bar area, cribbage, and dominoes.

Bar food (12-9.30(9 Sun)) ~ Restaurant ~ (01892) 862419 ~ Well behaved children in restaurant ~ Open 11-11; 12-10.30 Sun

LAVENHAM Map 2 A5
Angel
Market Place

This carefully renovated Tudor inn is an incredibly popular pub. As well as being an excellent place to eat and stay it also remains popular with locals popping in for just a drink and a chat. The long bar area, facing on to the charming former market square, is light and airy, with a buoyantly pubby atmosphere, plenty of polished dark tables, a big inglenook log fire under a heavy mantelbeam, and some attractive 16th-c ceiling plasterwork (even more elaborate pargeting in the residents' sitting room upstairs). Round towards the back on the right of the central servery is a no-smoking family dining area with heavy stripped pine country furnishings. The very good food can be eaten in either the bar or restaurant, and might include starters such as sweet potato and ginger soup (£3.50), game terrine with cumberland sauce (£4.95), half a dozen fresh oysters (£5.50), snacks such as pork pie and pickles or ploughman's (£4.95) and main courses such as steak and ale pie (£7.95), grilled salmon fillet with prawn and lemon sauce, lamb chops grilled with onion and rosemary gravy (£8.95), pot roast guinea fowl with apple and ginger sauce (£9.25), and puddings such as strawberry meringue roulade, steamed syrup sponge pudding or raspberry crème brûlée. Well kept Adnams Bitter, Greene King IPA and Abbot, and Nethergate Bitter on handpump, quite a few malt whiskies, and several decent wines by the glass or part bottle (you get charged for what you drink). They have shelves of books, dominoes, and lots of board games; classical piped music. There are picnic-sets out in front overlooking the square, and white plastic tables under cocktail parasols in a sizeable sheltered back garden; it's worth asking if they've time to show you the interesting Tudor cellar.

Bar food (12-2.15, 6.45-9.15) ~ Restaurant ~ (01787) 247388 ~ Children in eating area of bar and restaurant ~ Classical piano Fri evenings ~ Open 11-11; 12-10.30 Sun; closed 25-26 Dec ~ Bedrooms: /£70B

LEYBURN Map 3 B3

Sandpiper

Just off Market Place

This is an enjoyable little 17th-c stone cottage, whether you are dropping in for a quick drink (which in good weather can be had at white cast-iron tables on the front terrace amidst the lovely hanging baskets and flowering climbers), or planning a more leisurely meal. The bar has a couple of black beams in the low ceiling, antlers, and a few tables and chairs, and the back room up three steps has attractive Dales photographs. Down by the nice linenfold panelled bar counter there are stuffed sandpipers, more photographs and a woodburning stove in the stone fireplace; to the left is the no-smoking restaurant. At lunchtime, the good food might include sandwiches (from £2.10; steak with coleslaw £4.25), sausage and mash (£5.60), smoked chicken and caesar salad (£5.95), omelettes (from £6.25), chicken in red wine with button onions, mushrooms, and black bacon (£6.75), and crispy duck leg salad with oriental dressing (£9.50); in the evening there might be game terrine with warm brioche (£4), seared scallop with a celeriac purée (£6.50), pasta with wilted greens and feta (£8.75), pot roasted rabbit with wild mushrooms (£8.95), grilled tuna with caramelised shallots (£10.75), Moroccan spiced lamb with couscous (£10.95), and roasted salmon salad with lemon (£6.95). Puddings like raspberry and almond tart with clotted cream, crème brûlée or sticky toffee pudding with butterscotch sauce (from £3.30). Well kept Black Sheep Bitter, Dent Aviator, and Theakstons Bitter on handpump, around 100 malt whiskies, and a decent wine list; piped music.

Bar food (lunchtime) ~ Restaurant ~ (01969) 622206 ~ Children in eating area of bar but must leave restaurant by 8pm ~ Open 11.30-3, 6.30-11; 12-2.30, 7-10.30 Sun; closed Mon (except bank holidays) ~ Bedrooms: /£55S(£60B)

LITTLE HADHAM Map 2 B4
Nags Head

Hadham Ford; just S of A120 W of Bishops Stortford, towards Much Hadham

You can choose from around 20 fresh fish dishes every day in this sociable 16th-c country dining pub. Meat eaters and vegetarians shouldn't feel left out, though, as there are plenty of other dishes on the themed blackboards around the pub. Generous helpings of good reasonably priced bar food could include farmhouse grill (£5.75), poached skate in black butter, large battered cod, plaice or haddock or grilled bass (from £7.95), lots of good steak cuts (from £8.95) and seafood platter (£9.75), some of the ten vegetarian choices a day might be Thai red curry, moussaka or roasted vegetable torte (from £5.25); puddings (from £3) such as sticky toffee pudding. The linked heavily black-beamed rooms feel cosy and there are old local photographs, guns and copper pans in the small bar on the right, which has well kept Greene King IPA, Abbot, Ruddles and a guest such as Marstons Pedigree tapped from the cask, decent house wines, and freshly squeezed orange juice. The atmosphere is warm and relaxing and staff are friendly and efficient. The no-smoking restaurant is down a couple of steps (it's best to book for their good Sunday lunch). There are tables in a pleasant garden area, and Hopleys nursery specialising in unusual hardy perennials is just down the road; darts, fruit machine, TV.

Bar food (standard food times) ~ Restaurant ~ (01279) 771555 ~ Children in eating area of bar and restaurant ~ Open 11-2.30(3 Sat), 6-11; 12-3, 7-10.30 Sun

LLANDUDNO JUNCTION Map 3 D2
Queens Head

Glanwydden; heading towards Llandudno on B5115 from Colwyn Bay, turn left
into Llanrhos Road at roundabout as you enter the Penrhyn Bay speed limit;
Glanwydden is signposted as the first left turn off this

The enjoyable, generous bar food is what draws customers to this modest-
looking village pub. Served by polite efficient staff, the weekly changing
menu (made with lots of fresh local produce) might include dishes such as
soup (£2.95; local fish soup £3.25), open sandwiches (from £4.10), smoked
goose breast with peach and apple chutney (£5.25), fresh potted Conwy
crab (£4.95), pancakes filled with mushrooms and asparagus with napoli
sauce (£7.25), steak and mushroom pie (£7.95), lamb cutlets with plum
and port sauce (£9.50), steaks (from £11.75) and seafood platter (£13.50).
Tempting puddings include pecan pie and oranges in Cointreau (£3.50).
Though there is quite an emphasis on dining, locals do come in for a drink;
well kept Ind Coope Burton and Tetleys and maybe a guest on handpump,
decent wines including several by the glass, several malts, and good coffee
(maybe served with a bowl of whipped cream and home-made fudge or
chocolates). The spacious and comfortably modern lounge bar has brown
plush wall banquettes and windsor chairs around neat black tables and is
partly divided by a white wall of broad arches and wrought-iron screens;
there's also a little public bar; the dining area has a no-smoking section;
unobtrusive piped music. There are some tables out by the car park. No
dogs.

*Bar food (12-2.15, 6-9; 12-9 Sun) ~ Restaurant ~ (01492) 546570 ~
Children over 7 welcome in eating area of bar and restaurant ~ Open
11.30-3, 6-11; 11.30-10.30 Sun; closed 25 Dec*

CENTRAL LONDON Map 13
Eagle

159 Farringdon Road, EC1; opposite Bowling Green Lane car park;
⊖ Farringdon/Old Street

As ever, the distinctive Mediterranean-style meals here have delighted readers over the last year, but there's also been much praise for the atmosphere – it buzzes with life, and despite the emphasis on eating, always feels chatty and pubby. Made with the finest quality ingredients, the food still ranks among the very best you'll find in any London pub, effortlessly superior to those in the welcome imitators that have sprung up all over the city. Typical dishes might include Florentine pea soup (£4.50), poached ham hock with chickpeas, spinach and chives, marinated rump steak sandwich, or linguini with crab, lemon, garlic, chilli and parsley (£8.50), roast spring chicken with celeriac, celery and cream or shoulder of lamb with chilli, caraway seeds, couscous and dried fruits (£9.50), and grilled tuna with an Italian herb and olive oil sauce (£11.50); they also do Spanish and goats milk cheeses (£6), and Portuguese custard tarts (£1). Though they don't take credit cards, they do accept debit cards. On weekday lunchtimes especially, dishes from the blackboard menu can run out or change fairly quickly, so it really is worth getting here as early as you possibly can if you're hoping to eat. The open kitchen forms part of the bar, and furnishings in the single room are simple but stylish – school chairs, a random assortment of tables, a couple of sofas on bare boards, and modern paintings on the walls (there's an art gallery upstairs, with direct access from the bar). Quite a mix of customers, but it's fair to say there's a proliferation of young media folk (the *Guardian* is based just up the road). It gets particularly busy in the evening (and can occasionally be slightly smoky then), so this isn't the sort of place you'd go for a quiet dinner, or a smart night out. Well kept Charles Wells Bombardier and IPA on handpump, good wines including a dozen by the glass, good coffee, and properly made cocktails; piped music (sometimes loud). There are times during the week when the Eagle's success means you may have to wait for a table, or at least not be shy about sharing; it can be quieter at weekends.

Bar food (12.30-2.30(3.30 Sat, Sun), 6.30-10.30; not Sun evening) ~ Restaurant ~ (020) 7837 1353 ~ Children in eating area of bar ~ Open 12-11(5 Sun); closed Sun evening, bank holidays, one week at Christmas

NORTH LONDON Map 2 C4
Duke of Cambridge

30 St Peter's Street, N1; ⊖ Angel, though some distance away

London's first completely organic pub, this very well refurbished cornerhouse caused quite a stir when it first appeared, but has now comfortably settled into its role of right-on gastropub – so successfully that its owners have opened similar ventures in other parts of town. Don't be fooled into thinking it's at all faddy: the food and drink here are excellent, the extra attention put into sourcing everything simply meaning standards end up higher. The one downside is that so do the prices, particularly for the drinks, but it's worth the extra to enjoy choices and flavours you simply won't find anywhere else. There are four organic real ales on handpump, not cheap but tasty (though we haven't yet personally verified the claim that organic drinks are less likely to cause a hangover): from London's small Pitfield Brewery Eco Warrior and Singhboulton (named for the pub's two owners), St Peters Organic Ale, and Shoreditch Organic Stout. They also have organic draught lagers and cider, organic spirits, and a very wide range of organic wines, many of which are available by the glass; the full range of drinks is chalked up on a blackboard, and also includes good coffees and teas, and a spicy ginger ale. The big, busy main room is simply decorated and furnished, with lots of chunky wooden tables, pews and benches on bare boards, a couple of big metal vases with colourful flowers, daily papers, and carefully positioned soft lighting around the otherwise bare dark blue walls. The atmosphere is warmly inviting, with the constant sound of civilised chat from a steady stream of varied customers, many of whom do fit the Islington stereotypes: on our last visit, conversations on neighbouring tables revolved around the latest TV commissions and Italian Renaissance art. No music or games machines. Another blackboard lists the changing choice of well presented food: things like pumpkin, pear and celery soup (£4.50), chicken liver pâté (£6), four-cheese risotto with leek (£7), Moroccan vegetable stew (£8), roast pheasant with bean and bacon cassoulet and thyme jus (£12), fried hake with Portuguese potato and pepper stew (£12.50), and pear and almond tart (£6.50); children's helpings. A note explains that though they do all they can to ensure their game and fish have been produced using sustainable methods, these can't officially be classed as organic. They take credit cards. A corridor leads off past a few tables and an open kitchen to a couple of smaller candlelit rooms, more formally set for eating; there's also a small side terrace. The company's other pubs are the Crown in Victoria Park, and the Pelican in Ladbroke Grove.

Bar food (12.30-3, 6.30-10.30(9 Sun); not Mon am) ~ (020) 7359 3066 ~ Children welcome ~ Open 12(5 Mon)-11; 12-10.30 Sun

SOUTH LONDON Map 2 C4
Fire Station

150 Waterloo Road, SE1; ✆ Waterloo

Best known for the imaginative food served from the open kitchen in the back dining room, this remarkable conversion of the former LCC central fire station is the favoured choice for the area's after-work drinkers. It's hardly your typical local, but it does a number of traditionally pubby things better than anyone else nearby. The décor in the two vibrantly chatty rooms at the front is something like a cross between a warehouse and a schoolroom, with plenty of wooden pews, chairs and long tables (a few spilling on to the street), some mirrors and rather incongruous pieces of dressers, and brightly red-painted doors, shelves and modern hanging lightshades; the determinedly contemporary art round the walls is for sale, and there's a table with newspapers to read. Well kept Adnams Broadside, Brakspears, Youngs, and a beer brewed for them by Hancocks on handpump, as well as a number of bottled beers, variously flavoured teas, several malt whiskies, and a good choice of wines (a dozen by the glass). They serve a short range of bar meals between 12 and 5.30, which might include several interestingly filled ciabattas (from £4.45), and a daily pasta dish (£6.50), but it's worth paying the extra to eat from the main menu. Changing daily, this has things like tagliatelle with a cheese, leek, pea and asparagus sauce, with rocket and parmesan (£9.95), chicken breast stuffed with mozzarella, sun-blushed tomato and sage risotto with pesto dressing (£11.95), marinated pork fillet with celeriac and bacon mash and rhubarb jus (£12.25), tandoori seared tuna fillet with sag aloo, raita, aubergine chutney and curry oil (£12.50), and puddings such as peach and almond tart with custard sauce; some dishes can run out, so get there early for the best choice. They also do a simpler set menu between 5.30 and 7.30 (£10.95 two courses, £13.50 three). You can book tables. Piped modern jazz and other music fits into the good-natured hubbub; there's a TV for rugby matches. Those with quieter tastes might find bustling weeknights here a little too hectic (it can get noisy then) – it's calmer at lunchtimes and during the day. At the busiest times in the bar, it's a good idea to keep your belongings firmly to hand. The pub is very handy for the Old Vic, Waterloo Station and the Imperial War Museum a bit further down the road.

Bar food (11-5.30) ~ Restaurant ~ (020) 7620 2226 ~ Children welcome ~ Open 11-11; 12-10.30 Sun; closed 25, 26 Dec, 1 Jan, Easter wknd

WEST LONDON Map 2 C4
Anglesea Arms

35 Wingate Road, W6; ✪ Ravenscourt Park

One of the best known of London's gastropubs (despite its out-of-the-way location), and with good reason: the food really is top notch. Changing every lunchtime and evening, the inventive menu might include several starters like goats curd, courgette and oregano tart (£4.50), Catalan-style chorizo, garlic and eel gratin (£4.95), and pigeon, foie gras and chicken liver terrine with brioche and onion marmalade (£5.25), and half a dozen or so main courses such as wilted wild garlic leaf and morel risotto (£7.25), stuffed saddle of rabbit 'cock a leekie' (£7.50), chargrilled chump of lamb (£9.75), and delicious red mullet on saffron mash with Mediterranean vegetables (£9.95); good puddings, and some unusual farmhouse cheeses (£4.50). The bustling eating area leads off the bar but feels quite separate, with skylights creating a brighter feel, closely packed tables, and a big modern mural along one wall; directly opposite is the kitchen, with several chefs frantically working on the meals. You can't book, so best to get there early for a table, or be prepared to wait. A couple of readers have found it rather smoky. It feels a lot more restaurranty than, say, the Eagle, though you can also usually eat in the bar: rather plainly decorated, but cosy in winter when the roaring fire casts long flickering shadows on the dark panelling. Neatly stacked piles of wood guard either side of the fireplace (which has a stopped clock above it), and there are some well worn green leatherette chairs and stools. Courage Best, Fullers London Pride, Greene King Old Speckled Hen and Marstons Pedigree on handpump, with a wide range of carefully chosen wines listed above the bar. Several tables outside overlook the quiet street (not the easiest place to find a parking space).

Bar food (12.30-2.45, 7.30-10.45; 1-3.30, 7.30-10.15 Sun) ~ Restaurant ~ (020) 8749 1291 ~ Children in eating area of bar and restaurant ~ Open 11-11; 12-10.30 Sun; closed 24 Dec-1 Jan

WEST LONDON Map 2 C4
Atlas

16 Seagrave Roadd, SW6; ✆ West Brompton

Once the kind of place that deserved a fleeting visit at best, the Atlas has been transformed by two brothers (one of whom used to be a chef at the Eagle) into an unexpectedly rewarding food pub. The imaginative meals have quickly gained quite a reputation, and there's a nicely buzzing atmosphere in the evenings. Tables are highly prized, so if you're planning to eat – and most people do – arrive early, or swoop quickly. Listed on a blackboard above the brick fireplace, and changing every day, the shortish choice of excellent meals might include cauliflower and saffron soup with parmesan crostini (£3.50), fresh marinated anchovies on bruschetta with cucumber relish (£6), calves liver risotto with onion, carrot and sage (£7.50), grilled Tuscan sausages with roast shallots, baked polenta, porcini and field mushrooms (£8), Moroccan chicken with sweet potatoes and couscous salad (£8.50), pan-fried lemon sole with puy lentils and salsa verde (£11), and grilled rib-eye steak with spiced black beans (£11.50); they sometimes have a nice chocolate cake, or good cheeses. The long knocked-together bar has been nicely renovated without removing the original features; there's plenty of panelling and dark wooden wall benches, with a mix of school chairs and well spaced tables. Smart young types figure prominently in the mix, but there are plenty of locals too, as well as visitors to the Exhibition Centre at Earls Court (one of the biggest car parks is next door). Charles Wells Bombardier, Fullers London Pride, and Greene King IPA on handpump, and a well chosen wine list, with a changing range of around ten by the glass; friendly service. The piped music is unusual – on various visits we've come across everything from salsa and jazz to vintage TV themes. Down at the end is a TV, by a hatch to the kitchen. At the side is a narrow yard with lots of tables and colourful plants (and heaters for winter).

Bar food (12-3, 7-10.30(10 Sun)) ~ (020) 7385 9129 ~ Children in eating area of bar till 7pm ~ Open 12-11(10.30 Sun); closed 24 Dec-2 Jan

WEST LONDON Map 2 C4
Havelock Tavern

Masbro Road, W14; ☻ Kensington (Olympia)

A blue-tiled cornerhouse in an unassuming residential street, this out-of-the-way place is worth tracking down for its excellent quality food. Changing every day, the menu might include things like spiced red bean and bacon soup with coriander and crème fraîche (£4), rabbit rillettes with gherkins, toast and chutney (£5.50), warm feta, courgette, red onion and tomato tart (£6.50), cod fishcake with spinach, tomato aïoli and lemon (£8), poached gammon with yellow split peas, green peppercorns and mint (£8.50), and roast sirloin of beef with polenta, savoy cabbage and anchovy and lemon butter (£10.50); you can't book tables, and they don't take credit cards. On our last visit they had an unusual way of spotting where you were sitting – upon ordering we were given a vase of fresh flowers marked with the table number. Until 1932 the building was two separate shops (one was a wine merchant, but no one can remember much about the other), and it still has huge shop-front windows along both street-facing walls. The L-shaped bar is plain and unfussy: bare boards, long wooden tables, a mix of chairs and stools, a few soft spotlights, and a fireplace; a second little room with pews leads to a small paved terrace, with benches, a tree, and wall climbers. Well kept Brakspears, Marstons Pedigree and Wadworths 6X on handpump from the elegant modern bar counter, and a good range of well chosen wines, with around 10 by the glass; mulled wine in winter, and home-made elderflower soda. Service is particularly friendly and attentive, and the atmosphere relaxed and easy-going; no music or machines, but plenty of chat from the varied range of customers. Dominoes, Scrabble and other board games. Though evenings are always busy (you may have to wait for a table then, and some dishes can run out quite quickly), it can be quieter at lunchtimes, and in the afternoons can have something of the feel of a civilised private club. On weekdays, parking nearby is metered.

Bar food (12.30-2.30(3 Sun), 7-10(9.30 Sun)) ~ No credit cards ~ (020) 7603 5374 ~ Children welcome ~ Open 11-11; 12-10.30 Sun; closed Easter Sun, Christmas

WEST LONDON Map 2 C4
White Horse

1 Parsons Green, SW6; ⊖ Parsons Green

Busy, friendly and meticulously run, this splendidly organised pub has earned lots of praise from readers over the last year, not least for its continued emphasis on an impressively eclectic range of drinks. Seven perfectly kept real ales include Adnams Broadside, Bass, Harveys Sussex, Highgate Mild, Roosters Ranger (brewed to their specification) and changing guests like Dark Star Spiced Vice and Roosters Yankee; they also keep 15 Trappist beers, 45 other foreign bottled beers, a dozen malt whiskies, and a broad range of good, interesting and not overpriced wines. Every item on the menu, whether it be scrambled egg or raspberry and coconut tart, has a suggested accompaniment listed beside it, perhaps a wine, or maybe a bottled beer. They're keen to encourage people to select beer with food in the same way you might do wine, and organise regular beer dinners where every course comes with a recommended brew. The often inventive bar food might include sandwiches (from £4), ploughman's (with some unusual cheeses, £5), chicken liver and foie gras parfait (£5.25), cucumber sushi with Hoegaarden tempura prawns (£6.75), salmon fishcakes with tarragon mayonnaise or arancini with mozzarella, chargrilled vegetables and pesto dressing (£7.75), beer-battered cod and chips (£8.25), and pan-fried sea bass with Thai green curry, sticky rice and bok choi (£12.75). There's usually something to eat available all day; at weekends there's a good brunch menu, and in winter they do a very good Sunday lunch. The stylishly modernised U-shaped bar has plenty of sofas, wooden tables, and huge windows with slatted wooden blinds, and winter coal and log fires, one in an elegant marble fireplace. The pub is usually busy (sometimes very much so, with an obvious part of the mix the sort of people that once earned the pub its hated nickname, the Sloaney Pony), but there are usually enough smiling, helpful staff behind the solid panelled central servery to ensure you'll rarely have to wait too long to be served. All the art displayed is for sale; they have a small gallery upstairs, with bi-monthly exhibitions. The back restaurant is no smoking. On summer evenings the front terrace overlooking the green has something of a continental feel, with crowds of people drinking al fresco at the white cast-iron tables and chairs; there may be Sunday barbecues. They have monthly beer festivals (often spotlighting regional breweries), as well as lively celebrations on American Independence Day or Thanksgiving.

Bar food (12-10.30; sandwiches only 4-6) ~ Restaurant ~ (020) 7736 2115 ~ Children in eating area of bar and restaurant ~ Open 11-11; 12-10.30 Sun; closed 24-27 Dec

LONG COMPTON Map 1 A6
Red Lion
A3400 S of Shipston-on-Stour

This attractive former coaching inn has been well refurbished, to make the most of its old features without introducing too much olde-worlde clutter. The roomy lounge bar has brown panelling and stripped stone, with a lot of old local photographs and other pictures and a high Delft shelf with antique bottles. In its rambling corners there are old-fashioned built-in settles among pleasantly assorted and comfortable old seats and tables on the flagstones, and there are good log fires. Good value food includes sandwiches (from £1.95), soup (£2.60), warm smoked trout (£3.50), ploughman's (from £4.40), chilli (£6.15), cashew nut paella (£6.25), steak and kidney pie (£6.75) and daily specials such as grilled sardines (£3.95), leek and stilton sausages and mash (£6.75), salmon fishcakes on noodles with sweet chilli sauce and coriander (£8.25) and fried pork tenderloin with calvados, apples and cream (£8.50). Well kept Adnams, Courage Directors, Hook Norton and Websters on handpump; the landlord is warmly welcoming and attentive, and his staff are efficient and helpful. The simple public bar has pool; unobtrusive piped music. There are tables out in the garden, with a play area.

Bar food (standard food times) ~ Restaurant ~ (01608) 684221 ~ Children welcome ~ Open 11-2.30, 6-11; 12-3, 7-10.30 Sun

LONGRIDGE Map 3 C3
Derby Arms

Chipping Road, Thornley; 1½ miles N of Longridge on back road to Chipping

This very welcoming old stone-built country pub has been run by the same family for over a century; the current licensee's great-grandmother was married from here in 1898. Though the thoughtful personal service stands out, it's particularly well liked for its very good food, excellently presented, and making splendid use of fresh local ingredients. A typical choice includes sandwiches, Bury market black pudding (£3.95), vegetarian hotpot (£6.95), roast chicken with bacon, stuffing and apple sauce (£7.50), an impressive steak and kidney pudding (£7.95), steaks (from £8.95), roast shank of lamb with redcurrant gravy (£9.95), and usually a wide choice of changing fish specials such as dressed crab (£5.75), fillet of fresh sea bream with a Thai red curry sauce (£11.95), scallops in a cream and mushroom sauce or monkfish in batter (£12.95), and turbot with parma ham and asparagus (£14.50). Potatoes and vegetables come in separate dishes. They do various set menus, including a bargain Lancashire special, with three local dishes for £7.95; prompt, efficient and friendly waitress service. The main bar has something of a hunting and fishing theme, with old photographs commemorating notable catches, some nicely mounted lures above the comfortable red plush seats, and a stuffed pheasant that seems to be flying in through the wall. To the right is a smaller room with sporting trophies and mementoes, and a regimental tie collection, while off to the left are a couple of no-smoking dining areas. Well kept Bass, Greenalls and Marstons Pedigree on handpump, and a good range of wines including several half-bottles and a dozen or so by the glass, particularly strong on South African. The gents' has dozens of riddles on the wall; you can buy a sheet of them in the bar (the money goes to charity). There are a few tables out in front, and another two behind the car park, enjoying fine views across to the Forest of Bowland.

Bar food (12-2.15, 6.30-9.30(6-10 Sat); 12-9.15 Sun) ~ Restaurant ~ (01772) 782623 ~ Children in restaurant ~ Open 12-3.30, 6-11; 12-10.30 Sun

LOWER ODDINGTON Map 1 A6
Fox

Near Stow-on-the-Wold

The licensees are still enthusiastically making improvements to this smart, very popular inn. A custom-built awning has been installed with outdoor heaters to cover the terrace in the newly planted cottage garden – this will enable customers to dine out on the chilliest of summer evenings. Improvements and new ideas have been added to the wine list and menu. A third bedroom with antiques has been opened, and a local artist and specialist painter has decorated the lavatories. The Red Room houses a collection of wine-related antiques and corkscrews, and the other simply and spotlessly furnished rooms have fresh flowers and flagstones, an inglenook fireplace, hunting scene figures above the mantelpiece, a display cabinet with pewter mugs and stone bottles, daily newspapers, and hops hanging from the ceiling; dominoes, cribbage, backgammon, chess and cards. Served by staff in uniform shirts, the good, interesting food might include tomato and red pepper soup (£3.95), courgette and blue cheese risotto (£4.25), griddled ciabatta sandwiches (weekday lunchtimes only; from £4.50), baked sardines with lemon and herb butter (£5.25), super salmon fishcakes with a chive cream sauce, chicken, leek and mushroom pie, smoked haddock with spinach and a poached egg, and duck leg with shi-itake mushroom sauce, potato and parsnip mash (all £8.50), rib-eye steak (£10.75), daily specials such as roast shoulder of lamb with garlic, sage and cider sauce (£9.75) or griddled tuna loin with roasted peppers and aubergines (£11.50), and puddings like apple tart with calvados cream, plum and frangipane tart with plum sauce or white and dark chocolate iced terrine with amaretti biscuits (£3.75); every Tuesday, they have special fish starters and main courses; Sunday roast sirloin of beef (£9.50). The wine list is excellent (they have daily and monthly specials), and they keep Badger Tanglefoot, Hook Norton Best, and a changing guest like Goffs Jouster or Shepherd Neame Spitfire on handpump. A good eight-mile walk starts from here (though a stroll around the pretty village might be less taxing after a fine meal).

Bar food (till 10pm) ~ Restaurant ~ (01451) 870888 ~ Children welcome if quiet and well behaved ~ Open 12-3, 6.30-11; 12-3, 7-10.30 Sun; closed 25 Dec, evenings 26 and 31 Dec, 1 Jan ~ Bedrooms: /£58B

LUDLOW Map 1 A5
Unicorn

Corve Street, off main road to Shrewsbury

Even when this 17th-c inn is really busy – which it often is – the staff manage to cope with the rush with friendly efficiency; best to get there early. The appetising range of food remains one of the main draws: home-made soup (£2.75), chicken liver pâté (£4.25), pasta, artichoke and blue cheese bake or home-cooked ham with parsley sauce (£6.75), lamb cutlets with onion and rosemary sauce (£7.25), Mediterranean-baked vegetables with brie and garlic bread (£8.25), beef in ale with herb dumplings (£8.50), bacon-wrapped chicken and creamy mushroom sauce (£8.95), mixed grill (£9.25), steaks (from £9.25), bass with pink peppercorn sauce (£12.25), half a roast duck with cumberland sauce (£13.25), and home-made puddings (£3.50); friendly and obliging service. There's a good social buzz in the solidly beamed and partly panelled bar, with a mix of friendly locals and visitors, and a huge log fire in a big stone fireplace; the timbered, candlelit restaurant is no smoking. Well kept Flowers IPA and Wadworths 6X on handpump; cribbage and dominoes. Outside, tables shelter pleasantly among willow trees on the pretty little terrace right next to the modest River Corve. This is a picturesque town. Please note, they no longer do bedrooms.

Bar food (12-2.15, 6(7 Sun)-9.15) ~ Restaurant ~ (01584) 873555 ~ Children in eating area of bar and restaurant ~ Open 12-2.30(3.30 Sat), 6-11; 12-3.30, 7-10.30 Sun; closed 25 Dec

LYDDINGTON Map 3 E4
Old White Hart

Village signposted off A6003 N of Corby

It's the very good food that draws most customers to this really friendly old country inn. The menu and specials board change all the time, but might include home-made soups such as french onion, tomato and tarragon (£2.95), celery and parmesan tart (£3.95), fresh sardines on garlic and tomato toast (£4.25), lunchtime baguettes (from £4.95), sautéed sweetbreads glazed in honey and rosemary in puff pastry (£4.95), seared king scallops with cherry tomatoes and red onions on mixed leaves with balsamic dressing (£5.95), home-made chicken, bacon and herb pie, cod with herb crust and chive butter sauce or home-made sausages with fresh horseradish mash (£8.95), turbot in chive butter sauce (£11.95), half crispy duck with blackcurrant sauce (£13.95), and puddings such as lemon crème brûlée and hot sticky toffee pudding (£2.75). An original 17th-c window in the passage to the cosy bar is a discreet reminder that this pub was once part of the Burghley Estate. The softly lit low-ceilinged bar has just three close-set tables in front of the warm log fire, with heavy bowed beams and lots of attractive dried flower arrangements. The bar opens into an attractive restaurant, and on the other side is a tiled-floor room with some stripped stone, cushioned wall seats and mate's chairs, and a woodburning stove; one restaurant is no smoking. Well kept Greene King IPA, Abbot and Triumph and a guest such as Timothy Taylors Landlord on handpump; piped music. There are picnic-sets in the safe and pretty walled garden, which has twelve floodlit boules pitches – on Thursday you can listen to the church bell ringers. There are good nearby walks and the pub is handy for Bede House.

Bar food (12-2(2.30 Sun), 6-9; not Sun evening) ~ Restaurant ~ (01572) 821703 ~ Well behaved children welcome ~ Open 12-3, 6-11; 12-4, 7-10.30 Sun ~ Bedrooms: £45B/£65B

MACCLESFIELD Map 3 D3
Sutton Hall Hotel

Leaving Macclesfield southwards on A523, turn left into Byrons Lane signposted Langley, Wincle, then just before canal viaduct fork right into Bullocks Lane; OS Sheet 118 map reference 925715

Peacocks strut among the tables on the tree-sheltered lawn, and ducks and moorhens swim in the pond in front of this elegant but unstuffy 16th-c baronial hall. Inside, the bar is divided into separate areas by tall black oak timbers, with some antique squared oak panelling, lightly patterned art nouveau stained-glass windows, broad flagstones around the bar counter (carpet elsewhere), and a raised open fire. It is mostly furnished with straightforward ladderback chairs around sturdy thick-topped cast-iron-framed tables, and there are a few unusual touches such as a suit of armour by a big stone fireplace, a longcase clock, a huge bronze bell for calling time and a brass cigar-lighting gas taper on the bar counter itself. Reasonably priced home-made bar food includes soup (£1.95), sandwiches (from £3.50), moules marinières (£4.75), broccoli and cheese bake (£5.75), tasty steak, kidney and oyster pie (£6.95), daily specials such as roast turkey with tarragon cream sauce (£6.45), grilled halibut in teriyaki marinade (£7.95), venison steak with cream, brandy and peppercorn sauce (£8.50), and puddings such as blueberry crème brûlée and chocolate, hazelnut and rum flan (£3). Well kept Bass, Greene King IPA, Marstons and a guest beer on handpump, 40 malt whiskies, decent wines, freshly squeezed fruit juice, and a proper Pimms. They can arrange clay shooting, golf or local fishing for residents, and there's access to canal moorings at Gurnett Aqueduct on the Macclesfield Canal 200 yards away.

Bar food (12-2.30(2 Sun), 7-10) ~ Restaurant ~ (01260) 253211 ~ Children in restaurant and family room wknd and bank hol lunchtimes only ~ Open 11-11(10.30 Sun) ~ Bedrooms: £75S(£75B)/£90S(£90B)

MAIDENSGROVE Map 2 C3
Five Horseshoes

W of village, which is signposted from B480 and B481; OS Sheet 175 map reference 711890

Set on a lovely common high up in the Chiltern beechwoods and close to good local walks, this highly regarded 17th-c brick pub has a separate bar set aside for walkers (and their boots). Readers are full of praise for the imaginative bar food here, which includes lunchtime dishes such as home-made soup (£3.85; their popular stilton soup £4.35), ploughman's (£5.45), filled baked potatoes (from £6.50), pancakes with fillings such as smoked chicken and mushroom in a creamy sauce or spicy Thai vegetables (from £6.95), warm smoky bacon and stilton salad (£6.95), braised lamb shank with provençale sauce (£9.95), and daily specials. Also, the à la carte menu can be taken at any time: chargrilled vegetables (£5.95), prawn and crab ravioli or tagliatelle with provençale sauce (£7.50), pork fillet in honey and mustard sauce with deep-fried vegetables (£10.95), rack of lamb with minted apricot sauce (£14.50) and halibut with a herb crust (£15.50), with home-made puddings such as warm citrus sponge or cookies and fudge cheesecake (from £4.50). On Sundays in winter they do set meals (£15.95) and in summer they hold barbecues. The atmosphere in the rambling main bar is really welcoming. Furnished with mostly modern wheelback chairs around stripped wooden tables (though there are some attractive older seats and a big baluster-leg table), it has a proper log fire in winter; the low ceiling in the main area is covered in bank notes from all over the world, mainly donated by customers. Well kept Brakspears PA, SB and seasonal ales on handpump, and a dozen wines by the glass, including champagne. There are fine views from the sheltered back garden, which has a rockery and some interesting water features. Look out for the red kites which now patrol the surrounding countryside – if you're as lucky as one reader, you might even be able to spot one from your table in the extended restaurant.

Bar food (standard food times) ~ Restaurant ~ (01491) 641282 ~ Children welcome in top bar ~ Open 11-2.30, 6-11; 12-9 Sun; closed 26 Dec

MAWDESLEY Map 3 C2
Red Lion

Heading N on B5246 from Parbold, turn right into Maltkiln Lane at Bispham
Green signpost, then keep on, bearing right after 1.6 miles into Mawdesley High
Street, and thence into New Street

The splendid food in the brightly painted conservatory is what draws so
many people to this otherwise busily traditional village local. Even
ordinary-sounding dishes are prepared with real flair, and the quality and
presentation truly are outstanding. The choice might include ravioli with
prosciutto, sun-dried tomatoes and mozzarella (£4.50), warm smoked
salmon and anchovy salad with seed mustard vinaigrette (£5.50), roasted
bell pepper with Mediterranean vegetables and mozzarella melt or
delicious salmon stuffed with prawns and spinach with a tomato and
cheddar glaze (£9), bass with red pepper and basil vinaigrette (£9.50),
roast Goosnargh duck with honey and star anise jus (£12), and saddle of
wild boar with smoked bacon crackling and game sauce (£14); excellent
puddings. At lunchtimes (not Sunday) they also do bar snacks such as
sandwiches (from £3.25), and there are various set menus and themed
events. Booking is recommended at weekends. The colourful décor in the
dining room is quite a shock after the far more conventional bar, which
has wooden tables, a brick bar counter, standing timbers, a few plants, a
nice old clock, and a good chatty atmosphere; a separate public bar has a
TV and fruit machine. Service is friendly and particularly helpful; the
landlady first worked here as a barmaid 30 years ago, and the landlord
works hard to make everyone feel at home. Well kept Theakstons Best
and Websters, and several well chosen wines by the glass; piped music.
There are tables in a courtyard behind, and more in front – surrounded
by hanging baskets and flowering tubs. The two big lions standing guard
by the main door are white, rather than red (and that's not a suggestion
to the local Young Farmers!).

*Bar food (lunchtimes only; not Sun) ~ Restaurant ~ (01704) 822208/822999
~ Children in restaurant ~ Jazz Sun afternoon monthly and Sun evening
twice monthly in summer ~ Open 12-11(10.30 Sun)*

MELLOR Map 3 D3
Oddfellows Arms

Heading out of Marple on the A626 towards Glossop, Mellor is the next road after the B6102, signposted off on the right at Marple Bridge; keep on for nearly 2 miles up Longhurst Lane and into Moor End Road

An absence of piped music and games, and nice open fires, encourages a cosy chatty atmosphere in the low-ceilinged flagstoned bar at this pleasantly civilised old country pub. Although those just after a drink are made perfectly welcome, most people come here for the enjoyable food, which includes soup (£2), sandwiches (from £2.25), mozzarella and tomato salad (£3.95), garlic tiger prawns on ciabatta bread (£4.45), Peking duck (£4.95), salads (from £5.95), daily roast or various curries (£6.45), yoghurt marinated garlic chicken or cassoulet (£7.95), steaks (from £9.95), daily specials such as marinated goats cheese on ciabatta (£4.75), baked trout with lime leaves, chilli and white wine (£7.95), brill fillet with thyme-seasoned olive oil and warmed seafood salad (£10.95), cajun swordfish steak (£11.95), and puddings (£2.95). Well kept Adnams, Flowers IPA, Marstons Pedigree and a weekly changing guest such as Shepherd Neame Spitfire on handpump served with or without a sparkler; prompt friendly service. There's a small no-smoking restaurant upstairs, and a few tables out by the road. Parking can be difficult when busy.

Bar food (12-2.30, 6.30-9.30) ~ Restaurant ~ (0161) 449 7826 ~ Children welcome lunchtime and early evening ~ Open 12-3, 5.30-11; 7-10.30 Sun

MELLS Map 1 C5
Talbot

W of Frome; off A362 W of Buckland Dinham, or A361 via Nunney and Whatley

Although much emphasis is placed on the good, imaginative food in this rather smart place, there is a 15th-c tithe barn with a high beamed ceiling which locals head for to enjoy the well kept Butcombe and Fullers London Pride tapped from the cask. Taken in the restaurant, the lunchtime food might include home-made soup (£3.95), ham and eggs (£7.65), hot ratatouille and cheese flan, various omelettes, ploughman's, griddled bratwurst sausages with garlic mash and onion gravy or baked mushrooms stuffed with stilton and walnuts (all £7.50), and daily specials like chicken curry (£7.95), sweet and sour stir-fried duck (£8.25), and beef casserole (£8.95); evening dishes such as steamed asparagus in puff pastry (£5.50), grilled scallops (£7.25), fillet of pork stuffed with leek and stilton (£13.50), breast and confit leg of Gressingham duck marinated in ginger, plum sauce and lime (£13.95), lots of fresh daily delivered fish (from around £9.95), and puddings (£4.25); they also offer a two-course menu (£9.95). The licensee is friendly and helpful, and the attractive main room has stripped pews, mate's and wheelback chairs, fresh flowers and candles in bottles on the mix of tables, and sporting and riding pictures on the walls, which are partly stripped above a broad panelled dado, and partly rough terracotta-colour. A small corridor leads to a nice little room with an open fire; piped music, table skittles, TV, cribbage and dominoes. Sunday roast, and nice breakfasts; good wines, and well chosen staff. There are seats in the cobbled courtyard. The village was purchased by the Horner family of the 'Little Jack Horner' nursery rhyme and the direct descendants still live in the manor house next door. The inn is surrounded by lovely countryside and good walks.

Bar food (standard food times) ~ Restaurant ~ (01373) 812254 ~ Children welcome ~ Open 12-2.30(3 Sat), 6.30-11; 12-3, 7-10.30 Sun; closed evening 25 Dec ~ Bedrooms: £45B/£75B

MELROSE Map 4 E3
Burts Hotel
B6374, Market Square

Melrose is perhaps the most villagey of the Border towns, and this comfortably civilised hotel is an ideal place to stay while you discover its charms. Always busy and cheerful, the friendly L-shaped lounge bar has lots of cushioned wall seats and windsor armchairs on its turkey carpet, and Scottish prints on the walls; the Tweed Room and the restaurant are no smoking. Well kept Belhaven 80/-, Caledonian Deuchars IPA and a guest such as Broughton Greenmantle on handpump, over 80 malt whiskies, and a good wine list; dominoes. Food here is consistently good, but it's best to arrive early or book. Promptly served by professional, hard-working staff, the inventive bar menu might include soup (£2.50), fried cod and smoked haddock fishcakes with spiced red pepper cream or carpaccio with parmesan flakes and dressed leaves (£4.25), breaded haddock or vegetable tortilla (£7.25), chicken breast wrapped in bacon sliced over a tomato and pesto fondue or warm pork salad with cherry tomato, mushrooms and grapes with sweet mustard dressing (£8.25) and puddings such as warm treacle tart or dark chocolate and orange marquise with a ragoût of seasonal fruits and minted mascarpone (£4.25); extremely good breakfasts. The owners here have been providing personal, attentive service for more than 30 years now, and have attracted a good few loyal devotees along the way. There's a well tended garden (with tables in summer). An alternative if distant way to view the town's striking abbey ruins is from the top of the tower at Smailholm.

Bar food (12-2, 6-9.30(6-10 Fri, Sat)) ~ Restaurant ~ (01896) 822285 ~ Children welcome ~ Open 11-2.30, 5-11; 12-2.30, 6-11 Sun; closed 26 Dec ~ Bedrooms: £52B/£92B

MICKLEHAM Map 2 D4
King William IV

Byttom Hill; short but narrow steep track up hill just off A24 Leatherhead—
Dorking by partly green-painted restaurant – public car park down here is best
place to park; OS Sheet 187 map reference 173538

Cut into a steep hillside – it's quite a climb up – this unusually placed pub
has panoramic views from its snugly atmospheric plank-panelled front bar.
The more spacious back bar is quite brightly lit, with kitchen-type chairs
around its cast-iron-framed tables, log fires, fresh flowers on all the tables,
and a serviceable grandfather clock. Enjoyable bar food might include
weekday sandwiches, ploughman's (from £5.25), filled baked potatoes
(from £5.50), brie and leek in filo pastry with apricot purée, steak, kidney
and mushroom pie or seafood pie (£8.25), tandoori chicken (£8.95),
chargrilled tuna (£9.25), rump steak (£10.25), and puddings such as hot
chocolate fudge cake or fruit crumble (£3.75); the choice is more limited on
Sundays and bank holidays, and they don't take bookings in summer. Well
kept Adnams Best, Badger Best, Hogs Back TEA and a guest such as
Ringwood Fortyniner on handpump; quick and friendly service; light piped
music. At the back, the lovely terraced garden is neatly filled with sweet
peas, climbing roses and honeysuckle and plenty of tables (some in an
extended open-sided wooden shelter with gas heaters); a path leads straight
up through woods where it's nice to walk after lunch – quite a few walkers
do come here. No children inside.

Bar food (12-2, 7-9.30) ~ (01372) 372590 ~ Open 11-3, 6-11; 12-3, 7-10.30
Sun; closed 25 Dec, evening 31 Dec

MILTON BRYAN Map 2 B3
Red Lion

Toddington Road, off B528 S of Woburn

This comfortably relaxing pub, handy for Woburn Abbey and Safari Park, is changing, so we cannot guarantee that it will continue to be run along the same lines. Up to now it's been one of the county's best pubs, with a good range of food at sensible prices, from chunky sandwiches to typical pub dishes, fresh fish specials and a good value pensioners' lunch. The beamed bar area has white-painted walls, some exposed brickwork, big fading rugs on the part wood and part flagstoned floors, a case of sporting cups, and fresh flowers on the round wooden tables; piped music. Well kept Greene King IPA and Old Speckled Hen and a fortnightly changing guest on handpump. There are plenty of tables, chairs and picnic-sets out on the terrace and lawn, which looks across to a delightfully thatched black and white timbered house; there's a climbing frame out here too.

Bar food (12-2.30, 6.30-10) ~ Restaurant ~ (01525) 210044 ~ Children welcome ~ Open 11-3(4 Sat), 6-11; 12-4, 6-10.30 Sun

MONKSILVER Map 1 C4
Notley Arms
B3188

As popular as ever, this bustling, friendly pub does tend to fill up quickly with customers keen to enjoy the good, reasonably priced food – and in proper pub fashion, they don't take reservations, so you do have to get there pretty promptly. The beamed and L-shaped bar has small settles and kitchen chairs around the plain country wooden and candlelit tables, original paintings on the black-timbered white walls, fresh flowers, a couple of woodburning stoves, and maybe a pair of cats. Bar food includes sandwiches (from £2.75), home-made soup (£2.75), very good ploughman's (from £3.95), home-made tagliatelle with ham, mushrooms, cream and parmesan cheese (£4.75), warm stilton flan with balsamic pear (£5.50), fresh asparagus and parmesan feuilleté or bacon, leek and cider pudding (£5.75), beef in ale pie (£7.75), fresh cod fillet with shrimp butter (£8.25), sirloin steak (£8.95), puddings such as strawberry cheesecake, brown bread ice cream or banana and pecan nut cake with toffee sauce (from £2.75), and winter roast Sunday lunch; very good cheerful staff. Well kept Exmoor Ale, Smiles Best, Wadworths 6X, and maybe Youngs Special on handpump, and country wines; cribbage, dominoes, chess, Scrabble, trivia, table tennis (in alley), and alley skittles. Families are well looked after, with colouring books and toys in the bright no-smoking little family room. There are more toys outside in the immaculate garden, running down to a swift clear stream.

Bar food (standard food times; no food for 2 wks end Jan-beg Feb) ~ (01984) 656217 ~ Children in family room ~ Open 11.30-2.30, 6.30-11; 12-2.30, 7-11(10.30 in winter) Sun; closed 25 Dec

MOULTON Map 3 B3
Black Bull

Just E of A1, 1 mile E of Scotch Corner

Particularly handy for the A1, this decidedly civilised place makes an excellent stop for lunch or dinner. The bar has a lot of character – as well as a huge winter log fire, fresh flowers, an antique panelled oak settle and an old elm housekeeper's chair, built-in red-cushioned black settles and pews around the cast-iron tables (one has a heavily beaten copper top), silver-plate Turkish coffee pots and so forth over the red velvet-curtained windows, and copper cooking utensils hanging from black beams. A nice side dark-panelled seafood bar has some high seats at the marble-topped counter. Good lunchtime bar snacks include lovely smoked salmon in sandwiches (£3.25), on a plate (£5.50), and in pâté (£5.75); they also do very good home-made soup served in little tureens (£2.75), fresh plump salmon sandwiches (£3.25), chicken, bacon and avocado baguette, ploughman's or bangers and mash (£4.95), linguini with tomato sauce, pancetta and parmesan (£5.25), queenie scallops in garlic with wensleydale and thyme crumb (£5.75), carpaccio of peppered rump with caper and cornichon salad or smoked haddock, walnut and gruyère quiche (£5.95), warm salad of asparagus, pancetta, parmesan and quails' eggs (£6), and puddings such as hot orange liqueur pancakes or crème brûlée (£3.50). In the evening (when people do tend to dress up), you can also eat in the polished brick-tiled conservatory with bentwood cane chairs or in the Brighton Belle dining car. Good wine, a fine choice of sherries, and around 30 malt whiskies, and 30 liqueurs. There are some seats under trees in the central court.

Bar food (lunchtime; not Sun) ~ Restaurant (evening) ~ (01325) 377289 ~ Children welcome if over 7 ~ Open 12-2.30, 6-10.30(11 Sat); 12-2 Sun; closed Sun evening and 24-26 Dec

NAILSWORTH Map 1 B5
Egypt Mill

Just off A46; heading N towards Stroud, first right after roundabout, then left

This is a stylish conversion of a three-floor stonebuilt mill, which still has
working waterwheels and the millstream flowing through. The brick and
stone-floored split-level bar gives good views of the wheels, and there are
big pictures and lots of stripped beams in the comfortable carpeted lounge,
along with some hefty yet elegant ironwork from the old mill machinery.
Although it can get quite crowded on fine weekends, it's actually spacious
enough to feel at its best when it's busy – with good service to cope, and
the atmosphere is almost bistro-ish; piped music. There's a civilised upstairs
restaurant, and a no-smoking area. Well kept Tetleys, Wadworths 6X, and
a guest beer on handpump, and a wide choice of nicely presented good
generous food such as lunchtime sandwiches (from £3), filled baguettes
(from £3.80), omelettes (£5), and ploughman's (£5.50), as well as soup
(£3.20), prawns on Mediterranean couscous (£4.50), pasta and broccoli
bake, fresh haddock and chips or home-made steak and kidney pudding
(£7.95), chicken tikka (£8.95), steaks (from £11.95), fish from Cornwall
such as lemon sole (£11.45), and puddings like bread and butter pudding
or chocolate roulade (£4.50). The floodlit terrace garden by the millpond is
pretty, and there's a little bridge over from the car park; no dogs.

Bar food (standard food times) ~ Restaurant ~ (01453) 833449 ~ Children
in eating area of bar and restaurant ~ Open 11-3, 6.30(6 Sat)-11; 12-3, 6-11
Sun ~ Bedrooms: £49.50B/£75B

NORTON Map 3 E3
Hundred House

A442 Telford—Bridgnorth

Of course the attractively presented, good food in this popular family-run inn is a major draw, but the very well established cottagey gardens are worth a visit in themselves, with old-fashioned roses, trees, and herbaceous plants, and a very big working herb garden that supplies the kitchen. The neatly kept interior, prettied up with lots of dried and fresh flowers, herbs and hops, is divided into several separate areas, with old quarry tiles at either end and modern hexagonal ones in the main central high beamed part. Steps lead up past a little balustrade to a partly panelled eating area where stripped brickwork looks older than that elsewhere. Handsome fireplaces have log fires or working Coalbrookdale ranges (one has a great Jacobean arch with fine old black cooking pots), and around sewing-machine tables are a variety of interesting chairs and settles with some long colourful patchwork leather cushions; the main dining room is no smoking. Enjoyable bar food includes home-made soup (£3.95), chicken liver pâté with cream and brandy (£4.95), pork sausages with onion gravy (£6.95), charlotte of carrot wrapped in courgette with roast shallots and tomato coulis (£8.50), steak and kidney pie or chargrilled chicken with sweet red pepper coulis, mint yoghurt and fennel salad (£8.95), and daily specials such as assiette of ham terrine with cured duck breast (£7.95), braised lamb casserole (£11.95), local sirloin steak (£12.95), chargrilled salmon fillet with tarragon cream sauce (£13.95), chargrilled swordfish loin with tomato salsa and smoked paprika mayonnaise (£14.95), and home-made puddings such as hot chocolate pudding or raspberry crème brûlée (from £4.95). Well kept Heritage Bitter (brewed for them by a small brewery: light and refreshing and not too bitter), with three or four guests such as Batemans XB, Everards Tiger, Highgate Saddlers, and Robinsons Bitter on handpump, an extensive wine list with house wines by the carafe, half carafe, and big or small glass, farm cider and lots of malt whiskies; pretty bedrooms.

Bar food (12-2.30, 6-10(7-9 Sun)) ~ Restaurant ~ (01952) 730353 ~ Children in eating area of bar and restaurant ~ Open 11-2.30, 6-11; 11-11 Sat; 11-3, 7-10.30 Sun ~ Bedrooms: £75B/£99B

NORWICH Map 3 E6
Adam & Eve

Bishopgate; follow Palace Street from Tombland, N of cathedral

Well situated in the town centre and near the cathedral, this characterful place is the oldest pub in Norwich, and is thought to date back to at least 1249 – though the striking Dutch gables were added in the 14th and 15th c. The little old-fashioned bars quickly fill at lunchtime with a good mixed crowd of people, and there are antique high-backed settles (one handsomely carved), cushioned benches built into partly panelled walls, and tiled or parquet floors; the snug room is no smoking at lunchtime; piped music. Enjoyable, good value bar food under the cheery new landlady includes sandwiches, granary baps or filled french bread (from £2.55), cheese and ale soup with pastry top (£3.75), ploughman's (from £4.50), chilli or chicken curry (£4.75), ham and egg (£4.85), daily specials such as home-made ratatouille (£3.85), king prawns in garlic sauce (£5.25), crispy chicken in batter with a spicy dip (£4.85), a roast of the day with Yorkshire pudding (£4.95), and puddings like home-made spicy bread and butter pudding (from £2.70). Well kept Adnams Bitter, Greene King IPA, Charles Wells Bombardier and Theakstons Old Peculier, and a guest such as Adnams Broadside on handpump, a wide range of malt whiskies, about a dozen decent wines by the glass, Addlestone's cider and freshly squeezed orange juice. There are wooden picnic-sets in front of the pub and very pretty summer tubs and hanging baskets.

Bar food (12-7; 12-2.30 Sun) ~ (01603) 667423 ~ Children welcome in snug ~ Open 11-11; 12-10.30 Sun; closed 25, 26 Dec, 1 Jan

ODELL Map 2 A3
Bell

High Street/Horsefair Lane; off A6 S of Rushden, via Sharnbrook

The five small homely low-ceilinged rooms in this pretty stone and thatched village pub – some with shiny black beams – loop around a central servery and are furnished with handsome old oak settles, bentwood chairs and neat modern furniture; there's a log fire in one big stone fireplace, and two coal fires elsewhere, with well kept Greene King IPA, Abbot, Triumph and seasonal ales on handpump. Reasonably priced bar food includes sandwiches (from £2.20), ploughman's (from £4.40), omelettes (£4.10), ham, egg and chips (£4.65), vegetable pie (£4.50), liver and bacon (£5.50), and daily specials from the board such as asparagus and mushroom pasta (£5.20), smoked bacon steak with cumberland sauce (£7.25), vegetable lasagne (£5.60), braised lamb shank (£8.95) or lamb or chicken curry (£7.50); usual children's dishes (from £2.30) and puddings such as crunchy Dime bar gateau and cheesecake (from £2.20). Picnic-sets on the flower-filled terrace overlook a wooded garden, and from here there's an attractive walk down through a wild area to a bridge over the Great Ouse. Children will enjoy watching the garden roamings of Lucy the ten-year-old goose, and golden pheasants, cockatiels and canaries. Further along the road is a very pretty church, and the pub is handy for the local country park.

Bar food (standard food times; not Sun evening) ~ (01234) 720254 ~ Children in eating area of bar and in separate family room ~ Open 11-3, 6-11; 12-3, 7-10.30 Sun

OLD DALBY Map 3 D4
Crown

By school in village centre turn into Longcliff Hill

It's worth going to the trouble to find this tucked away, quite sophisticated creeper-covered former farmhouse. Three or four intimate little rooms have black beams, one or two antique oak settles, a mix of carvers and wheelback chairs, hunting and other rustic prints, open fires, darts and cribbage; the snug is no smoking. Made from fresh local produce wherever possible, the choice of good imaginative food changes every three months, but might include soup or sandwiches (£3.95), caesar salad or watermelon and mozzarella (£4.50), cold vegetable terrine (£4.95), filled ciabatta (from £5.95), sausage and mash (£6.95), chicken, ham and mushroom pie (£7.50), lamb shank or chicken supreme with orange and cream sauce (£10.95), pork escalope filled with mozzarella and ham with apple and cider sauce (£11.25), roast loin of lamb stuffed with basil and garlic with cherry tomatoes, courgettes, layered potatoes and rosemary jus (£13.75), fillet steak on a croûton topped with pâtés with a red wine sauce (£17.50), and puddings such as key lime pie, summer pudding or hot apple lattice (£4.50); good service. The dining room has a pleasantly relaxed bistro feel. Outside, there is cast-iron furniture and rustic tables and chairs on the terrace, hanging baskets and urns of flowers, and steps lead down through the sheltered sloping lawn where you can practise your boules with the pub's two teams. Well kept Banks's and three changing guest ales such as Courage Directors, Morrels Varsity and Theakstons Old Peculier either on handpump or tapped straight from the cask, and two dozen or more malt whiskies.

Bar food (standard food times; not Sun evening or Mon lunchtime) ~ Restaurant ~ (01664) 823134 ~ Children over 5 at lunchtime, over 10 evenings ~ Open 12-3, 6-11(7.30-10.30 Sun); 12-2.30, 6.30-11(7.30-10 Sun) in winter; closed Mon lunchtime except bank hols

OWSLEBURY Map 2 D2
Ship

Whites Hill; village signposted off B2177 between Fishers Pond and Lower Upham; can also be reached from M3 junction 10 via Morestead, or from A272 2½ miles SE of A31 junction

What was the family room here has been refurbished, with pine tables and chairs on old pine floorboards, hops and wooden blinds, and is now a bustling, friendly restaurant. The old bars on the right of the front entrance have varnished black oak 17th-c ship's timbers as beams and wall props, sporting and naval mementoes, wheelback chairs around wooden tables, and a big central fireplace; on the left is a comfortable dining area. Good bar food at lunchtime includes filled baguettes, home-cooked ham and eggs (£6.75), steak and kidney pie or warm goats cheese salad with fig chutney (£6.95), Thai prawn and crab cakes with hot chilli relish or calves liver sautéed in port with toasted brioche (£7.95), beef curry (£8.95), and steaks (from £10.50); also, home-made soup (£3.50), warm honey-glazed duck with oriental dressing (£5.25), spinach, mushroom and pepper parcel or pork with thyme, caramelised peaches and calvados (£9.95), lamb rosettes with brandy and mint sauce, cranberry and apricot compote (£10.25), and daily specials such as poached egg florentine (£4.25), giant tiger prawns with coriander butter (£6.95), locally made speciality sausage (duck and hoisin, wild boar, lamb and mint, £7.25), venison stew with red wine and bubble and squeak (£9.95), chargrilled butterfish with lemon cream sauce (£9.50), and braised shank of lamb with rosemary and red wine (£10.25); children's menu (£3.75). Well kept Cheriton Pots Ale, Greene King IPA and a couple of guests such as Bass or Flowers Original on handpump, and a decent wine list; cribbage, dominoes, piped music, and pétanque. Particularly in good weather, this is a fine place for families as they have a children's play area, a weekend bouncy castle, a pets corner, an aviary, and a summer marquee; both garden areas have fine views – one side looks right across the Solent to the Isle of Wight, the other gives a view down to Winchester. Lots of good surrounding walks.

Bar food (standard food times; all day Sun) ~ (01962) 777358 ~ Children welcome ~ Occasional jazz ~ Open 11-3, 6-11; 11-11 Sat; 12-10.30 Sun; 11-3, 6-11 Sat in winter; closed winter Mon lunchtimes

PAGLESHAM Map 2 C5
Plough & Sail

East End; on the Paglesham road out of Rochford, keep right instead of heading into Church End

The big log fires inside this beautifully kept 17th-c dining pub are a welcome contrast to the bitter winds that bite in across the marshes in winter. Covered in white weatherboarding (like many of the older buildings around here), it's friendly and cosy inside, with pine tables and seats under its rather low beams, lots of brasses and pictures, and pretty flower arrangements. Good food includes sandwiches (from £2.75), soup (£2.75), ploughman's (£4.25), lasagne (£7.50) and steak and kidney pie (£7.95), with interesting daily specials such as field mushrooms topped with brie (£3.95), fresh prawns, crab and salmon on mixed leaves with balsamic dressing (£6.25), home-made curries (£6.95), and fresh fish such as fried skate or monkfish (from £8.95); home-made puddings such as fruit crumble and coconut and lime pudding with coconut ice cream (£3.25). The staff are friendly and attentive. Well kept Greene King IPA and a guest such as Mighty Oak Burntwood on handpump; decent house wines; cribbage, dominoes and unobtrusive piped music. There are tables and an aviary in the attractive and neatly kept garden. It's in a pretty spot and so can get very busy on warm summer evenings.

Bar food (12-2, 7-9.30; 12-9 Sun) ~ Restaurant ~ (01702) 258242 ~ Children in eating area of bar ~ Open 11.30-3(3.30 Sat), 6.30-11; 12-10.30 Sun

PHILLEIGH Map 1 E2
Roseland
Between A3078 and B3289, just E of King Harry ferry

Handy for Trelissick Gardens and the King Harry ferry, this charming little place remains as consistently friendly and as popular as ever. The two bar rooms (one with flagstones and the other carpeted) have wheelback chairs and built-in red-cushioned seats, open fires, old photographs and some giant beetles and butterflies in glasses, and a relaxed chatty atmosphere; the little back bar is used by locals. Enjoyably good bar food includes home-baked pasty (£2.60), sandwiches (from £3.50; bocatta bread with chargrilled chicken, hummus, mint and tzatziki £6.50), ploughman's or filled baked potatoes (from £4.50), crevettes sautéed in lime and chilli butter (small £5.95, large £7.95), beef and stilton pie (£8.25), braised shank of lamb (£8.95), crab cakes with a tomato and basil dressing (£9.95), daily specials like pork and stilton pâté (£5.95), scallops with brandy and coriander with a herb crust (£9.95), and Aberdeen Angus steak (£12.50), puddings (£3.95), and children's menu; you must book to be sure of a table. The restaurant is no smoking. Well kept Bass, Ringwood Best, Marstons Pedigree, and Sharps Own and Doom Bar on handpump, local cider, quite a few wines by the glass, and several malt whiskies; dominoes and cribbage. The pretty paved front courtyard is a lovely place to sit in the lunchtime sunshine beneath the cherry blossom, and the back garden has a small outdoor children's play area.

Bar food (standard food times) ~ Restaurant ~ (01872) 580254 ~ Children welcome ~ Open 11-3, 5.30-11; 12-3, 6-10.30 Sun

PICKERING Map 3 B4
White Swan

Market Place, just off A170

This former coaching inn is on a winning streak these days. As well as its flourishing gently upmarket hotel side, with very comfortable recently reworked bedrooms, it has a charming country atmosphere in its small and civilised front bar, with panelling, dark plush cushions and a log fire; the snug, with another fire, is no smoking. They use as much carefully sourced local produce as possible, which at lunchtime might run from sandwiches (from £4.75; Yorkshire rarebit with pear chutney and watercress salad £4.95; chicken breast with guacamole, bacon and lemon dressing £5.50), home-made soup (£3.95), creamed mushrooms with garlic and dry cured bacon (£4.10), chicken liver pâté (£4.25), grilled swaledale goats cheese (£4.95) through Whitby crab or grilled sausages with mash and onion gravy (£6.95), ploughman's (£7.25), lambs liver (£7.80), salmon fishcakes with lemon sauce (£7.95), to chargrilled sirloin steak (£10.95), with more elaborate or heartier evening dishes such as assiette charcuterie with parmesan and lemon (£6.95), potted Whitby lobster and crab with watercress and mustard seed salad (£7), marinated vegetables with fresh herb salad and polenta (£10), parma ham-wrapped pork fillet with porcini stuffing, baby leeks, thyme potatoes and pan juices (£13.50), roast rack of spring lamb with chargrilled courgettes, olive oil mash and mint sauce (£14.25), and roast monkfish with tomato and coriander curry and green sauce (£14.50), and puddings such as lemon tart with lime and mascarpone ice cream, rich chocolate cake with clotted cream and macerated cherries or crème brûlée with apple crisps and chantilly cream (from £3.50). The same menu is available (with a small surcharge) in the small and attractive no-smoking dining room. If you stay, the breakfast is good. Well kept Black Sheep Bitter and Special and a local guest beer on handpump, nine good house wines (by two sizes of glass) and an impressive wine list, good coffee, friendly helpful staff. There's a busy but comfortable family room.

Bar food (12-4, 5-6.30; 12-5, 7-9 Sun) ~ Restaurant ~ (01751) 472288 ~ Children in eating area of bar and restaurant ~ Open 10.30-3, 6-11; 10-11 Mon and Sat; 12-5, 7-10.30 Sun ~ Bedrooms: /£100B

PITLOCHRY Map 4 D2
Moulin

Kirkmichael Roadd, Moulin; A924 NE of Pitlochry centre

The traditional pubby atmosphere at this imposing white-painted 17th-c inn owes much to the well kept real ales on handpump, which are brewed in the little stables across the street: Braveheart, Moulin Light, Ale of Atholl and the stronger Old Remedial; group brewery tours by arrangement. Although the building has been much extended over the years, the bar, in the oldest part of the building, still seems an entity in itself. Above the fireplace in the smaller room is an interesting painting of the village before the road was built (Moulin used to be a bustling market town, far busier than Pitlochry), while the bigger carpeted area has a good few tables and cushioned banquettes in little booths divided by stained-glass country scenes, another big fireplace, some exposed stonework, fresh flowers, and local prints and golf clubs around the walls; bar billiards, shove-ha'penny, cribbage, dominoes and fruit machine. A wide choice of enjoyable bar food includes soup (£2.25), lunchtime sandwiches and baked potatoes (from £3.75), ploughman's (£3.95), Isle of Skye mussels (£4.50/£6.50), haggis and neeps (£5.45), stuffed peppers (£6.50), game casserole or grilled salmon (£6.95), and puddings such as chocolate and nut ice-cream cake or honey sponge and custard (£2.50); prompt friendly service. They keep around 40 malt whiskies. Picnic-sets outside are surrounded by tubs of flowers, and look across to the village kirk. They offer good value three-night breaks out of season. Rewarding walks nearby.

Bar food (12-9.30) ~ Restaurant (6-9) ~ (01796) 472196 ~ Children in eating area of bar and restaurant ~ Open 12-11(11.45 Sat) ~ Bedrooms: £25B/£50B

RAGLAN Map 1 B5
Clytha Arms
Clytha, off Abergavenny road – former A40, now declassified

Very reasonably priced considering the high quality, and made using lots of fresh local ingredients, the delicious bar food at this graciously comfortable, fine old country inn is really enjoyed by readers. Generously served dishes could include soup (from £4.50), bacon, laverbread and cockles, black pudding with apple and potato mash, faggots and peas with beer and onion gravy (£5.95), three cheese ploughman's or wild mushroom ragoût with pasta (£6.50), wild boar sausages with potato pancakes (£6.75), smoked salmon and scrambled egg (£7.20), daily specials such as spaghetti with bacon and cockles (£6.25) and grilled salmon and prawn salad (£7.25). Not content with serving really good bar food, they have a well stocked bar too, with well kept Bass, Bulmastiff Gold, Felinfoel Double Dragon and three interesting changing guest beers on handpump, as well as Weston's farm cider, a changing guest cider, and home-made perry, and the extensive wine list has a dozen or so by the glass. There are usually a couple of locals in the carefully refurbished ba,r which has a good bustling atmosphere, solidly comfortable furnishings and a couple of log fires; darts, shove-ha'penny, boules, table skittles, cribbage, dominoes, draughts and chess. The exceptionally helpful staff and interested licensees make this such a nice place to stay; the two labradors, Beamish and Stowford, are nicely welcoming too. Don't miss the murals in the lavatories. This lovely building stands in its own extensive well cared for grounds, which are a mass of colour in spring.

Bar food (standard food times; not Mon lunchtime or Sun evening) ~ Restaurant ~ (01873) 840206 ~ Children in eating area of bar and restaurant ~ Open 12-3.30, 6-11; 12-11 Sat; 12-4, 7-10.30 Sun; closed Mon lunchtime except bank holidays ~ Bedrooms: £45B/£60B

READING Map 2 C3
Sweeney & Todd
10 Castle Street; next to Post Office

Though you'd never guess it from the street, a lively bar is hidden behind the baker's shop in this unique patisserie-cum-pub, selling pies, soft drinks and even fresh eggs. Behind the counter and down some stairs, a surprising number of tiny tables are squeezed into one long thin room, most of them in rather conspiratorial railway-carriage-style booths separated by curtains, and each with a leather-bound menu to match the leather-cushioned pews. Old prints line the walls, and the colonial-style fans and bare-boards floor enhance the period feel. Among the impressive choice of pies might be chicken, honey and mustard, hare and cherry, duck and apricot, goose and gooseberry, partridge and pear, or the rugby-influenced five nations – a medley of beef, Guinness, garlic, mustard and leeks (all £3.60), with other bar food such as soup (£2.50), sandwiches (from £2.50), casseroles (£5.10), and roasts (£6). Helpings are huge, and excellent value. Well kept Adnams Best, Badger Tanglefoot, Wadworths 6X and a changing guest are served on handpump from the small bar, with various wines and a range of liqueurs and cigars. You can buy the pies in the shop to take away.

Bar food (standard food times) ~ Restaurant ~ (0118) 958 6466 ~ Children welcome away from bar ~ Open 11-11; closed Sun, 25 and 26 Dec, and bank holidays

REIGATE HEATH Map 2 D4
Skimmington Castle

3 miles from M25 junction 8: through Reigate take A25 Dorking (West), then on edge of Reigate turn left past Black Horse into Flanchford Road; after ¼ mile turn left into Bonny's Road (unmade, very bumpy track); after crossing golf course fork right up hill

It's well worth the journey to find this rather remote – though often busy – quaint old country pub. The bright main front bar leads off a small central serving counter with dark simple panelling. There's a miscellany of chairs and tables, shiny brown vertical panelling, a brown plank ceiling, well kept Greene King IPA, Wadworths 6X, Youngs Special and a guest such as Adnams Broadside on handpump, with several wines by the glass, and cask-conditioned cider. The cosy back rooms are partly panelled too, with old-fashioned settles and windsor chairs; one has a big brick fireplace with its bread-oven still beside it – the chimney is said to have been used as a highwayman's look-out. There's another small room down steps at the back; shove-ha'penny, cribbage, dominoes, ring the bull, board games, and piped music. Good popular bar food includes soup and sandwiches (from £2.85, smoked salmon £3.95), ploughman's (from £4.50), fresh breaded haddock (£6.25), pork in cider pie (£6.50), roast chump of lamb with couscous (£8.50), beef wellington (£10.50), daily specials such as moules marinières (£5.50), venison steak (£8.95), and monkfish wrapped in seaweed (£10.50), and puddings (£2.95); to be sure of a table, you must book ahead. There are nice views from the crazy-paved front terrace and tables on the grass by lilac bushes, with more tables at the back overlooking the meadows and the hillocks. There's a hitching rail outside for horses, and the pub is handy for ramblers on the North Downs.

Bar food (12-2.15, 7-9.30; 12-2.30, 7-9 Sun) ~ (01737) 243100 ~ Children welcome ~ Folk second Sun of month ~ Open 11-3, 5.30(6 Sat)-11; 12-10.30 Sun; closed evenings 25 and 26 Dec and 1 Jan

ROMALDKIRK Map 3 B3
Rose & Crown
Just off B6277

Still on tremendously good form, this immaculately kept 18th-c coaching inn goes from strength to strength year after year, with continual care and attention given to the details that mark this place out from other pubs. The cosy beamed traditional bar has old-fashioned seats facing the warming log fire, a Jacobean oak settle, lots of brass and copper, a grandfather clock, and gin-traps, old farm tools, and black and white pictures of Romaldkirk on the walls. The smart Crown Room, where bar food is served, has more brass and copper, original etchings of game shooting scenes and farm implements. The hall is hung with wine maps and other interesting prints and a photograph of the Hale Bopp comet over Romaldkirk church that was taken by a guest; no-smoking oak-panelled restaurant. As well as making their own marmalades, jams, chutneys and bread, they also change the very imaginative bar menu weekly. It is very popular so you will need to book. In addition to lunchtime baps (from £3.35) and ploughman's (£5.50), excellent food might include home-made soup (£2.95), baked cheddar soufflé with green herb sauce (£4.50), fried black pudding with leek and bacon risotto and balsamic jus (£4.95), sautéed chicken livers with roasted pepper brioche and salad (£7.95), confit of duck leg with spiced red cabbage and red wine jus (£9.50), baked smoked haddock with wilted spinach, poached egg and hollandaise (£10.50), steak, kidney and mushroom pie (£8.50), fried pigeon with root rösti, onion confit and juniper berry sauce (£10.95) and puddings such as sticky toffee pudding or walnut and syrup tart (£3.25). Well kept Black Sheep and Theakstons Best on handpump; good, friendly service. Tables outside look out over the village green, still with its original stocks and water pump. The village is close to the superb Bowes Museum and the High Force waterfall, and has an interesting old church. The recently decorated charming bedrooms have fresh flowers, hair dryers, and trouser presses – and on the top floor are three rooms (two are suites and one has a sitting area) with hi-fi systems.

Bar food (12-1.30, 6.30-9.30) ~ Restaurant ~ (01833) 650213 ~ Children welcome; must be over 6 in restaurant ~ Open 11-3, 5.30-11; 12-3, 7-10.30 Sun; closed 24-26 Dec ~ Bedrooms: £62B/£86B

SALT Map 3 D3
Holly Bush

Village signposted off A51 S of Stone (and A518 NE of Stafford)

Readers are enthusiastic about the home-made bar food at this white-painted thatched house set in a pretty village, and you should arrive early if you want to eat here as it fills up very quickly. The menus are prepared from as much fresh local produce as possible, and include sandwiches (from £1.75, triple deckers £2.95), filled baked potatoes (from £2.25) breaded mushrooms or pâté (£3.25), steaks (from £5.95), poached plaice (£7.25), steak and ale pie or Greek lamb (£7.95), and daily changing specials such as grilled black pudding with poached egg (£3.25), fresh Scottish mussels steamed in cider with cream and onion sauce (£5.95), wild mushroom stroganoff (£6.25), cod with a herb and goats cheese crust (£8.45), and duck breast in green peppercorn and sherry sauce (£10.50); home-made puddings (from £2.75); Sunday roasts. The oldest part of the building dates back to the 14th c, and has a heavy beamed and planked ceiling (some of the beams are attractively carved), a salt cupboard built in by the coal fire, and other nice old-fashioned touches such as an antique pair of clothes brushes hanging by the door, attractive sporting prints and watercolours, and an ancient pair of riding boots on the mantelpiece. Around the standing-room serving section several cosy areas spread off, including a modern back extension which blends in well, with beams, stripped brickwork and a small coal fire; there are comfortable settees as well as more orthodox seats. Well kept Bass, Boddingtons and Courage Directors on handpump, friendly and efficient service, maybe piped nostalgic pop music; darts, shove-ha'penny, cribbage, backgammon, Jenga, fruit machine. The big back lawn has rustic picnic-sets and a busy dovecote; they may have traditional jazz and a hog roast in summer as well as a fireworks display on 5 November.

Bar food (12-2, 6-9.30) ~ (01889) 508234 ~ Children in eating area of bar ~ Open 12-3, 6-11; 12-11 Sat; 12-10.30 Sun

SAPPERTON Map 1 B6
Bell

Village signposted from A419 Stroud—Cirencester; OS Sheet 163 map reference 948033

After a year of renovations, this 250-year-old pub has an entirely new look. There are three separate, cosy rooms with a nice mix of wooden tables and chairs, country prints on stripped stone walls, log fires and woodburning stoves, fresh flowers, and newspapers and guidebooks to browse. Imaginative bar food, using local produce whenever possible and no frozen food at all (except ice cream), might include cold home-cooked ham, home-made piccalilli and a basket of hot crusty bread (£3.95), saffron and dolcelatte risotto cakes, tomato and garlic pulp (£4.25), Welsh rarebit with red onion marmalade (£4.95), a platter of pork pie and cheese with home-made chutney and fruit (£5.95), roasted mushrooms with leeks, gorgonzola rarebit and a sweet pepper dressing (£8.95), slow honey-roast belly of pork with apple and mustard mash (£9.95), pine nut-crusted chicken breast filled with basil butter (£10.95), and daily specials such as roast parsnip and curry soup (£3.25), spicy crab fritters with a coconut and mint dip (£5.95), warm salad of pigeon breast with black pudding and bacon (£7.95), roasted breast of duck with stir-fried noodles and home-made plum sauce or roasted hake steak on crushed chickpeas with fresh basil oil and bacon lardons (£12.95), and home-made puddings like rhubarb and cinnamon crumble, chocolate and brandy mousse or amaretto bread and butter pudding (£3.95); Sunday roast rib of Shorthorn beef (£9.95). A basket of home-made bread and butter accompanies every meal. Well kept Hook Norton Best, Uley Best and Old Spot and a guest such as Arkells Summer Ale or Bath Gem on handpump, up to 10 wines by the glass, champagne by the glass, and Weston's cider; cribbage and dominoes. Harry the springer spaniel likes to greet everyone. There are tables out on a small front lawn, and a partly covered back courtyard garden for eating outside. Good surrounding walks, and horses have their own tethering rail.

Bar food (standard food times; not Mon except bank hols) ~ (01285) 760298 ~ Children in eating area of bar ~ Open 11-2.30, 6.30-11; 12-3, 7-10.30 Sun; closed Mon except bank hols

SCAYNES HILL Map 2 D4

Sloop

Freshfield Lock; at top of Scaynes Hill by petrol station turn N off A272 into
Church Road, keep on for 1½ miles and then follow Freshfield signpost

After a visit to Sheffield Park Gardens or the Bluebell Steam Railway, this
pleasantly set country pub is a good spot for lunch. The long saloon bar
has wheelbacks and other chairs around pubby tables, a warmly friendly
atmosphere, well kept Greene King IPA, Abbot, Dark Mild, Ruddles
County, and a couple of guests such as Black Sheep Bitter, Gales HSB or
Charles Wells Bombardier on handpump, and a decent wine list with 8 by
the glass; there are benches in the old-fashioned brick porch. Good home-
made bar food includes soups such as stilton and broccoli or vegetable with
garlic croûtons (£3.95; popular New Hampshire fish stew £6.95), roast
peppers filled with onion, mushroom and bacon, topped with cheese
(£4.50), lunchtime ploughman's (£4.95), vegetable lasagne or home-made
steak, stout and mushroom pie (£6.95), liver and bacon with onion gravy
(£7.95), maple and mustard chicken, pheasant braised in blackcurrant and
winter ale (£8.95), steaks (from £9.95), grilled whole bass with olives,
garlic and tomato (£11.95), daily specials such as devilled kidneys (£6.95),
marlin tagliatelle with tomato and brie (£8.95), sautéed venison in port,
thyme and honey (£9.95), and fillet of beef stroganoff (£10.95), and
puddings such as home-made apple crumble, crème brûlée or bread
pudding with maple and cream (£3.50); best to book. Good service from
chatty, welcoming staff. The basic but airy public bar has restored
woodwork, settles and cushioned stools on the bare boards, and railway
memorabilia on the walls; bar billiards (in a small room leading off the
bar), piped music, darts, shove-ha'penny, cribbage and dominoes. There
are lots of tables in the sheltered garden.

*Bar food (12-2.15, 6.30-9.15 Mon-Sat, 12-8.30 Sun) ~ (01444) 831219 ~
Children in eating area of bar ~ Live music first Fri of month ~ Open 12-3,
6-11; 12-10.30 Sun*

SEAVIEW Map 2 E3
Seaview Hotel

High Street; off B3330 Ryde—Bembridge

There are sea views from the continental-style terraces on either side of the path to the front door of this comfortably bustling hotel. Popular with locals, the nautical back bar is a lot pubbier than you might imagine from the outside, with traditional wooden furnishings on the bare boards, lots of seafaring paraphernalia around its softly lit ochre walls, and a log fire. The civilised airier bay-windowed bar at the front has an impressive array of naval and merchant ship photographs, as well as Spy nautical cartoons for *Vanity Fair*, original receipts for Cunard's shipyard payments for the *Queen Mary* and *Queen Elizabeth*, and a line of close-set tables down each side on the turkey carpet. Using local ingredients wherever possible, good well presented generous bar food includes soup (£2.95), hot crab ramekin (£4.95), warm crispy duck and nut salad with tangy mango dressing (£6.50), spinach and ricotta puff with wholegrain mustard mash or pork and leek sausages and mash (£7.50), grilled swordfish steak with red wine reduction (£11.95), changing blackboard specials such as local crab and lobster, and puddings such as steamed treacle pudding with cream (£3.50) and iced lemon brûlée (£3.95); children's menu; the restaurant is no smoking. Service is generally good and the staff are friendly. Goddards and Greene King Abbot are kept on handpump, and there's a good wine list (the landlord used to be a director of Corney and Barrow wine merchants) and choice of malt whiskies; darts, cribbage, dominoes, shove-ha'penny and piped music. Some of the bedrooms have sea views.

Bar food (12-2, 7-9.30) ~ Restaurant ~ (01983) 612711 ~ Children in eating area of bar and restaurant; no under 5s in restaurant after 7.30pm ~ Open 11-2.30(3 Sat), 6-11; 12-3, 7-10.30 Sun; closed three days at Christmas ~ Bedrooms: £65B/£75B

SELLACK Map 1 A5
Lough Pool

Back road Hoarwithy—Ross-on-Wye

The new licensee at this lovely old black and white timbered country cottage is well known in the gastronomic world as a talented chef/licensee. He plans to build on the best aspects of this already well liked place and bring up the areas where it's been lagging. Many readers will be pleased to hear that as a starting point he's banished the piped music. Improvements to the kitchen should help plans to gear up the food by using fresh local and where possible organic produce, but at the same time keeping the menu nice and pubby in the bar, with a more elaborate imaginative choice in the redecorated no-smoking restaurant. There are now two guest beers such as Hook Norton and Wadworths 6X alongside well kept John Smiths and Wye Valley Bitter and Butty Bach on handpump, a good range of malt whiskies, local farm ciders and a well chosen reasonably priced wine list. The beamed central room has kitchen chairs and cushioned window seats around wooden tables (some now replaced by nicer ones) on the mainly flagstoned floor, sporting prints and bunches of dried flowers, and a log fire at each end. Other rooms lead off, with attractive individual furnishings and nice touches like the dresser of patterned plates. A good balanced bar menu includes soup (£3.25), black pudding fritters with beetroot relish (£4.25), ploughman's (£5.50), charcuterie (£4.50/£7.50), sausages, or steak and kidney pie (£6.25), spaghetti with tomato, basil and caper sauce (£6.95), battered cod with mushy peas and home-made tartare sauce (£9.50) and roast crispy duck with limes (£22 for two). There are plenty of picnic-sets on the neat front lawn, and pretty hanging baskets.

Bar food (standard food times) ~ Restaurant ~ (01989) 730236 ~ Children in eating area of bar and restaurant ~ Open 11.30-2.30, 6.30-11; 12-5 (2 in winter), 7-10.30 Sun; closed Sun eve Nov-Feb

SHALFLEET Map 2 E2
New Inn

Main Road (A3054 Newport—Yarmouth)

The good fresh fish served at this welcoming former fishermen's pub is bought from the quay only a short walk away. A brief menu with sandwiches (from £2.95), filled baguettes (from £3.75) and ploughman's (from £5.25) is supplemented by changing blackboard specials (with up to 16 types of fish) which might include grilled sardines with garlic and black pepper butter (£3.95), mushrooms in white wine and stilton (£4.50), moules marinières (£4.95/£8.95), pork fillet with apple and cider sauce, chicken breast with honey and cream sauce or Thai-style swordfish (£8.95), lobster salad (£11.95), and their famous fish platter for two (£45); it's a good idea to book. The partly panelled, flagstoned public bar has yachting photographs and pictures, a boarded ceiling, scrubbed deal tables, windsor chairs, and a roaring log fire in the big stone hearth, and the carpeted beamed lounge bar has more windsor chairs, boating pictures, and a coal fire. The snug is no smoking. Well kept Badger Best, Bass, Ventnor Golden and a couple of guests such as Goddards Fuggle-Dee-Dum and Jennings Cocker Hoop on handpump, and around 60 wines; piped music.

Bar food (12-2.30, 6-9.30) ~ Restaurant ~ (01983) 531314 ~ Children away from main bar ~ Open 12-3, 6-11(10.30 Sun)

SHAVE CROSS Map 1 D5
Shave Cross Inn

On back lane Bridport—Marshwood, signposted locally; OS Sheet 193 map
reference 415980

The original timbered bar at this charming, partly 14th-c flint and thatch
inn is a lovely flagstoned room, surprisingly roomy and full of character,
with country antiques and an enormous inglenook fireplace. The no-
smoking dining area and restaurant are stylishly decorated with crimson
walls, Renaissance drawings in red chalk and candles on the tables. They
have three well kept real ales on handpump such as Adnams Broadside,
Bass and Otter Ale, and several wines by the glass; piped music. Very good
imaginative bar food includes home-made soup (£3.25), lunchtime
baguettes (from £3.45), grilled sardines (£4.95), fresh salmon fishcakes
(£5.75), confit of duck leg or wild mushrooms with a cream, herb and
cheese sauce, smoked pigeon breast, ploughman's or home-made burger
(£5.95), Greek-style marinated pork, fresh haddock or vegetable risotto
(£7.50), chicken breast with a stuffing of smoked mozzarella cheese and
pesto wrapped in parma ham, or salmon fillet with lemon butter (£10.95)
and duck breast with an orange and herb glaze or lamb cutlets with a
redcurrant and red wine sauce (£13.95). The sheltered flower-filled garden
with its thatched wishing-well and goldfish pool is very pretty.

*Bar food (standard food times; not Sun evening, Mon) ~ Restaurant ~
(01308) 868358 ~ Children in restaurant ~ Open 11.30-3, 7-11; 12-3,
7-10.30 Sun; closed winter Mon*

SHEEPSCOMBE Map 1 B5
Butchers Arms

Village signposted off B4070 NE of Stroud; or A46 N of Painswick (but narrow lanes)

This is the sort of friendly, relaxed pub where a good mix of customers mingles very happily in the chatty atmosphere – unspoilt by noisy games machines or piped music. They still have their popular policy of not reserving tables in the bar so casual diners and locals have a welcoming area in which to enjoy their drinks. The bar has log fires, seats in big bay windows, flowery-cushioned chairs and rustic benches, and lots of interesting oddments like assorted blow lamps, irons, and plates. Good lunchtime bar food includes home-made soup (£3.25), lots of filled rolls (from £3.50; bacon and egg £4.25; steak and mushrooms £4.95), chicken and bacon caesar salad topped with parmesan croûtons (£4.75; main course £6.75), filled baked potatoes (from £4.75), home-made chicken liver pâté (£4.95), ploughman's (from £5.50), local beef and Guinness sausages with onion gravy or vegetable and nut hotpot bake (£6.50), and mixed game in a cranberry and red wine sauce topped with puff pastry (£7.75), with evening extras such as fresh local rainbow trout (£6.75), chicken simmered in a sherry, mushroom, onion and tomato sauce (£8.75), and duck breast with an orange and Grand Marnier glaze (£11.95), and daily specials like salmon and haddock fishcakes with parsley and dill sauce (£6.75), braised lamb in a leek, mint and red wine sauce (£7.25), pork escalope topped with bacon, pineapple and melted cheese (£7.85), and grilled fresh monkfish medallions with a redcurrant dressing (£8.95). The restaurant and a small area in the bar are no smoking. Well kept Hook Norton Best, and two changing guests such as Wickwar Old Arnold or Wychwood Fiddler's Elbow on handpump, decent wines with several by the glass, and country wines; darts, cribbage, cards, and dominoes. The views are marvellous and there are teak seats below the building, tables on the steep grass behind, and a cricket ground behind on such a steep slope that the boundary fielders at one end can scarcely see the bowler. This pub is one of little Blenheim Inns group.

Bar food (12-2.30, 7-9.30) ~ Restaurant ~ (01452) 812113 ~ Children in eating area of bar and restaurant ~ Occasional morris men ~ Open 11.30-3, 6-11; 12-3.30, 7-10.30 Sun

SHEFFIELD Map 3 C4
Fat Cat
23 Alma Street

A huge draw to this well run pub is the big choice of well kept real ales on handpump. They keep around 10 ales, including their own, and have a popular Brewery Visitor's Centre (you can book brewery trips (0114) 249 4804) with framed beer mats, pump clips, and prints on the walls. As well as their own-brewed and cheap Kelham Island Bitter, Pale Rider, another Kelham Island beer, and Timothy Taylors Landlord, there are seven interesting guest beers on handpump from breweries like Coach House, Cropton, Durham, Glentworth, Lloyds, Titanic, and so forth, plus continental and British bottled beers, a Belgian draught beer, fruit gin, country wines, and farm cider. Incredibly cheap, enjoyable bar food includes sandwiches, lentil soup (£1.30), ploughman's, spinach pasta, courgette and potato pie, pork casserole or quiche (all £2.50), and puddings such as rhubarb crumble or jam roly-poly (£1); well liked Sunday lunch (£3). There's always a good, friendly bustle and a wide mix of customers from far and wide, and the two small downstairs rooms have brewery-related prints on the walls, coal fires, simple wooden tables and cushioned seats around the walls, and jugs, bottles, and some advertising mirrors; the one on the left is no smoking; cribbage and dominoes, and maybe a not-so-fat-cat wandering around. Steep steps take you up to another similarly simple room (which may be booked for functions) with some attractive prints of old Sheffield; there are picnic-sets in a fairylit back courtyard.

Bar food (12-2.30, 6-7.30; not Sat or Sun evening, not 1 Jan) ~ No credit cards ~ (0114) 249 4801 ~ Children in upstairs room (if not booked up) ~ Open 12-3, 5.30-11; 12-3, 7-10.30 Sun; closed 25 and 26 Dec

SHINCLIFFE Map 3 A3
Seven Stars

High Street North; A177 a mile or so S of Durham

The relaxed and comfortably welcoming interior of this early 18th-c village inn is quite civilised but still largely unspoilt, so although the food here is very good there's still a nice local atmosphere. The lounge bar has a coal fire in its handsome Victorian fireplace, with a pair of big Staffordshire dogs on the mantelpiece below a big mirror, old brewery advertisements, copper kettles hanging from the beams, and cushioned wall banquettes and stools around cast-iron-framed tables. Very enjoyable imaginative bar food from a changing menu might include home-made soup (£3.50), salad of calamari and monkfish or New Zealand mussels marinated in oriental spices with tempura batter (£5.50), wild mushroom, spinach and ricotta pancake (£9.50), fried salmon escalope on spring onion, lemon and crab risotto (£10.50), chicken breast stuffed with Toulouse sausage and black pudding (£11.50). Well kept Marstons Pedigree and a couple of guests such as Charles Wells Bombardier and Courage Directors on handpump, 25 malt whiskies, friendly staff; chess, draughts, dominoes and piped music. The candlelit dining room and half the lounge are no smoking. Parking can be a problem but it's just 10 minutes' or so drive from central Durham, with fairly frequent buses passing the door. Pretty window boxes, creepers, and seats out at the end of the attractive village street.

Bar food (12-2.30, 6-9.30) ~ Restaurant ~ (0191) 384 8454 ~ Children in eating area of bar and restaurant ~ Open 12-11 ~ Bedrooms: £40S/£50S

SHREWSBURY Map 3 E2

Armoury

Victoria Quay, Victoria Avenue

By the time this book is published, the area in front of this former warehouse will have been pedestrianised and there will be tables out there for summer dining. You can take boats out on the River Severn, escorted past rows of weeping willows by swans and gently quacking ducks – it does get busy, particularly at weekends. Big arched windows overlooking the river light up the single airy room, which is packed with old prints, documents and other neatly framed ephemera, with glass cabinets showing off collections of explosives and shells as well as corks and bottle openers, and one entire wall covered with copiously filled bookshelves. There's a mix of good heavy wooden tables, chairs and high-backed settles, interspersed by the occasional green-painted standing timber, and colonial fans whirring away on the ceiling. Tables at one end are laid out for eating, with a grand stone fireplace at the other end. An eye-catching range of varied drinks served from behind the long bar counter includes well kept Boddingtons, Wadworths 6X, Woods Shropshire Lad, and up to five changing guests on handpump, as well as a good wine list with several by the glass, around 70 malt whiskies, a dozen different gins, lots of rums and vodkas, a wide choice of brandies, and some unusual liqueurs. Alongside soup (£3.95), sandwiches (from £3.25) and ploughman's (£5.75), bar food includes chilli crab and potato cakes with cucumber and coriander yoghurt (£3.95), chicken liver and smoked bacon pâté with a pineapple and onion chutney (£4.25), cumberland sausage with horseradish mash and red wine gravy (£6.95), lambs liver with mashed sweet potato, crispy smoked bacon and stilton gravy (£7.45), crispy pancake filled with oyster mushrooms, spring greens and ginger served on stir-fried lemon and spinach noodles (£8.25), cold poached salmon fillet with asparagus mousse (£8.50), rib-eye steak with peppercorn sauce (£12.75), and puddings such as treacle tart or chocolate chip sponge (£4.25). The pub doesn't have its own parking but they sell vouchers for parking up nearer the Quarry.

Bar food (12-2.30, 6-9.30; 12-9.30(9 Sun) Sat) ~ (01743) 340525 ~ Children till 9pm ~ Open 12-11(10.30 Sun); closed 25 and 26 Dec

SLAPTON Map 1 E4
Tower

Signposted off A379 Dartmouth—Kingsbridge

This atmospheric old place is a good all-rounder. There's a good choice of real ales, a decent wine list, particularly good food and a warm, friendly atmosphere. The low-ceilinged bar has armchairs, low-backed settles on the flagstones, and open log fires, and up to five well kept real ales such as Adnams Best, Badger Tanglefoot, Dartmoor Best, and Exmoor Bitter, with a guest such as Exmoor Gold or Wells Bombardier on handpump; farm cider. Under the new chef, the good, imaginative food at lunchtime includes soups such as parsnip and cranberry or green bean and aubergine (£2.95), sandwiches (from £3.40), mushrooms sautéed with stilton and cream sauce (£4.25), warm ratatouille tartlet with basil dressed leaves (£4.95), local pork sausages with wholegrain mustard mash and onion gravy (£5.95), lightly spiced crab cakes with a seafood nage (£6.95), and braised lamb shank with mash and a redcurrant and rosemary gravy (£7.95), with evening dishes such as home-made chicken liver pâté with spiced pears (£4.50), sautéed scallops with sweet chilli and crème fraîche (£6.95), poached guinea fowl with broad beans, garlic and pear couscous (£8.95), plaice fillets with tomato and chilli ham and spinach (£9.75), and crusted beef fillet with pepper sauce (£14.95), and puddings like chocolate and orange baked mousse, apricot and brandy bread and butter pudding or apple and toffee pie (£3.50); lots of interesting daily specials too using local game and fish. The dining room is no smoking; cribbage, dominoes, chess, backgammon, Scrabble, draughts, and piped music. There are picnic-sets on the neatly kept back lawn, which is overhung by the ivy-covered ruin of a 14th-c chantry. The lane up to the pub is very narrow.

Bar food (12-2.30, 7-9.30; not winter Sun evening or Mon) ~ Restaurant ~ (01548) 580216 ~ Children in eating area of bar and restaurant ~ Live folk and jazz ~ Open 12-3, 6-11; 12-3, 7-10.30 Sun ~ Bedrooms: /£50S

SNETTISHAM Map 3 D5
Rose & Crown

Village signposted from A149 King's Lynn—Hunstanton Road, just N of Sandringham

There's massive confirmation in our postbag this year that the licensees of this ancient white pub are making their philosophy really work: they aim to make you feel thoroughly at home from the moment you arrive until the end of a memorably satisfying visit. Freshly cooked seasonal bar food using local produce where possible is from a changing menu which might include lunchtime dishes such as smoked gammon and pearl barley broth (£3.50), toasted filled focaccia (£4.95), fried sardines with bok choi salad (£5.50) and beef, Guinness and mushroom casserole or Portuguese-style salt cod with roast peppers, aïoli and parmesan (£8.50), with evening dishes such as roasted red pepper and tomato soup with vanilla oil (£3.50), Greek tapas with pitta bread (£5.75), roast chicken breast with spinach polenta and crab and lime bisque (£10.95), grilled black bream with Asian leaves, strawberry stilton and toasted pecan nuts (£13.25), and daily specials such as braised lamb shank and chorizo and bean stew with sweet potato chips (£9.95), additional vegetables (£1.50); they have a pudding chef so expect these to be good, and where practical they will do small helpings of menu items for children. The interior has been very thoughtfully put together, with several separate areas each with its own character: an old-fashioned beamed front bar with black settles on its tiled floor, and a great log fire; another big log fire in a back bar with the landlord's sporting trophies and old sports equipment; a no-smoking bar with a colourful but soothing décor and white linen tablecloths (this room is favoured by people eating); and another warmly decorated room, nice for families, with painted settles and big old tables. Some lovely old pews and other interesting furniture sit on the wooden floor of the dining room, and there are shelves with old bottles and books, and old prints and watercolours. Well kept Adnams Bitter and Broadside, Bass, Greene King IPA and maybe a guest such as Fullers London Pride on handpump, quite a few wines by the glass and freshly squeezed orange juice. The colourful enclosed garden has picnic-sets among herbaceous borders and flowering shrubs, and two spectacular willow trees; also a great wooden fort, swings, a playhouse and chipmunks. The bedrooms are most attractive. Well behaved dogs welcome.

Bar food (12-2(2.30 wknds), 7-9(9.30 Fri, Sat)) ~ Restaurant ~ (01485) 541382 ~ Children in eating area of bar, restaurant, and family room ~ Open 11-11; 12-10.30 Sun ~ Bedrooms: £50B/£80B

SPARSHOLT Map 2 D2
Plough

Village signposted off A272 a little W of Winchester

The popular food at this busy country dining pub is really very good. It's all neatly kept, with friendly staff, and the main bar has a bustling atmosphere, an interesting mix of wooden tables and chairs, with farm tools, scythes and pitchforks attached to the ceiling; one area is no smoking. From quite a choice, the bar food includes lunchtime sandwiches, baguettes such as prawn, tomato and chive mayonnaise (£5.75), marinated salmon salad with crusty bread (£8.50), chicken breast in lime and coriander with tomato and red onion salsa (£8.95), and tossed salad with strips of beef fillet in an oriental dressing (£9.50); also, three bean and vegetable casserole with pesto croûtes (£6.95), tagliatelle with mushrooms, rosemary and cream (£7.95), braised ham with celeriac mash and roasted vegetables (£8.50), roasted pork tenderloin wrapped in smoked bacon with apricot and ginger sauce (£11.95), and whole red snapper with shallots on a bed of roasted tomatoes (£13.95). To be sure of a table you must book beforehand. Well kept Wadworths IPA, 6X, Farmers Glory, and a seasonal guest on handpump, and an extensive wine list. There's a children's play fort, and plenty of seats on the terrace and lawn.

Bar food (12-2, 6-9(9.30 Fri, Sat)) ~ (01962) 776353 ~ Children in eating area of bar ~ Murder mystery evenings March and Oct; Jazz first Sun in August ~ Open 11-3, 6-11; 12-3, 6-10.30 Sun; closed 25 Dec

ST KEW Map 1 D3
St Kew Inn

Village signposted from A39 NE of Wadebridge

'A thoroughly enjoyable place' is how several readers describe this rather grand-looking old stone building. The neatly kept bar has winged high-backed settles and varnished rustic tables on the lovely dark Delabole flagstones, black wrought-iron rings for lamps or hams hanging from the high ceiling, a handsome window seat, and an open kitchen range under a high mantelpiece decorated with earthenware flagons. At lunchtime, the good, popular bar food includes sandwiches, soup (£2.50), filled baked potatoes or good ploughman's (£4.25), leeks and bacon in a cheese sauce or plaice and chips (£5.95), and sirloin steak (£11.95), with evening dishes like home-made chicken liver pâté (£3.50), vegetarian curry (£5.95), beef in Guinness with herb dumplings or lambs liver in a crème fraîche, mushroom and sherry sauce (£7.50), and honey-roast duck with a red wine and orange sauce (£11.95); daily specials such as gruyère and onion tart, several fresh fish dishes, seasonal game or steak and kidney pie, and children's menu (from £3.50). Well kept St Austell Tinners, HSD, and Summer Ale tapped from wooden casks behind the counter (lots of tankards hang from the beams above it), a couple of farm ciders, a good wine list, and several malt whiskies; darts, cribbage, and dominoes. The big garden has seats on the grass and picnic-sets on the front cobbles. Parking is in what must have been a really imposing stable yard. The church next door is lovely.

Bar food (standard food times) ~ Restaurant ~ (01208) 841259 ~ Children in restaurant ~ Open 11-11; 12-10.30 Sun; 11-2.30, 6-11 winter wkdys; 12-3, 7-10.30 Sun in winter

STAPLEFORD TAWNEY Map 2 B4

Mole Trap

Tawney Common, which is signposted off A113 just N of M25 overpass; OS Sheet
167 map reference 550013

It's a true sign of quality when a tucked-away pub pulls in plenty of people:
tracking this one down on a weekday lunchtime inspection trip, along
narrow country lanes to what seemed the back of beyond, we opened the
door (mind your head as you go in!) to find it simply humming with
customers. The smallish carpeted bar has black dado, beams and joists,
brocaded wall seats, library chairs and bentwood elbow chairs around
plain pub tables, and steps down through a partly knocked-out timber stud
wall to a similar area; keeping those three coal fires blazing must be nearly
a full-time job. There are a few small pictures, 3-D decorative plates, some
dried-flower arrangements and (on the sloping ceiling formed by a staircase
beyond) some regulars' snapshots, and also a few dozen beermats stuck up
around the serving bar. The beers on handpump do change interestingly,
and on our visit were Attleborough Wolf and Granny Wouldn't Like It; the
piped radio was almost inaudible under the gentle wash of contented
chatter. In the food line, the lamb curry is strongly tipped, and other home-
made dishes include liver and bacon, chicken and ham pie, quiche or fresh
fish (£5.50) and steaks (£6.95). There are some plastic tables and chairs
and a picnic-set outside, and the cat we met is a friendly creature – in fact
one of quite a tribe of resident animals, many rescued and most wandering
around outside, including rabbits, more cats, a couple of dogs, hens, geese,
a sheep, goats and horses.

*Bar food (standard food times; not Sun evening) ~ Restaurant ~ No credit
cards ~ Children in eating area of bar ~ Open 11.30-3, 6.30-11; 12-3.30,
7-10.30 Sun; 12-3, 7-11(10.30 Sun) in winter*

STARBOTTON Map 3 B3
Fox & Hounds

B6160 Upper Wharfedale road N of Kettlewell; OS Sheet 98 map reference 953749

As well as being an enjoyable place to stay, this warmly friendly and prettily placed little Upper Wharfedale village inn has a good crowd of chatty locals (though visitors are made very welcome, too) and offers imaginative food and well kept real ales. The bar has traditional solid furniture on the flagstones, a collection of plates on the walls, whisky jugs hanging from the high beams supporting ceiling boards, and a big stone fireplace (with an enormous fire in winter). To be sure of a seat, it's best to get here early as the food is so popular: lunchtime baguettes and ploughman's, soup with home-made brown bread (£3), stilton, sun-dried tomato and sweet roast pecan salad or blue cheese soufflé with tomato and onion salad (£3.75), mixed bean and apple casserole or lamb and mint burger in a bap (£6.75), steak and mushroom pie (£7.25), chicken, leek and mushroom crumble (£7.50), bacon steaks with cumberland sauce (£7.75), Moroccan-style lamb (£8.75), and home-made puddings such as chocolate ginger pudding with chocolate fudge sauce, brown sugar chestnut meringues, and sticky toffee pudding (£3); hard-working, cheerful staff. Well kept Black Sheep Bitter, Theakstons Old Peculier, and Timothy Taylors Landlord on handpump, and around 60 malt whiskies. Dominoes, cribbage, and well reproduced, unobtrusive piped music. Seats in a sheltered corner enjoy the view over the hills all around this little hamlet.

Bar food (standard food times) ~ (01756) 760269 ~ Children in eating area of bar ~ Open 11.30-3, 6.30-11; 12-3, 7-10.30 Sun; closed Mon (except bank hol lunch) and Jan-mid Feb ~ Bedrooms: /£55S

STOCKLAND Map 1 D5

Kings Arms

Village signposted from A30 Honiton—Chard; and also, at every turning, from N end of Honiton High Street

There's always a good mix of customers in this bustling 16th-c pub because despite the emphasis on the good, enjoyable food, there's a proper locals' bar with well kept real ales, pub games, and live weekend music. The dark-beamed, elegant dining lounge has solid refectory tables and settles, attractive landscapes, a medieval oak screen (which divides the room into two), and a great stone fireplace across almost the whole width of one end; the cosy restaurant has a huge inglenook fireplace and bread oven. Bar food is served at lunchtime only: sandwiches (from £1.75), home-made soup (£2.50), smoked mackerel pâté or vegetable mousse (£4), omelettes (from £4), various pasta dishes (£4.50), and steak and kidney pie or scrumpy pork (£5.50); there might be Portuguese sardines (£4), moules marinières or confit of duck with a plum sauce (£5), mushroom stroganoff or pasta carbonara (£7.50), supreme of guinea fowl or king prawn madras (£9.50), Cotley rack of lamb (£10.50), and puddings such as apple and treacle crumbly, crème brûlée or chocolate truffle torte (£3.50). In the evening, only the restaurant menu is available. Well kept Courage Directors, Exmoor Ale and Gold, and Otter Ale on handpump, over 40 malt whiskies (including island and west coast ones; large spirit measures), a comprehensive wine list, and farm ciders. At the back, a flagstoned bar has cushioned benches and stools around heavy wooden tables, and leads on to a carpeted darts room with two boards, another room with dark beige plush armchairs and settees (and a fruit machine), and a neat ten-pin skittle alley; dominoes, quiz machine, TV, and quiet mainly classical piped music. There are tables under cocktail parasols on the terrace in front of the white-faced thatched pub and a lawn enclosed by trees and shrubs.

Bar food (lunchtime only) ~ Restaurant ~ (01404) 881361 ~ Children in eating area of bar and restaurant ~ Live music Sat and Sun evenings and bank hols ~ Open 12-3, 6.30-11; 12-3, 6.30-10.30 Sun; closed 25 Dec ~ Bedrooms: £30B/£50B

STOKE ST GREGORY ST3527 Map 1
Rose & Crown

Woodhill; follow North Curry signpost off A378 by junction with A358 – keep on
to Stoke, bearing right in centre

As well as being a friendly place for an enjoyable meal or drink, this
country cottage is a comfortable and popular place to stay, and has been
run for 22 years by the same hard-working licensees. The bar is decorated
in a cosy and pleasantly romanticised stable theme: dark wooden loose-box
partitions for some of the interestingly angled nooks and alcoves, lots of
brasses and bits on the low beams and joists, stripped stonework, and
appropriate pictures including a highland pony carrying a stag; many of the
wildlife paintings on the walls are the work of the landlady, and there's an
18th-c glass-covered well in one corner. Using fresh local produce, fresh
fish from Brixham, and their own eggs, the bar food at lunchtime might
include sandwiches in home-made granary bread (from £2.50),
ploughman's (£4.20), ham and egg or omelettes (£5), grilled liver and
bacon, scrumpy chicken or gammon and pineapple (£6.50), vegetarian
dishes such as nut roast chasseur or stir-fry vegetables (£7.50), grilled skate
wings (£8), steaks (from £9), and puddings (£2.75); evening dishes are
similar (but cost a bit more) with extras such as prawn stir-fry (£7.50) and
excellent grilled 8oz rib-eye steak (£9), and they also offer a three-course
meal for £13.50 with more elaborate dishes like stuffed burgundy snails,
lobster soup, roast duckling with cherry or roast rack of lamb. Plentiful
breakfasts, and a good three-course Sunday lunch (£8.25). The attractive
dining room is no smoking. Well kept Hardy Royal Oak, and guests like
Black Sheep or Exmoor Ale on handpump, Thatcher's farm cider, and a
good wine list; unobtrusive piped classical music and dominoes. Under
cocktail parasols by an apple tree on the sheltered front terrace are some
picnic-sets; summer barbecues and a pets corner for children. The pub is in
an interesting Somerset Levels village with willow beds still supplying the
two basket works.

*Bar food (standard food times) ~ Restaurant ~ (01823) 490296 ~ Children
welcome ~ Open 11-2.30, 7-11; 12-3, 7-10.30 Sun ~ Bedrooms:
£25(£35B)/£38(£50B)*

STOKENHAM Map 1 E4
Tradesmans Arms

Just off A379 Dartmouth—Kingsbridge

This charming thatched village pub is the sort of place people always think of when friends want a recommendation. The little beamed bar has a warm, friendly atmosphere, plenty of nice antique tables and neat dining chairs – with more up a step or two at the back – window seats looking across a field to the village church, and a big fireplace; the no-smoking room to the left of the door offers the same food as the bar. Good food at lunchtime includes snacks such as home-made soup (£2.75; fish soup with garlic flutes £3.25), sandwiches (from £2.65), and home-made pâté (£3.50), plus specials like home-made fishcakes with a spicy tomato sauce or mixed seafood in a white wine sauce topped with breadcrumbs and cheese (£5.50), venison stew (£6.75), and beef and mushroom casserole (£6.95); in the evenings, there might be prawns flamed in brandy with a garlic dip (£3.75), tartare of smoked salmon and puy lentils (£3.95), mussels provençale (£4.25), aubergine stuffed with roasted peppers and mushrooms, topped with breadcrumbs and cheese (£7.75), sauté of rabbit with fresh horseradish (£9.25), braised leg of barbary duck with orange and lemon sauce (£11.25), and fried halibut with lime and ginger sauce (£11.95), and puddings such as fresh pineapple and black pepper flamed in rum and served with coffee ice cream, apple and walnut pudding or fresh lemon soufflé (from £2.95); Sunday roast lamb or beef (£6.95). Well kept Adnams Southwold and Broadside, and a guest such as Butcombe or Exmoor Ale on handpump, and quite a few malt whiskies. Dogs are welcome on a lead in the main bar area. There are some seats outside in the garden.

Bar food (standard food times; not Mon, Tues or Sat lunchtimes; not Sun or Mon evenings) ~ Restaurant ~ (01548) 580313 ~ Children in back room lunchtimes only ~ Open 12-3, 6.30-11; closed Sun evening, Mon, Tues and Sat lunch; but open full time bank hols

STONEHAVEN Map 4 C3
Lairhillock

Netherley; 6 miles N of Stonehaven, 6 miles S of Aberdeen, take the Durris turn-off
from the A90

A good place to come for a decent meal, this friendly extended country pub
is smart but relaxed, with a traditional atmosphere that remains
welcoming, even at its busiest. The cheerful beamed bar has panelled wall
benches, a mixture of old seats, dark woodwork, harness and brass lamps
on the walls, a good open fire, and countryside views from the bay
window; there's an unusual central fire in the spacious separate lounge. A
good choice of well kept ales might include Courage Directors, Belhaven
80/-, Marstons Pedigree and Timothy Taylors Landlord and guests such as
Heather Ale on handpump, over 50 malt whiskies, and an extensive wine
list; cheery efficient staff, a nice pub cat, darts, cribbage and dominoes.
Good, freshly prepared bar food might include soup (£2.25), king prawns
gambas (£5.75), a changing terrine or pâté (£4.35), filled baguettes (£4.65),
lunchtime ploughman's (£5.95), steak and ale pie (£7.95), stir-fry of
monkfish and crayfish tails (£9.75), chicken stuffed with haggis in light
whisky sauce or braised leg of lamb with red wine, rosemary and root
vegetables (£8.95), maybe ostrich fillet steaks (£10.95), and puddings such
as cheesecake or banana and butterscotch sundae (from £2.95); Sunday
buffet lunch (£7.95). A separate thoughtful children's menu is now
available, including wild boar sausages and mash (£3.50) and spicy spare
ribs (£2.95). The cosy, highly praised restaurant is in an adjacent building.
There are panoramic views from the no smoking conservatory.

*Bar food (6-9.30 wkdys and 6-10 Fri, Sat) ~ Restaurant ~ (01569) 730001 ~
Children welcome ~ Open 10.30-2.30, 5-11; 11-12 Sat; 11-11 Sun*

STOW BARDOLPH Map 3 E5

Hare Arms

Just off A10 N of Downham Market

The sort of place you wish for as a local, this neatly kept creeper-covered pub has a timelessly traditional village atmosphere. The welcoming bar is decorated with old advertising signs and fresh flowers, with plenty of tables around its central servery, and a good log fire; maybe two friendly ginger cats and a sort of tabby. This bar opens into a spacious heated and well planted no-smoking conservatory. Bar food includes sandwiches (from £2.50), ploughman's (£6.75), mushroom stroganoff (£7.25), steak and mushroom pie, turkey breast wrapped in bacon with creamy mustard sauce, spare ribs, chestnut and parsnip bake or spinach and mixed pepper tart (£7.50), swordfish steak with black bean sauce or red snapper fillet with garlic butter (£8.95) and steaks (from £10.75). Well kept Greene King IPA and a couple of guests such as Badger Tanglefoot and Ruddles County on handpump' a decent range of wines, and quite a few malt whiskies; maybe cockles and whelks on the bar counter; fruit machine. The pretty garden has picnic-sets under cocktail parasols and wandering peacocks and chickens.

Bar food (12-2, 7-10) ~ Restaurant ~ (01366) 382229 ~ Children in conservatory and family room ~ Open 11-2.30, 6-11; 12-2.30, 7-10.30 Sun; closed 25, 26 Dec

SUTTON GAULT Map 2 A4
Anchor

Village signposted off B1381 in Sutton

Although this very special old place is mainly popular for dining, the licensees are determined to keep a relaxed and informal pubby atmosphere. The four heavily timbered stylishly simple rooms have three log fires, antique settles and well spaced scrubbed pine tables on the gently undulating old floors, good lithographs and big prints on the walls, and lighting by gas and candles. As well as a thoughtful wine list (including a wine of the month and eight by the glass), winter mulled wine and freshly squeezed fruit juice, they have a real ale tapped from the cask which could be from a fairly local brewer like City of Cambridge, Nethergate or Humpty Dumpty. The new head chef here was formerly head chef at the Old Bridge Hotel in Huntingdon, and we're already detecting signs of even warmer than usual approval for the good imaginative food. It currently includes Thai chicken and coconut soup (£3.95), chicken liver and brandy pâté with red onion marmalade (£4.95), fried quail with fresh rhubarb chutney (£5.50), venison carpaccio with pesto dressing and parmesan shavings (£6.95), crisp risotto cake with baby sweetcorn and oyster mushrooms (£10.75), steak, kidney and Guinness pie (£11.95), roast fillet of salmon, vermouth sauce and fennel purée (£12.50), roast loin of wild rabbit with sherry sauce (£12.95), barbary duck breast with braised red cabbage (£14.95), and calves liver with potato rösti (£13.95); home-made puddings such as hot sticky toffee pudding, home-made bakewell tart, and chocolate and brandy terrine with raspberry coulis (£4.45), and a particularly good changing British cheeseboard (£5.50). From Monday to Friday lunchtimes (not bank holidays), there's a very good value two-course menu (£7.95), and children can have most of their dishes in smaller helpings; three-course Sunday lunch (£16.50); booking advised. In summer you can sit outside and there are good walks and birdwatching near here as the pub is well set by the high embankment of the New Bedford river; no dogs.

Bar food (12-2, 7-9(6.30-9.30 Sat); not 26 Dec) ~ Restaurant ~ (01353) 778537 ~ Children welcome ~ Open 12-3, 7-11(10.30 Sun) ~ Bedrooms: £50S(£65B)/£66.50S(£95B)

SWILLAND Map 2 A6
Moon & Mushroom

Village signposted off B1078 Needham Market—Wickham Market, and off B1077

They keep only independent East Anglian beers such as Buffys Hopleaf and Norwich Terrier, Nethergates Umbel, Wolf Bitter and Coyote and Woodfordes Norfolk Nog and Wherry, all tapped straight from casks racked up behind the long counter at this cosy little place. It's run by cheerful, genuinely helpful people and there's a good mix of chatty customers – all of which creates a bustling but relaxed atmosphere. The homely interior is mainly quarry tiled with a small coal fire in a brick fireplace, old tables (with lots of board games in the drawers) arranged in little booths made by pine pews, and cushioned stools along the bar. An unusual touch is the four hearty hotpots in the no-smoking dark green and brown painted cottagey dining room through a small doorway from the bar. These are served to you from Le Creuset dishes on a warming counter and might include coq au vin, pork with peppers, minted lamb, pheasant au vin (all £6.55). You then help yourself to a choice of half a dozen or so tasty vegetables. Another couple of dishes might include ploughman's (£4.25), halibut mornay and stilton and pasta bake (£5.95), with proper home-made puddings like raspberry and apple crumble, bread and butter pudding and toffee and ginger pudding with butterscotch sauce (£2.95). This is still a real local so food service ends quite early. They have about 10 decent wines by the glass and 20 malt whiskies. You approach the pub through an archway of grapevines and creepers, and a little terrace in front has flower containers, trellis and nice wooden furniture under parasols. No children inside.

Bar food (12-2, 6.30-8.15; not Sun, Mon) ~ No credit cards ~ (01473) 785320 ~ Open 11-2.30, 6-11; 12-2.30, 7-10.30 Sun

SWINTON Map 4 D3
Wheatsheaf

A6112 N of Coldstream

Extremely well run, this has excellent food, service to match, and a nice setting in a pretty village surrounded by rolling countryside, just a few miles away from the River Tweed. At lunchtime, the daily changing menu might include sandwiches, soup (£2.80), aubergine and parmesan melanzane (£4.25), sautéed mushrooms and bacon in a filo pastry basket (£4.70), fillet of salmon with tomato salsa (£8.95), corn-fed chicken in a red wine and mushroom sauce (£7.90), local wild boar sausages with red wine and mushroom sauce (£7.90), and deep-fried fillet of haddock in a crispy beer batter (£6.75), with evening dishes such as roast loin of highland venison in a juniper and quince sauce with spiced poached pear (£14.90), chargrilled Scotch fillet steak on a Glenmorangie whisky and honey mustard sauce (£15.85), filo pastry gateau with grilled goats cheese, pine nuts and stir-fried vegetables on a cream, mushroom and brandy sauce (£9.45), and scrumptious puddings such as lemon and almond cake with mascarpone ice cream (£4). Booking is advisable, particularly from Thursday to Saturday evening. Caledonian Deuchars IPA and a guest such as Broughton Clipper on handpump, a decent range of malt whiskies and brandies, good choice of wines, and cocktails. Service is helpful, unhurried and genuinely welcoming. The carefully thought-out main bar area has an attractive long oak settle and some green-cushioned window seats, as well as wheelback chairs around tables, a stuffed pheasant and partridge over the log fire, and sporting prints and plates on the bottle-green wall covering; a small lower-ceilinged part by the counter has pubbier furnishings, and small agricultural prints on the walls – especially sheep. The front conservatory has a vaulted pine ceiling and walls of local stone, while at the side is a separate locals' bar; cribbage and dominoes. The garden has a play area for children. The dining areas are no smoking. They do very good breakfasts.

Bar food (12-2, 6-9.30) ~ Restaurant ~ (01890) 860257 ~ Children in eating area of bar and restaurant ~ Open 11-2.30, 6-11; 12.30-2.30, 6.30-10.30 Sun; closed Sun evening in winter; closed Mon ~ Bedrooms: £50S(£50B)/£80S(£80B)

TARRANT MONKTON Map 1 D6
Langton Arms
Village signposted from A354, then head for church

A very good, well balanced all-rounder, this charmingly set 17th-c thatched pub is doing very well at the moment. As well as two beer festivals a year, they have what they describe as a mini beer festival going on all the time, with well kept Ringwood Best and four quickly changing guests from lots of interesting little brewers such as Cottage, Cannon Royall, Moor and Tring on handpump. Very enjoyable bar food from a traditionally imaginative menu includes home-made soup (£2.95), deep-fried cod or four bean stew (£5.95), faggots in onion sauce (£6.50), fried lambs liver with bacon and sausage (£6.50), smoked trout salad or braised rabbit with tarragon and mustard (£6.95), chicken breast in oriental spices with peanut and chilli sauce or pigeon breast in cranberry and red wine sauce (£7.95) and puddings such as jam roly-poly, treacle tart or local ice creams (from £3); Sunday roast (£6). The fairly simple beamed bar has a huge inglenook fireplace, settles, stools at the counter and other mixed dark furniture, and the public bar has a juke box, darts, pool, a fruit machine, TV, cribbage, and dominoes; piped music. There's a no-smoking bistro restaurant in an attractively reworked barn, and a skittle alley that doubles as a no-smoking family room during the day. The garden has a very good wood-chip play area, and there are good nearby walks.

Bar food (11.30-2.30, 6.30-9.30; 12-3, 6-9 Sun) ~ Restaurant ~ (01258) 830225 ~ Children welcome in family room and restaurant ~ Open 11.30-11; 12-10.30 Sun ~ Bedrooms: £50B/£70B

TAYVALLICH Map 4 D1
Tayvallich Inn

B8025, off A816 1 mile S of Kilmartin; or take B841 turn-off from A816 2 miles N of Lochgilphead

Fresh seafood brought in by local fishermen from the bay of Loch Sween just across the lane is the highlight of the menu at this simply furnished café/bar, with lovely views over the yacht anchorage and loch from its terrace. The choice typically includes good haddock and chips (£4.95), fried scallops (£13.50), mussels (£7.90), cajun salmon with black butter (£10.50), specials such as fillet of beef stroganoff (£11) and a variety of white fish, depending on what's been caught; other bar food includes soup (£2.20), chicken liver pâté (£3.85), stir-fried vegetables (£4.95), home-made burgers (from £5.20), chicken curry (£6.25), sirloin steak (£12.95) and puddings (£3.20); children's helpings. All the whiskies are Islay malts; they also do fresh milk shakes. Service is friendly, and people with children are very much at home here. The small bar has local nautical charts on the cream walls, exposed ceiling joists, and pale pine upright chairs, benches and tables on its quarry-tiled floor; darts, dominoes, cards. It leads into a no-smoking (during meal times) dining conservatory, from where sliding glass doors open on to the terrace; there's a garden, too.

Bar food (12-2, 6-8.30) ~ Restaurant (from 7) ~ (01546) 870282 ~ Children welcome ~ Open 11-12(1 Fri); 11-1 Sat; 12.30-12 Sun; 11-2.30, 6-11 (winter wkdys); 11-2.30, 5-1 (winter Fri, Sat) 12.30-2.30, 5-12 (winter Sun)

TETBURY Map 1 B5

Gumstool

Part of Calcot Manor Hotel; A4135 W of town, just E of junction with A46

Although attached to a well thought of country hotel, this civilised dining bar does have a welcoming and informally relaxed atmosphere. There are some concessions to those wanting just a drink, but most people do come to enjoy the good, interesting food. The layout is well divided to give a feeling of intimacy without losing the overall sense of contented bustle, the lighting is attractive, and materials are old-fashioned (lots of stripped pine, flagstones, gingham curtains, hop bines) though the style is neatly modern. Beyond one screen there are a couple of marble-topped pub tables and a leather armchair by the big log fire; daily papers; well kept Bath Gem Bitter, Courage Best, Uley Hogshead, and Wickwar BOB on handpump, 60 malt whiskies, and a dozen interesting wines by the glass, spanning a wide price range. Several dishes on the menu sensibly come in two sizes: stilton and port rarebit on an apple, celery and grape salad (£4.75; generous £6.75), caramelised red onion tart with slow baked tomatoes, and taleggio on a rocket salad (£5.25; generous £7.50), devilled lambs kidney in pastry (£5.75; generous £8), and Thai-spiced crab cakes with cucumber and crème fraîche (£5.50; generous £8). They also offer soup (£3.25), a plate of local cheeses with celery, grapes and pickle (£5.50), Gloucestershire Old Spot pork and beer sausages with spring onion mash and onion gravy (£8.50), smoked haddock fishcakes with lemon and dill (£8.80), breast of chicken with button mushrooms, bacon, caramelised red onions and a red wine sauce or slow roasted duck salad with sweet and sour dressing, coriander and pickled Japanese ginger (£9), shepherd's pie with a garlic gratin crust (£9.30), chargrilled rib-eye steak with deep-fried onions and tarragon shallot butter (£11), long braised lamb shank with pickled lemon, tomato and oregano (£11.25), and puddings like steamed lemon upside-down pudding with custard, spiced apple pie with cinnamon ice cream or crème brûlée (from £4); extra vegetables £1.50. To be sure of a table, you must book beforehand. Most of the restaurant is no smoking; piped music. The neat side lawn has a couple of picnic-sets; Westonbirt Arboretum is not far away.

Bar food (all day summer wknds) ~ Restaurant ~ (01666) 890391 ~ Children in eating area of bar ~ Open 12-2.30, 6-11; 12-11 Sat, Sun; 12-2.30, 6-11 wknds in winter ~ Bedrooms: /£130B

THORGANBY Map 3 B4
Jefferson Arms
Off A163 NE of Selby, via Skipwith

The rösti menu in this friendly pub is very popular with customers, and is prepared by Mrs Rapp's husband, who is Swiss. A rösti is a speciality with grated, fried potatoes: with Swiss pork sausages in onion sauce or spinach, cheese and fried egg (£5.80), with ham and cheese gratinated and a fried egg, grilled lamb croquettes with herb oil and onion or with tuna, prawns, black olives, tomatoes and cheese (all £6.40), and pork in a cream of mushroom sauce (£7.90). Also, sandwiches (from £2.60; filled baguettes from £3.20), fluffy omelette filled with ham, cheese or mushrooms (£5.40), home-made ostrich burger (£6.40), vegetable lasagne (£6.80), haddock in beer batter with home-made chips (£6.90), chicken breast in a light creamy curry sauce with peaches (£9.90), halibut steak with herbs and butter (£10.90), and puddings such as hot chocolate fudge cake or lemon sponge pudding (from £3); the restaurant is no smoking. The spacious main bar is relaxed and stylish, with brick pillars and bar counter, dark wooden cushioned pews, several big mirrors on the green fleur-de-lys patterned walls, and a couple of decorative chairs. A delightful little beamed lounge is more comfortable still, full of sofas and armchairs, as well as fresh flowers and potted plants, a fireplace with logs beside it, an antique telephone, and a pile of *Hello!* magazines. The long narrow no-smoking conservatory is festooned with passion flowers. Well kept Black Sheep Bitter and John Smiths on handpump, and a thoughtful wine list; piped music, dominoes, chess and backgammon. There are tables in a porch area, and more in a side garden with roses and a brick barbecue. It's a nice, peaceful place to stay.

Bar food (standard food times) ~ Restaurant ~ (01904) 448316 ~ Children in eating area of bar ~ Open 12-3, 6-11; 12-10.30 Sun; closed Mon, closed Tues lunchtime ~ Bedrooms: £35S/£55S

THORINGTON STREET Map 2 B5
Rose

B1068 Higham—Stoke by Nayland

It's the smiling welcome from the cheery landlady and her daughter, the properly pubby atmosphere and the nice mix of customers that readers really enjoy at this welcoming village pub. The building is partly Tudor, and has been knocked through into a single longish partly divided room, with old beams, pine tables and chairs, and enough pictures, prints and brasses to soften the room without overdoing the décor. Among them are old photographs of the landlady's family who were in the fishing trade. Food is not over-fancy, but good and well thought out. Frequent fresh fish deliveries mean fish and seafood are particularly tasty: fish and chips (£5.95), whole baby squid, Dover and Torbay sole, whole plaice, jumbo haddock, skate wing, and mussels, lobsters, oysters, crab and Mediterranean prawns (£7.95-£12.95). Other dishes might include sandwiches (from £2.20), home-made soup (£3.95), ploughman's (from £3.75), lunchtime lasagne, chilli or quiche (£5.95), chicken goujons in sesame seeds with garlic mayonnaise (£7.95), steaks (from £8.95) and puddings such as pineapple upside-down cake, popular melt-in-the-mouth meringues filled with fruit and cream, and blackberry and apple pie (£2.50). The top end of the restaurant is no smoking. Well kept Adnams, Greene King Abbot and IPA, Woodfordes Wherry, and a guest beer on handpump, and decent wines; dominoes, cribbage, cards, dice, and piped music. The fair-sized garden has picnic-sets and summer barbecues, and overlooks the Box valley.

Bar food (standard food times) ~ Restaurant ~ No credit cards ~ (01206) 337243 ~ Children welcome ~ Open 12-3, 7-11(10.30 Sun); closed Mon

TIRRIL Map 3 A2
Queens Head

3½ miles from M6 junction 40; take A66 towards Brough, A6 towards Shap, then B5320 towards Ullswater

Although this pub has many attributes, it's the genuinely warm and friendly welcome from the helpful staff that our readers comment on so often. Their beer also draws favour, and in their own little brewery in one of the old outhouses behind the pub they brew Bewshers Best (after the landlord in the early 1800s who bought the inn from the Wordsworths and changed its name to the Queens Head in time for Victoria's coronation), Academy Ale, and Old Faithful, and keep guest beers such as Dent Aviator, and Jennings Cumberland on handpump; they also hold a popular Cumbrian Beer & Sausage Festival during August. Over 40 malt whiskies, a good choice of brandies and other spirits, a carefully chosen wine list. The oldest parts of the bar have original flagstones and floorboards, low bare beams, black panelling, high-backed settles, and a roomy inglenook fireplace (once a cupboard for smoking hams); the little back bar has a lot of character; piped music. At lunchtime, good bar snacks include baguettes (from £3.25), hot sirloin steak and fried onions £4.25), filled baked potatoes (from £3.95), pasta dishes (£3.75 or £7.50), stuffed pitta breads (from £4.25; peppered beef strips and cooling cucumber dip £4.95), ploughman's (from £5.50), chilli (£7.25), home-made pie of the day (£7.50), chargrilled gammon and eggs (£7.75), OAP specials (from £4.75), and puddings such as banoffi pie, chocolate crush or summer pudding (from £2.75). Also, home-made soup (£2.50), steak in ale pudding or Mediterranean carrot roll (£7.95), Lakeland lamb shoulder in redcurrant gravy (£9.50), and daily specials such as grilled black pudding on coarse grain mustard sauce (£2.95), Thai fishcakes on hollandaise sauce (£8.75), crab, spinach and cream cheese strudel (£8.95), and tuna steak in lime and ginger butter (£9.25); the restaurant is no smoking. Pool, juke box, and dominoes in the back bar. The pub is very close to a number of interesting places, such as Dalemain House at Dacre.

Bar food (12-2, 6-9.30) ~ Restaurant ~ (01768) 863219 ~ Children in eating area of bar and in restaurant; for accommodation, under 3, over 13 ~ Open 12-3, 6-11; 12-11 Sat; 12-10.30 Sun; closed evening 25 Dec ~ Bedrooms: £35B/£50B

TREBURLEY Map 1 D3
Springer Spaniel
A388 Callington—Launceston

Now run by the same energetic licensee as the very popular Roseland at
Philleigh, this bustling pub remains well liked for its food. The relaxed bar
has a lovely, very high-backed settle by the woodburning stove in the big
fireplace, high-backed farmhouse chairs and other seats, and pictures of
olde-worlde stage-coach arrivals at inns; this leads into a room with
chintzy-cushioned armchairs and sofa in one corner, and a big solid teak
table. Up some steps from the main bar is the beamed, attractively
furnished, no-smoking restaurant. From the menu, there might be
sandwiches, mushroom pots (with bacon in a cream and brandy sauce
£4.50), Mediterranean tart (£5.60), steak and kidney pie or scallops
sautéed with bacon and shallots (£6.50), fresh vegetable risotto (£6.95),
chicken breast with a glaze of caramelised red onions and balsamic vinegar
(£8.95), cod steak baked with a cheesy herb crust on a provençale sauce
(£9.50), shank of lamb with fresh orange, red wine, garlic and rosemary or
local crab salad (£9.95), duck breast with a whisky and stem ginger sauce
(£11.95), and puddings like minted white chocolate cheesecake on a bitter
chocolate sauce, treacle and lemon tart with clotted cream or espresso
crème brûlée (from £4.25); children's dishes (from £3.75). Well kept
Sharps Doom Bar, Eden Ale, and a beer named for the pub on handpump,
a good wine list, and 20 malt whiskies.

*Bar food (standard food times) ~ Restaurant ~ (01579) 370424 ~ Children
welcome ~ Open 11-3, 5.45-11; 12-3.30, 6.30-10.30 Sun; closed 4 days over
Christmas*

TREVAUNANCE COVE Map 1 E2
Driftwood Spars
Quay Road, off B3285 in St Agnes

In a lovely spot just up the road from the beach and dramatic cove, this 17th-c building (originally a marine warehouse and fish cellar) was constructed from local slate and granite, and timbered with massive ships' spars – the masts of great sailing ships, many of which were wrecked along this coast. There's said to be an old smugglers' tunnel leading from behind the bar, up through the cliff. The two lower bars are bustling and popular, with a variety of wooden tables and chairs, old ship prints and lots of nautical and wreck memorabilia, a winter log fire, and a good mix of customers; one bar has a juke box, pool, fruit machine and TV. Upstairs, the comfortable dining areas offer plenty of space (and residents have the use of a similarly comfy gallery bar). Decent bar food includes sandwiches (from £1.90), filled baked potatoes (from £3), ploughman's (from £3.85), chilli crab cakes (£5.20), ham and eggs (£5.40), steaks (from £7.50), and daily specials like local boar burgers (£4.50), honey mustard chicken, or lamb and mint casserole (£6.25), fish pie (£6.30), steak in ale pie (£6.50), a carvery on summer evenings and winter Sundays, and puddings such as banoffi pie, bread and butter pudding or sherry trifle (£2.50). They have their own microbrewery where they produce Cuckoo Ale, and keep five guests from Bass, Sharps, Skinners and St Austell on handpump; over 100 malt whiskies, and friendly helpful staff. There are seats in the garden, and the summer hanging baskets are pretty. Readers have enjoyed staying here; plenty of surrounding coastal walks.

Bar food (12-2.30, 6.30-9.30) ~ (01872) 552428 ~ Children welcome ~ Live music Fri/Sat evenings ~ Open 10.30-11; 12-10.30 Sun; 11 opening in winter ~ Bedrooms: £32S/£64B

TROUBECK Map 3 B2

Queens Head

A592 N of Windermere

By the time this book is published, there will be two new dining areas here, built on the site of the former kitchen (which will be rebuilt in the back car park), and six new bedrooms. The dining rooms will also be somewhere you can drop into for a casual drink, and will have oak beams and stone walls, an open fire, settles along big tables, and similar décor to the existing bars. The big rambling original U-shaped bar has a little no-smoking room at each end, beams and flagstones, a very nice mix of old cushioned settles and mate's chairs around some sizeable tables (especially the one to the left of the door), and a log fire in the raised stone fireplace with horse harness and so forth on either side of it in the main part, with a woodburning stove in the other; some trumpets, cornets and saxophones on one wall, country pictures on others, stuffed pheasants in a big glass case, and a stag's head with a tie around his neck, and a stuffed fox with a ribbon around his. A massive Elizabethan four-poster bed is the basis of the finely carved counter where they serve Boddingtons, Coniston Bluebird, and Jennings Bitter, with guests such as Barngates Cracker, Dent Ramsbottom and Timothy Taylors Landlord on handpump. Very good, imaginative bar food includes light lunches such as a bowl of fresh mussels steamed with garlic and herbs and finished with cream (£4.95), confit of chicken leg on braised cabbage with roasted shallots or mixed bean and wild mushroom cassoulet served on pasta in a rich butter sauce (£5.95), and peppered venison and redcurrant casserole with a timbale of braised rice (£6.25), as well as soup with home-made bread (£2.75), wild mushroom, stilton and black olive terrine served on sun-dried tomato dressed leaves (£5.25), steak, ale and mushroom cobbler (£7.25), asparagus, courgette and spinach mousse set on sautéed mange tout and cherry tomatoes with a smoked garlic cream (£9.50), pieces of smoked haddock wrapped in filo pastry filled with a garlic cream and baked on to a tomato compote (£13.25), and calves liver seared on to creamed celeriac with a raspberry vinegar spiked jus (£14.25); puddings like sticky toffee pudding with crème anglaise, chocolate truffle cheesecake with a Baileys cream or mixed fruit parfait with fruit coulis (£3.75), and a thoughtful children's menu (from £3); they also have a three-course menu (£15.50); piped music. Seats outside have a fine view over the Trout valley to Applethwaite moors. This is a very nice place to stay, with excellent breakfasts – but check beforehand if you want an early start.

Bar food (standard food times) ~ Restaurant ~ (015394) 32174 ~ Children welcome ~ Open 11-11; 12-10.30 Sun; closed 25 Dec ~ Bedrooms: £51.50B/£75B

TUCKENHAY Map 1 D4
Maltsters Arms

Take Ashprington road out of Totnes (signposted left off A381 on outskirts), keeping on past Watermans Arms

This is a lovely spot by a peaceful wooded creek, with tables by the water and free overnight moorings for boats; plenty of bird life and surrounding walks. The hard-working licensees continue to hold all sorts of events: regular jazz sessions, various courses such as RYA navigation, barbecues in good weather, and lots of outside summer musical concerts such as Handel's *Water Music* played in the middle of the river on their pontoon. They keep a smashing range of drinks including well kept Blackawton 44, Princetown Dartmoor IPA and two changing guest beers on handpump, 17 good wines by the glass, local cider, a serious bloody mary, and items in the freezer like buffalo grass vodka and various eau de vies. And the daily changing bar food also continues to draw customers, with lunchtime dishes such as creamy onion and saffron or yellow pepper and sweetcorn soup (£3.50), sandwiches (from £3.95), ploughman's (from £4.75), squid flash-fried in balsamic vinegar (£4.95), smooth duck liver and orange pâté with a Grand Marnier dressing (£5.25), smoked salmon, mackerel and trout with a honey and mustard dressing (£5.75), cottage pie (£7.25), yam, spinach, mushroom and filo pie (£7.50), roast leg of lamb with rosemary gravy (£7.75), fillet steak with a creamy peppercorn and brandy sauce (£15.95), and grilled whole lemon sole with lemon and parsley butter (£17.50), with evening choices like fried herby salmon fishcakes with lemon, lime and dill dressing (£4.50), sautéed kidneys with onion, bacon and red wine (£5.25), spicy five bean chilli (£7.95), chicken supreme with creamy pesto sauce (£8.95), baked whole john dory with banana and balsamic vinegar (£9.95), and roast half Aylesbury duck with honey and five spice (£13.50), and puddings such as black forest crumble, chargrilled pineapple with butterscotch sauce or chocolate chip sponge pudding (£3.95); nice home-made bar nibbles, too. The long, narrow bar links two other rooms – a little snug one with an open fire, and plenty of bric-a-brac, and another with red-painted vertical seats and kitchen chairs on the wooden floor. Darts, shove-ha'penny, cribbage, dominoes, chess, backgammon, and TV for sports. There may be a minimum stay of two nights at weekends.

Bar food (12-3, 7-9.30) ~ Restaurant ~ (01803) 732350 ~ Children in separate family rooms ~ Jazz first and third Fri of month; outside music in summer ~ Open 11-11; 12-10.30 Sun; closed evening 25 Dec ~ Bedrooms: /£75S

TY'N-Y-GROES Map 3 D2

Groes

B5106 N of village

This well run old dining pub has magnificent views over scenic reaches of the Conwy River and the distant mountains, while the seats outside are a good place to sit and appreciate the pretty back garden with its flower-filled hayricks. First licensed in 1573, it claims to be the first licensed house in Wales. The homely series of rambling, low-beamed and thick-walled rooms are beautifully decorated with antique settles and an old sofa, old clocks, portraits, hats and tins hanging from the walls, and fresh flowers. A fine antique fireback is built into one wall, perhaps originally from the formidable fireplace which houses a collection of stone cats as well as winter log fires. A good range of bar food made with lots of local produce might include soup (£2.95), sandwiches (from £3), Welsh cheeseboard (£5.75), soup and a sandwich (£5.95), lasagne (£7.25), fishcakes (£7.50), steak and kidney pot with thyme dumplings (£7.75), crispy roast duck (£10.95) and steaks (from £12) with daily specials such as vegetable and mushroom pasta bake (£7.25), dijon chicken (£8.25), Welsh lamb steak (£9.25), salmon fillet with hollandaise sauce (£8.50) and seafood platter (£14); lots of delicious puddings such as lemon and ginger sponge and hot bara brith and butter pudding (£3.75); tempting home-made ice creams with unusual flavours such as honey and lemon or fragrant rose. Well kept Ind Coope Burton and Tetleys, a good few malt whiskies, kir, and a fruity Pimms in summer; cribbage, dominoes and light classical piped music at lunchtimes (nostalgic light music at other times). It can get busy but the friendly, efficient staff cope very well. It's a lovely place to stay with good views from the spotlessly kept bedrooms (some with terraces or balconies). There's an airy verdant no-smoking conservatory, seats on the flower-decked roadside.

Bar food (12-2.15, 6.30-9) ~ Restaurant ~ (01492) 650545 ~ Children under 10 in family room till 7.30pm, over 10 in restaurant ~ Open 12-3, 6.30 (6 Sat and Sun)-11 ~ Bedrooms: £64B/£81B

ULLINGSWICK Map 1 A5
Three Crowns

Village off A465 S of Bromyard (and just S of Stoke Lacy) and signposted off A417
N of A465 roundabout – keep straight on through village and past turn-off to
church; pub at Bleak Acre, towards Little Cowarne

What's nice about this place is that although you'll still find local farmers
in the very homely welcoming bar, the standard of imaginative cooking is
way above what you'd expect to find in a village local. Food is all cooked
with real flair, using local and organic products as much as possible. As a
consequence the seasonally changing menu is shortish but might include
starters such as asparagus and pea broth with goats cheese and prosciutto,
cheese and spinach soufflé, and warm duck liver mousse with port glaze
(all £4.95), main courses such as roast monkfish, scallop and langoustine
with laverbread sauce and crispy seaweed, tagliatelle with asparagus,
porcini and brown butter vinaigrette, and roast rack of lamb with
béarnaise sauce (all £12.95), puddings such as lemon tart with confit
orange or apple parfait (£3.95), and local cheeses (£3.95). They also do a
two- and three-course lunch (£8/£10). The charmingly traditional interior
has hops strung along the low beams of its smallish bar, a couple of
traditional settles besides more usual seats, a mix of big old wooden tables
with small round ornamental cast-iron-framed ones, open fires and one or
two gently sophisticated touches such as candles on tables and napkins;
half the pub is no smoking. They have well kept Hobsons Best and a
stronger guest ale from a small local brewer on handpump, farm ciders,
and up to 10 wines by the glass; cribbage. There are tables out on the
attractively planted lawn, with good summer views.

*Restaurant ~ (01432) 820279 ~ Well behaved children welcome in eating
area of bar ~ Open 12-2.30, 7-11; 12-3, 7-10.30 Sun; closed Tues and two
wks after Christmas*

ULVERSTON Map 3 B2
Bay Horse

Canal Foot signposted off A590 and then you wend your way past the huge Glaxo factory

Standing on the water's edge of the Leven Estuary with views of both the Lancashire and Cumbrian fells, this civilised hotel was once a staging post for coaches that crossed the sands of Morecambe Bay to Lancaster in the 18th c. It's at its most informal at lunchtime when the good, imaginative bar food might include sandwiches (from £3.70; smoked chicken with curry mayonnaise and toasted coconut £3.95), home-made soup (£3.25), cheese platter with home-made biscuits and soda bread (£5.95), home-made herb and cheese pâté, savoury terrine or button mushrooms in a tomato, cream and brandy sauce on a peanut butter croûton (£6.25), smoked haddock and sweetcorn chowder served with hot garlic and paprika bread (£6.75), strips of chicken, leeks and button mushrooms on savoury rice with a sweet and sour sauce or braised lamb, apricot and ginger puff pastry pie (£8.50), flakes of smoked haddock and brandied sultanas cooked in a rich cheddar cheese sauce and served in a puff pastry case, venison burger with onion marmalade, and sage and apple sauce or smoked salmon, leek and waterchestnut quiche (£9), and home-made puddings (£4.50); it's essential to book for the restaurant. Well kept Jennings and Thwaites and a guest such as Greene King Old Speckled Hen on handpump, a decent choice of spirits, and a carefully chosen and interesting wine list with quite a few from South Africa. The bar has a relaxed atmosphere and a huge stone horse's head, as well as attractive wooden armchairs, some pale green plush built-in wall banquettes, glossy hardwood traditional tables, blue plates on a Delft shelf, and black beams and props with lots of horsebrasses. Magazines are dotted about, there's a handsomely marbled green granite fireplace, and decently reproduced piped music; darts, bar billiards, shove-ha'penny, cribbage, and dominoes. The no-smoking conservatory restaurant has fine views over Morecambe Bay (as do the bedrooms) and there are some seats out on the terrace. Please note, the bedroom price includes dinner as well.

Bar food (lunchtime only; not Mon) ~ Restaurant ~ (01229) 583972 ~ Children in eating area of bar and in restaurant if over 12 ~ Open 11-11; 12-10.30 Sun ~ Bedrooms: /£170B

UPTON Map 3 D4
French Horn
A612

Picnic-sets on the big sloping back paddock of this popular dining pub look out over farmland, and the front is decorated with attractive flower displays in summer. Readers are as enthusiastic as ever about the good food here and most of the tables are laid for eating, even on weekday lunchtimes. The wide choice of bar food includes soup (£2.50), sandwiches (from £2.95, baguettes from £3.85), baked potatoes (from £4.25) and ploughman's (from £4.50) which are served only at lunchtime. Other dishes might be fried goats cheese (£3.95), crab claws with white wine and fish velouté (£4.95), chicken and cashew nut stir-fry (£7.50), English lamb saddle with mustard, thyme and redcurrant sauce (£12.50), potato and leek bake (£6.95) or Scottish salmon with tomatoes and mozzarella (£9.25) followed by puddings such as bread and butter pudding or blackcurrant cheesecake (£3.10); booking is usually necessary if you want to eat here. There's a nicely relaxed atmosphere in the neat and comfortable open-plan bar with cushioned captain's chairs, wall banquettes around glossy tables, and watercolours by local artists (some may be for sale). Well kept Adnams and Courage Directors and a guest such as Greene King IPA on handpump; piped music.

Bar food (12-2, 6-9; 12-10 Sun) ~ Restaurant ~ (01636) 812394 ~ Children welcome ~ Jazz alternate Sun evenings ~ Open 11-11; 12-10.30 Sun

USK Map 1 B5
Nags Head
The Square

Run by the warmly welcoming Key family for 35 years, this relaxed old coaching inn serves tasty, unusual bar food with lots of seasonal game. Daily specials might include pheasant in port and duck in Cointreau (£10.50), stuffed partridge, a brace of quail with appropriate eggs, superb venison steaks with sauté potatoes, or guinea fowl in wine (£12), and other dishes such as home-made rabbit pie (£6.80), local salmon or wild boar in apricot and brandy sauce (£12), while the bar menu includes such things as snails and frogs' legs (£4.80) alongside familiar staples like soup (£3), battered cod (£5.80), steak pie (£5.80) and vegetable pancake (£6.50). You can book tables, some of which may be candlelit at night; piped classical music. The traditional main bar is full of character, with a huge number of well polished tables and chairs packed under its beams, some with farming tools, lanterns or horsebrasses and harness attached, as well as leatherette wall benches, and various sets of sporting prints and local pictures, among which are the original deeds to the pub. Well kept Brains SA, Buckley Best and Reverend James on handpump, served by courteous, friendly staff – it's the sort of place where they greet you as you come in, and say goodbye when you leave. Hidden away at the front is an intimate little corner with some African masks, while on the other side of the room a passageway leads to the pub's own busy coffee bar, open between Easter and autumn. Built in the old entrance to the courtyard, it sells snacks, teas, cakes and ice cream. Tables from here spill out on to the pavement in front. A simpler room behind the bar has prints for sale, and maybe locals drinking. In summer, the centre of Usk is full of hanging baskets and flowers, many of them looked after by the landlord; the church is well worth a look.

Bar food (12-2, 6-9.30) ~ Restaurant ~ (01291) 672820 ~ Children welcome ~ Open 11-3, 5.30-11; 12-3, 6-10.30 Sun

VENTNOR Map 2 E3

Spyglass

Esplanade, SW end; road down very steep and twisty, and parking can be difficult

If it's too wet to appreciate the view from the terrace of this marvellously positioned pub, perched above the sea wall, there's plenty to look at inside. Among the really interesting jumble of mainly seafaring memorabilia are wrecked rudders, ships' wheels, old local advertisements, rope makers' tools, stuffed seagulls, an Admiral Benbow barometer and an old brass telescope. The bustling mainly quarry-tiled interior is snug and pubby, and the atmosphere is buoyant; fruit machine, piped music. Generous helpings of good, reasonably priced bar food are promptly served and include sandwiches (from £2.75, baguettes from £3.75), filled baked potatoes (from £4.25), ploughman's and burgers (from £4.95), vegetable moussaka (£5.75), cottage pie (£5.95), tuna steak (£6.95), garlic prawns (£7.25), 8oz sirloin steak (£9.95) or tasty seafood platter (£10.95), and daily specials such as pork and mushroom cider casserole and crab and prawn gratin; puddings such as cherry or apple pie (from £2.75). They usually have well kept Badger Best and Tanglefoot, Ventnor Golden and possibly a guest on handpump. They don't mind dogs or muddy boots; no smoking area. On special occasions such as a lifeboat support week, there may be half a dozen or more guest ales tapped from the cask.

Bar food (12-2.15, 7-9.30 (9 wknds)) ~ (01983) 855338 ~ Children in family room ~ Live entertainment most nights ~ Open 10.30-11(10.30 Sun); closed Mon-Fri 3-6.30 in winter ~ Bedrooms: /£50B

WADDESDON Map 2 B3
Five Arrows
A41 NW of Aylesbury

This is a lovely civilised place – part of the Rothschild Estate – with consistently friendly service, exceptionally good food, and a fine choice of drinks. A series of light and airy high-ceilinged rooms makes up the unstuffy open-plan pubby bar, with family portrait engravings, lots of old estate-worker photographs, heavy dark green velvet curtains on wooden rails, mainly sturdy cushioned settles and good solid tables on parquet flooring (though one room has comfortably worn-in armchairs and settees). Newspapers and copies of *Country Life* are kept in an antique magazine rack. From the interesting menu, there might be soups such as broad bean minestrone or tomato and orange (£4.95), Thai-marinated fillet of red mullet on a bed of soy noodles (£4.95; main course £8.95), spring vegetable risotto with lemon and parmesan (£5.25), crayfish tail salad with dill mayonnaise (£5.95; main course £11.95), chargrilled breast of chicken with mango vinaigrette (£8.95), roasted darne of salmon wrapped in parma ham with a citrus jus (£11.25), confit of duck with raspberry and red wine jus (£12.95), pigeon breasts with black pudding on potato rösti with a port and redcurrant jus (£13.50), and puddings such as bourbon mousse with a duo of mango and raspberry coulis, banoffi pie, and warm chocolate fudge cake with traditional custard (£4.15). No sandwiches or snacks on Sundays. The country-house-style restaurant is no smoking; must book at busy times. The formidable wine list runs to Rothschild first-growth clarets as well as lesser-known Rothschild estate wines. Well kept Fullers London Pride on handpump, many malt whiskies, champagne by the glass, proper cocktails, and freshly squeezed orange juice; efficient service, unobtrusive piped music. The sheltered back garden has attractively grouped wood and metal furnishings. This is an ideal base for visiting Waddesdon Manor.

Bar food (12-2.30, 7-9.30; 12-2, 7.30-9 Sun) ~ Restaurant ~ (01296) 651727 ~ Children welcome ~ Open 11-11; 11-3, 6-11 Sat; 12-3, 7-10.30 Sun ~ Bedrooms: £60S/£85S(£85B)

WALKERINGHAM Map 3 C4
Three Horse Shoes

High Street; just off A161, off A631 W of Gainsborough

In summer the rather ordinary frontage of this pleasant village pub is transformed into a blaze of colour by the licensees' spectacular hanging baskets and flower displays. The 9,000 plants they use complement the slight austerity of the simple old-fashioned décor inside. They've a wide choice of good value food and they have plans to extend their snack menu. Enjoyable dishes might include soup (£1.50), mushrooms and ham in creamy garlic sauce or home-made pâté (£3.25), pork medallions in a white wine, mustard and cream sauce (£7.75), home-made steak and kidney or mushroom, cheese, leek and nut pie (£6.25), grilled plaice or liver, bacon and sausage casserole (£5.95) and specials such as braised steak with red wine and mushrooms (£7.50). In the welcoming bar you'll find well kept Bass, Stones, Worthington Best and a guest beer such as Batemans XXXB on handpump. Darts, dominoes, fruit machine, video game, and piped music. Outside there are seats among the flowers and a Japanese-style millennium garden beside the top car park.

Bar food (standard food times; not Sun evening) ~ Restaurant ~ (01427) 890959 ~ Children welcome ~ Open 11.30-3, 7-11; 12-3, 7-10.30 Sun

WARSLOW Map 3 D3
Greyhound

B5053 S of Buxton

The genial landlord at this slated stone pub goes out of his way to make sure his punters feel welcome. Cosy and comfortable inside, the beamed bar has long cushioned oak antique settles (some quite elegant), houseplants in the windows and cheerful fires. The home-made, well cooked bar food in large helpings includes lunchtime sandwiches (from £2.25), soup (£2.30), spicy Thai fishcakes or ginger creel prawns (£3.50), and a choice of around 20 main meals which include lunchtime ploughman's (from £5.50), steak, mushroom and ale pie, spinach and red pepper lasagne or creamy chicken curry (£6.75), pork fillet in a brandy and cream sauce, tuna and pasta florentine or game pie (£7); children's meals. Well kept Marstons Pedigree, Worthingtons and a guest beer such as Charles Wells Bombardier or Black Sheep on handpump. In the side garden there are picnic-sets under ash trees, with rustic seats out in front where window boxes blaze with colour in summer. The simple bedrooms are clean and comfortable; good breakfasts. The pub is surrounded by pretty countryside and is handy for the Manifold Valley, Dovedale and Alton Towers. The licensees also run the Devonshire Arms in Hartington.

Bar food (standard food times) ~ (01298) 84249 ~ Children welcome ~ Live music Sat evenings, not bank or school holidays ~ Open 12-2.30, 7-11; 12-3, 7-10.30 Sun; closed lunchtime Mon (except bank holidays) and Tues ~ Bedrooms: £17.50/£35

WATTON-AT-STONE Map 2 B4
George & Dragon

Village signposted off A602 about 5 miles S of Stevenage, on B1001; High Street

Though the old licensees have just retired, this civilised country dining pub is still very much the old firm as before. The chef has taken over as landlord and the staff is largely unchanged. Good, beautifully presented dishes include sandwiches (from £2.10), soup (£2.95) and ploughman's (£4.75) as well as more unusual dishes such as prawn and mixed fish chowder (£5.75), Chinese-style crispy duck (£7.45), Mediterranean tomato filled with cracked wheat, aubergine, haloumi and mozzarella (£7.85), lemon sole poached in white wine, lemon and fresh herbs (£8.75), roast chicken breast filled with sage leaves with marsala, sage and mushroom cream sauce (£8.95) and daily specials like white anchovy fillets (£4.45), braised beef with brandy and green peppercorn sauce (£6.85) or john dory with chilli and spring onion butter (£8.25) and home-made puddings (£3.25); friendly, professional service. The atmosphere is gently sophisticated, with kitchen elbow-chairs around attractive old tables, dark blue cloth-upholstered seats in the bay windows, an interesting mix of antique and modern prints on the partly timbered ochre walls, and a big inglenook fireplace. A quieter room off the main bar has spindleback chairs and wall settles cushioned to match the green floral curtains, and a hunting print and old photographs of the village above its panelled dado. Proper napkins, antiques and daily newspapers add to the smart feel. As well as a good wine list they have well kept Greene King Abbot, IPA and Old Speckled Hen on handpump, and several malt whiskies; fruit machine, and boules in the pretty extended shrub-screened garden. The pub is handy for Benington Lordship Gardens.

Bar food (12-2, 7-10; not Sun evening) ~ Restaurant ~ (01920) 830285 ~ Children in eating area of bar and restaurant ~ Open 11-2.30, 6-11; 11-11 Sat; 12-3.30, 7-10.30 Sun; closed 25 Dec, evening 26 Dec

WELLAND Map 1 A5
Anchor

Drake Street; A4104 towards Upton

This pretty, fairy-lit Tudor cottage is much enjoyed by readers for its attentive staff and well made bar food. The welcoming L-shaped bar has country prints on the walls, some armchairs around chatty low tables, and more sitting-up chairs around eating-height tables. Beyond is a spreading comfortably furnished dining area, nicely set with candles, pink tablecloths and napkins. Besides soup (£2.95), filled baked potatoes (from £3.99), omelette or a variety of ploughman's (from £3.99), an extensive choice of changing food on blackboards by the bar might include garlic and herb-smoked mackerel (£3.99), mushrooms, bacon and black pudding (£4.10), steak, kidney and ale pie (£6.99), pork loin stuffed with apple in stilton sauce, garlic mushroom and mascarpone cheese lattice pie (£7.95), trout fillet with lemon and herb butter (£9.05) and half roast duck with orange and Cointreau (£13.99); tempting puddings (from £2.99). Six well kept changing beers such as Charles Wells Bombardier, Church End Anchor Bitter, Hook Norton Anchor Best and Malvern Hills Black Pear on handpump; shove-ha'penny, cribbage, chess, dominoes and maybe unobtrusive piped music. Handy for the Three Counties Showground, it has a field for camping with tents or caravans with electric hook-up points. In summer the front is festooned with colourful hanging baskets, with a passion flower and roses climbing the walls. There are picnic-sets on the lawn, with flower borders and a big old apple tree. Their two new bedrooms have garden views (we have not yet heard from readers who have stayed in them).

Bar food (standard food times) ~ Restaurant ~ (01684) 592317 ~ Children in restaurant ~ Open 11.45-3, 6.45(6.30 Sat)-11; 12-3 (7-10.30 for bookings only) Sun ~ Bedrooms: £30B/£50B

WEOBLEY Map 1 A5
Salutation

Village signposted from A4112 SW of Leominster; and from A44 NW of Hereford (there's also a good back road direct from Hereford – straight out past S side of racecourse)

Even the bus shelter in this quaint little medieval village is black and white timbered, and this heavily beamed 500-year-old hotel is one of the oldest buildings here. It's a quiet village in lovely lush countryside, so this is a nice place to stay, with well equipped comfortable bedrooms and breakfasts that won't leave you hungry. The two areas of the comfortable lounge – separated by a few steps and standing timbers – have a relaxed, pubby feel, brocaded modern winged settles and smaller seats, a couple of big cut-away cask seats, wildlife decorations, a hop bine over the bar counter, and logs burning in a big stone fireplace; more standing timbers separate it from the neat no-smoking restaurant area, and there's a separate smaller parquet-floored public bar with sensibly placed darts, juke box, and a fruit machine; dominoes and cribbage. Very fairly priced bar food includes soup (£3.95), ratatouille-filled grilled mushrooms (£4.95), lunchtime filled baguettes including warm chicken and red onion (from £5.10), lunchtime ploughman's (£5.25), daily roast or leek and mushroom strudel (£6.95), steak and stout pie (£7.25), salmon and coriander fishcakes or supreme of pheasant with mushrooms, red onions and thyme (£7.95), puddings such as lemon tart with raspberry coulis or hazelnut parfait with a rich chocolate sauce (£4.25); three-course Sunday lunch (£13.50); the restaurant is more elaborate and costs more. Well kept Hook Norton Best, Fullers London Pride and a guest such as Wye Valley Butty Bach on handpump, an extensive wine list with mainly new world bins, and a couple of dozen malt whiskies. There are tables and chairs with parasols on a sheltered back terrace.

Bar food (standard food times) ~ Restaurant ~ (01544) 318443 ~ Children in eating area of bar, restaurant and conservatory ~ Open 11-11; 12-10.30 Sun ~ Bedrooms: £45S(£48B)/£69S(£72B)

WHITEWELL Map 3 C3
Inn at Whitewell

Most easily reached by B6246 from Whalley; road through Dunsop Bridge from
B6478 is also good

Set deep in the Forest of Bowland, this enduringly popular hotel is
surrounded by well wooded rolling hills set off against higher moors, and is
perhaps most dramatically approached from Abbeystead. The hotel owns
several miles of trout, salmon and sea trout fishing on the Hodder, and
with notice they'll arrange shooting. All the spacious bedrooms are very
well appointed with good bathrooms, CD players, and even some with
their own peat fires in winter. The interior is impressively furnished: the
old-fashioned pubby bar has antique settles, oak gateleg tables, sonorous
clocks, old cricketing and sporting prints, log fires (the lounge has a very
attractive stone fireplace), and heavy curtains on sturdy wooden rails; one
area has a selection of newspapers, dominoes, local maps and guide books,
there's a piano for anyone who wants to play, and even an art gallery.
Although it gets very busy, it's spacious inside and out, so usually remains
tranquil and relaxing. Well liked bar food includes soup (£3.20), open
sandwiches (from £3.90), toasted walnut brioche (£5), seafood chowder
(£5.50), grilled Norfolk kipper (£6.50), fish and chips (£7.80), fish pie
(£8.40), warm spinach and ricotta tartlet (£9), fried lambs kidneys (£11),
home-made puddings such as sticky toffee pudding and home-made
honeycomb and butterscotch ice cream (£3.50) and hand-made farmhouse
cheeses (from £3.50); the evening menu is slightly different. Very polite
staff serve coffee and cream teas all day – you can buy jars of the home-
made jam (from £1.50). Well kept Boddingtons and Marstons Pedigree on
handpump, and around 180 wines – including a highly recommended
claret. Down a corridor with strange objects like a stuffed fox disappearing
into the wall is the pleasant suntrap garden, with wonderful views down to
the valley.

*Bar food (standard food times) ~ Restaurant ~ (01200) 448222 ~ Children
welcome ~ Open 11-3, 6-11; 12-2, 7-10.30 Sun ~ Bedrooms: £83B/£99B*

WIGGINTON Map 1 A6
White Swan

Village signposted off A361 SW of Banbury

This small tucked-away stone-built pub has not much more than half a dozen tables, but the new landlord's cooking is a big draw here. Booking in the evenings is already advisable, and though it was quiet on our anonymous lunchtime inspection visit we anticipate trade will build up quickly here as word gets around. We swithered over unusual and tempting sandwiches (from £3.25) such as black pudding with mango, stilton with pear, or tuna melt, then plumped for two dishes of the day. Swordfish (like tuna, all too easy to dry out) was grilled just right, nicely cooked and still succulent. Liver and bacon (£7.95) was a far cry from your coarse café variety: with its rich gravy this was full of flavours and – very rare for this dish – even looked pretty. At the end of March, this came with genuine new potatoes, nicely cooked string beans, carrots and calabrese, and a clever mix of little bits of sauté potatoes with red pepper and onion in a savourous pan reduction. For such individual cooking, the food came remarkably quickly. Other dishes could include soup (£2.95), feta and olive salad (£3.95), smoked salmon, tomato and mozzarella pancakes (£4.95), corned beef hash (£6.50) and pork spare ribs (£7.25), with specials such as rabbit in cider and mustard (£8.95), and guinea fowl, lemon sole or duck breast in strawberry sauce (£11.95); puddings such as chocolate bread pudding (£2.95). We sat at a table on old flooring tiles by a hot inglenook log fire opposite the bar counter (which has well kept Hook Norton Best, Best Mild and Double Stout on handpump); down a step from here is a simply decorated carpeted area with neat tables and wheelback chairs, and the main blackboard over another huge fireplace. Service is quietly pleasant; relaxed chatty atmosphere; piped Dean Martin on our visit. There are a few picnic-sets out on a little terrace and patch of lawn behind.

Bar food (12-2.30, 6-10) ~ Restaurant ~ (01608) 737669 ~ Children welcome ~ Open 12-3, 6-11; 12-4, 7-11 Sun

WINCHESTER Map 2 D2
Wykeham Arms

75 Kingsgate Street (Kingsgate Arch and College Street are now closed to traffic; there is access via Canon Street)

Although new licensees have taken over this rather civilised but friendly inn, readers are quick to tell us that things are as good as ever. It remains an extremely popular place with a fine choice of drinks and food, and is a super place to stay. A series of stylish bustling rooms radiating from the central bar has 19th-c oak desks retired from nearby Winchester College, a redundant pew from the same source, kitchen chairs and candlelit deal tables and big windows with swagged paisley curtains; all sorts of interesting collections are dotted around. A snug room at the back, known as the Watchmakers, is decorated with a set of Ronald Searle 'Winespeak' prints, a second one is panelled, and all of them have a log fire; several areas are no smoking. Served by neatly uniformed, efficient staff, the very good food at lunchtime might include sandwiches (from £3; pork sausage with onion marmalade £3.95), home-made soup such as butternut squash (£3.25), cheese terrine (£5.25), vegetable lasagne (£5.50), haddock kedgeree (£5.75), lamb casserole (£6.25), Thai chicken (£6.50), cassoulet (£6.75), and steaks (from £12.50), with evening dishes like salmon and dill terrine (£4.75), warm pigeon and bacon salad with grain mustard dressing (£5.25), garlic, wild mushroom and roasted pepper risotto with parmesan (£9.95), grilled fillets of red mullet marinated with chilli and garlic, served on warm couscous salad with red pepper coulis (£12.50), duck breast with bacon and a creamy wild mushroom sauce (£12.75), roast rack of Hampshire Down lamb with garlic and rosemary-roasted vegetables and a port and redcurrant jus (£13.75), and puddings such as chocolate nemesis, raspberry and Benedictine bavarois or pecan pie (£4.50). There's a fine choice of 20 wines by the glass (including sweet wines), and quite a few brandies, armagnacs and liqueurs. Also, well kept Bass, and Gales Bitter, Best, and HSB on handpump. There are tables on a covered back terrace, with more on a small but sheltered lawn. The lovely bedrooms in the pub are thoughtfully equipped, and the Saint George, a 16th-c annexe directly across the street (and overlooking Winchester College Chapel) has more bedrooms, a sitting room with open fire, a post office/general stores, and a Burgundian wine store; you can enjoy the good breakfasts either in your room there or at the pub. No children inside.

Bar food (12-2.30, 6.30-8.45; not Sun) ~ Restaurant ~ (01962) 853834 ~ Open 11-11; 12-10.30 Sun; closed 25 Dec ~ Bedrooms: £45S(£69.50B)/£79.50B

WING Map 3 E4
Kings Arms

Top Street, signposted off A6003 S of Oakham

This genuinely friendly and relaxing early 17th-c inn scores top marks for its consistently good food, well kept ales and courteous and efficient service. Very enjoyable meals from a changing menu might include soup (£3.50), filled baguettes (from £4.25), ploughman's (£6.50), sausage and garlic mash with red wine jus (£7.50), fish stew (£7.95), battered haddock (£8.50), chicken supreme wrapped in bacon with stilton sauce (£9.90), roast bass on wild rocket with citrus dressing (£11.50) and fried monkfish medallions wrapped in parma ham on tomato and garlic sauce (£12.90). The bar has a traditional feel with wooden beams and a flagstone floor, as well as two large log fires, captain's chairs around pine and darker wood tables, old local photographs and a collection of tankards and old-fashioned whisky measuring pots; in the snug there are fishing rods and tackle; piped music. Well kept Batemans and Grainstore Cooking and a guest on handpump. The restaurant and comfortable neatly kept bedrooms are no smoking. There are seats, swings and slides in the sheltered garden, and a medieval turf maze is just up the road.

Bar food (12-2, 6.30-9(8.30 Sun); not Mon lunchtime) ~ Restaurant ~ (01572) 737634 ~ Children welcome ~ Open 12-3, 6-11; 12-11(12-3, 6-11 in winter) Sat; 12-10.30 Sun; closed Sun evening and Mon lunchtime in winter ~ Bedrooms: /£65B

WINGFIELD Map 2 A6
De La Pole Arms

Church Road; village signposted off B1118 N of Stradbroke

This beautifully restored village inn which is tucked away off the beaten track in lovely countryside is one of only three St Peters pubs. They stock all the St Peters beers on handpump and their entire range of over a dozen bottled beers. The deliberately simple yet elegant décor is very traditional with interesting bric-a-brac, comfortable traditional seating, and no distraction by noisy games machines or piped music. Very good bar food, served by courteous, friendly staff, might include soup (£3.95), a bowl of mussels or prawns (£6.95), cheese, spinach and ham bake (£7.50), steak and stout pie (£7.95), cold seafood platter (£8.95), baked halibut (£9.25), grilled skate wings (£9.50), and puddings such as apple crumble and custard, mango and orange mousse and chocolate and rum pots (£3.95); the restaurant is no smoking.

Bar food (standard food times) ~ Restaurant ~ (01379) 384545 ~ Children in eating area of bar and restaurant ~ Open 11-3, 6-11; 12-3 Sun; closed Sun evening and Mon

WINTERBOURNE Map 1 B6
Winterbourne Arms

3½ miles from M4 junction 13; A34 N, first left through Chieveley and on to B4494, then left and right

With new licensees and a new chef, this country pub remains popular for its wide choice of interesting food – but also manages to keep its friendly pubby atmosphere. From the lunchtime snack menu, there might be soup (£4.50), oven-baked potatoes or ciabatta with fillings such as stilton, onion confit and crispy parma ham, mozzarella, Mediterranean vegetables and pesto sauce or turkey, brie and bacon (from £4.50), duck salad with orange segments and balsamic dressing (£7.25), and stir-fried vegetables in sesame oil with a selection of seafood (£7.50); weekly changing specials such as wild mushrooms in a sherry cream sauce with puff pastry topping (£5.25), terrine of foie gras and duck with home-made piccalilli (£7.25), breast of quail with potato pancake, mushroom duxelle and beetroot jus (£13.50), and ravioli of crab garnished with langoustines and shellfish sauce (£16.50), with home-made puddings like zesty lemon tart or chocolate marquise with white chocolate sauce. Well kept Bass with two guests such as Fullers London Pride and West Berkshire Good Old Boy on handpump, and a decent wine list with 12 wines by the glass. The bars have been gently refurbished but have kept the collection of old irons around the fireplace, early prints and old photographs of the village, and a log fire; you can see the original bakers' ovens in the restaurant area, which was once a bakery. The peaceful view over the rolling fields from the big bar windows cunningly avoids the quiet road, which is sunken between the pub's two lawns; flowering tubs and hanging baskets brighten up picnic-sets, and the garden boasts a big weeping willow. There are nearby walks to Snelsmore and Donnington.

Bar food (12-2.30(2 Sun), 7-9.30) ~ Restaurant ~ (01635) 248200 ~ Children in restaurant, over 7 in evenings ~ Open 11.30-3(4 Sat), 6-11; 12-4 Sun; closed Sun evening, all day Mon – exc bank holidays

WOOBURN COMMON Map 2 C3
Chequers

From A4094 N of Maidenhead at junction with A4155 Marlow road keep on A4094 for another ¾ mile, then at roundabout turn off right towards Wooburn Common, and into Kiln Lane; if you find yourself in Honey Hill, Hedsor, turn left into Kiln Lane at the top of the hill; OS Sheet 175 map reference 910870

Even when really busy, the enthusiastic young staff here remain friendly and efficient. It's a welcoming place with a good mix of customers – many drawn from its thriving hotel and restaurant side. The low-beamed, partly stripped-brick bar has standing timbers and alcoves to break it up, comfortably lived-in sofas on its bare boards, a bright log-effect gas fire, and various pictures, plates, a two-man saw, and tankards; one room is no smoking. Changing daily, enjoyable food includes sandwiches (from £3.75), soup (£3.95), ploughman's (£5.25), popular vegetarian dishes such as chilled melon with grapes, mint and muscat wine (£6.95) and glazed Swiss cheese soufflé with garlic cream sauce (£7.95), deep-fried calamari with sweet chilli dressing (£7.95), seared black bream with spinach and newburg sauce (£9.95), a nage of fish and shellfish with saffron and dill sauce (£10.95), fried calves liver with potato purée and onion jus (£11.95), and puddings (from £3.75); there's a more formal restaurant. Well kept Greene King IPA, Original, and Ruddles County on handpump, a sizeable wine list (champagne and good wine by the glass), and a fair range of malt whiskies and brandies. The spacious garden, set away from the road, has cast-iron tables. Attractive stripped-pine bedrooms are in a 20th-c mock-Tudor wing; breakfasts are good.

Bar food (12-2.30, 7-9.30(10 Fri and Sat)) ~ Restaurant ~ (01628) 529575 ~ Children welcome ~ Open 11-11; 11-10.30 Sun ~ Bedrooms: £97.50B/£102.50B

WOOLLEY MOOR Map 3 D4
White Horse

Badger Lane, off B6014 Matlock—Clay Cross

There are lovely views over the Ogston reservoir and the Amber Valley from this delightfully situated, attractive old pub. A sign outside shows how horses and carts carried measures of salt along the toll road in front – the toll bar still stands at the entrance of the road. The chatty tap room, still very much in its original state, serves well kept Bass and Ruddles and a couple of guests such as Greene King Abbot and Old Speckled Hen. They also do home-made lemonade and decent wines. There is piped classical music in the lounge, and the views are from the no-smoking conservatory. It's best to book for the restaurant. Using fresh local produce, very enjoyable bar food includes good soup (£2.95), toasted panini (from £3.25), meze plate (£3.75), sandwiches (from £3.95), steak sandwich (£4.95), steak and kidney pie (£5.75), creole sweetcorn fritter with jambalaya rice and salsa (£6.25), fish and chips (£6.75), roast pork leg with apricot and almond stuffing or roast red pepper and goats cheese strudel (£7.25), beef and prune tagine (£7.75), fried entrecote on mushroom ragoût with watercress butter (£8.25), fried tuna with niçoise salad (£8.95), duck breast with blackberry and apple sauce (£9.95); good children's meals come with a puzzle sheet and crayons. Picnic-sets in the garden have lovely views too, and there's a very good children's play area with wooden play train, climbing frame and swings, and boules.

Bar food (12-2, 6-9 Mon-Sat, 12-8 Sun) ~ No credit cards ~ (01246) 590319 ~ Children in eating area of bar and restaurant ~ Open 12-3, 6-11; 12-11 Sat; 12-10.30 Sun

YANWATH Map 3 A2
Gate Inn

2¼ miles from M6 junction 40; A66 towards Brough, then right on A6, right on
B5320, then follow village signpost

An engaging combination of really good inventive food with the welcoming
environment of an unpretentious village local, this remains a very popular
and friendly place. The simple turkey-carpeted bar, full of chatting
regulars, has a log fire in an attractive stone inglenook and one or two nice
pieces of furniture and middle-eastern brassware among more orthodox
seats; or you can go through to eat in a two-level no-smoking restaurant.
Carefully prepared, imaginative food might include home-made soup
(£2.50), good 'black devils' (sliced black pudding with cream and
peppercorn sauce £3.30), seafood pancake (£3.95), pies such as sweet
potato or chicken and leek (£6.25), good fish pie (£6.75), much enjoyed
steak baguette (£6.95), salmon and monkfish wrapped in parma ham with
a creamy prawn sauce (£9.95), steaks (from £9.95), daily specials such as
venison steak with mushroom and red wine sauce (£9.75) and breast of
barbary duck with cranberry and orange sauce (£10.95), and puddings like
sticky ginger pudding or rich chocolate pudding with hot chocolate fudge
sauce (£3); friendly, helpful service. Well kept Hesket Newmarket Skiddaw
Special Bitter and Theakstons Best on handpump, and a decent wine list;
darts, dominoes, cribbage, and shove-ha'penny; the friendly border collie is
called Domino and is good with children. There are seats on the terrace
and in the garden.

*Bar food (standard food times) ~ Restaurant ~ (01768) 862386 ~ Children
welcome ~ Open 12-3, 6.30(6 Sat and Sun)-11(10.30 Sun); 12-2.30, 6.30-11
in winter*

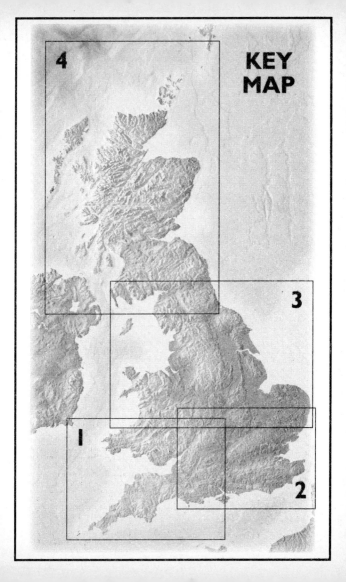

KEY
MAP

4

3

1

2

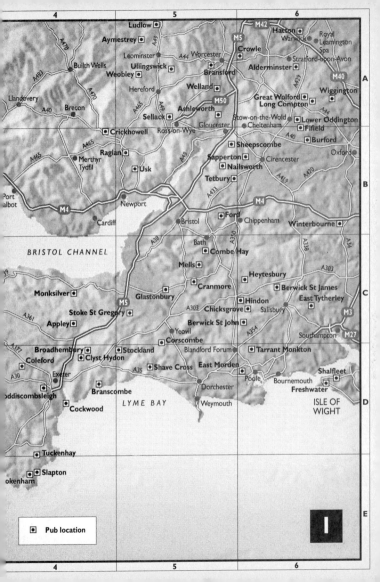

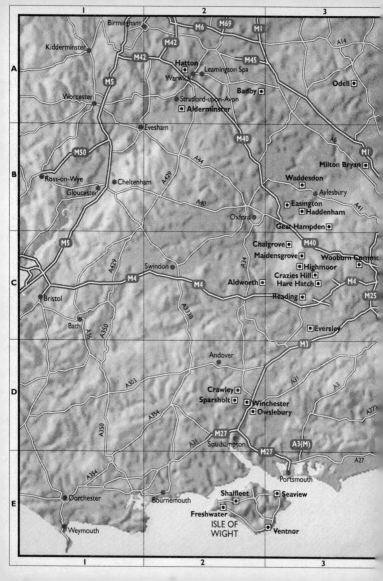

All Ebury titles are available in good bookshops or via mail order

TO ORDER
(please tick)

Pocket Good Guide to Great Family Days Out	£5.99	❑
The Good Pub Guide	£14.99	❑
The Good Britain Guide	£14.99	❑
The Good Hotel Guide to UK and Ireland	£15.99	❑
The Good Hotel Guide to Continental Europe	£16.99	❑

PAYMENT MAY BE MADE USING ACCESS, VISA, MASTERCARD, DINERS CLUB, SWITCH AND AMEX OR CHEQUE, EUROCHEQUE AND POSTAL ORDER (STERLING ONLY)

CARD NUMBER:...

EXPIRY DATE:........................   SWITCH ISSUE NO:..............

SIGNATURE:..

Please allow £2.50 for post and packaging for the first book and £1.00 thereafter

ORDER TOTAL: £.................................(INC P&P)

ALL ORDERS TO:

EBURY PRESS, BOOKS BY POST, TBS LIMITED, COLCHESTER ROAD, FRATING GREEN, COLCHESTER, ESSEX CO7 7DW, UK

Telephone: 01206 256 000   Fax: 01206 255 914

NAME:..

ADDRESS:..

....

....Post code...

Please allow 28 days for delivery. Please tick box if you do not wish to receive any additional information. ❑

Prices and availability subject to change without notice.